Corporate social reporting
accounting and accountability

Corporate social reporting
accounting and accountability

ROB GRAY
Department of Economics, University College of North Wales
DAVE OWEN
Faculty of Economic and Social Studies, University of Manchester
KEITH MAUNDERS
Department of Management Studies, University of Leeds

Prentice/Hall PHI International

Englewood Cliffs, NJ London Mexico New Delhi
Rio de Janeiro Singapore Sydney Tokyo Toronto

British Library Cataloguing in Publication Data

Gray, Rob
    Corporate social reporting: accounting and
    accountability.
    1. Industry – social aspects
    I. Title II. Owen, Dave   III. Maunders, Keith
    658.4'08   HD60
    ISBN 0–13–175464–5
    ISBN 0–13–175456–4 pbk

Prentice-Hall Inc., Englewood Cliffs, New Jersey
Prentice-Hall International (UK) Ltd, London
Prentice-Hall of Australia Pty Ltd, Sydney
Prentice-Hall Canada Inc., Toronto
Prentice-Hall Hispanoamericana S.A., Mexico
Prentice-Hall of India Private Ltd, New Delhi
Prentice-Hall of Japan Inc., Tokyo
Prentice-Hall of Southeast Asia Pte Ltd, Singapore
Editora Prentice-Hall do Brasil Ltda, Rio de Janeiro

Printed and bound in Great Britain for Prentice-Hall
International (UK) Ltd, 66 Wood Lane End,
Hemel Hempstead, Hertfordshire, HP2 4RG
by S R P Ltd, Exeter.

1 2 3 4 5 90 89 88 87 86

Contents

Preface

... because of the growing pressure for greater corporate accountability, I can forsee the day when, in addition to the annual financial statements certified by independent accountants, corporations may be required to publish a social audit similarly certified.

David Rockefeller, Chase Manhattan Bank, *New York Times*, 1 May 1972

... to think of the business corporation simply as an economic instrument is to fail totally to understand the meaning of the social changes of the last half century. D. Bell, Heinemann, London, 1974

Social reporting is the process of communicating the social and environmental effects of organizations' economic actions to particular interest groups within society and to society at large. As such it involves extending the accountability of organizations (particularly companies), beyond the traditional role of providing a financial account to the owners of capital, in particular, shareholders. Such an extension is predicated upon an assumption that companies *do* have wider responsibilities than simply to make money for their shareholders.

The nature of these responsibilities and the way in which the ensuing accountability might be discharged have become issues of widespread and often very heated debate – not just amongst extremists and pressure groups. In the UK, USA, Europe, Australasia and Japan, business executives, accountants, trade union officials, politicians, academics and professional organizations of varying hues and predispositions have locked horns over these complex and controversial issues. The interest shown in the area has generated literally hundreds of books and articles and it is now by no means uncommon for large organizations to produce experimental social reports alongside their more traditional financial reports.

Yet despite the extensive interest, social reporting remains outside the present orthodoxy of the predominantly capitalist economies of the West. There are two basic reasons for this. The first is that the different parties cannot agree on what 'social responsibility' really means and how any resultant accountability might be discharged. The second reason is more substantial. As Friedman notes, the extension of social responsibility and the development of social reporting are radical ideas with potentially far-reaching consequences for the relationship between society and its indigeneous organizations:

> few trends could so thoroughly undermine the very foundations of our free society as the acceptance by corporate officials of a social responsibility other than to make as much money for their stockholders as possible
>
> Friedman, 1962, p. 133

As a result, such developments are as strongly opposed by the political power of the status quo as they are hotly pursued by those of a more radical inclination.

One purpose in writing this book is to provide a means by which the issues involved, whether they be technical or political, are explicitly considered. This we do by focusing the core of the book on the concept of 'accountability'. With such an approach we believe we are able to provide a hitherto unavailable, cohesive framework for the subject area.

Nevertheless, a book such as this is inevitably influenced by the authors' 'world views' and in taking society's structure as given, as we choose to do for the main part, we should necessarily run the risk of doing violence to many important and articulate views that make no such assumption. Therefore, we also try to provide a substantial review of the whole spectrum of views, experiences and experimentation, both radical and non-radical, that have been generated in the subject's short history.

Chapter 1 is a 'ground clearing' exercise in which we seek to: clarify basic terminology such as accountability, responsibility, social accounting; analyze different underlying objectives of social reporting; and briefly outline different approaches to the subject. Chapters 2 and 3 review, in broad outline, the development of practice and its regulation in an international and UK context. Chapter 4 consists of an analysis of the basic elements of social reporting, including a review of the role of 'traditional' accounting theory in the development of corporate social reporting, the broad areas to be reported upon, the form which social reports might take and views on how they should be prepared. Chapters 5 to 7 review different approaches that have either been proposed or undertaken as methods of social reporting. They reflect the fact that there have been three main approaches: the presentation of reports in financial terms, reports in non-financial terms, and the so-called social audit approach. Chapters 8 and 9 focus on the specific and rather more developed area of reporting to and about employees – both to individual employees and to trade union officials for general information and collective bargaining purposes. Chapter 10 pulls together our arguments, draws out some conclusions and suggests possible ways forward.

By the end of the book we hope that the reader will have gained some understanding of the issues, have evolved an informed opinion about them and, if he or she be so minded, have some ideas about how and why an organization should disclose social information about its activities.

Finally, we should offer two mild words of warning. Most literature on social accountability concentrates on companies rather than other organizations, and although we have attempted to keep our brief as wide as possible, inevitably many of our examples are also company-based. Secondly, the study of the social accountability of organizations is not easy. Unlike financial accounting, say, it is not a simple, straightforward and traditional subject as most texts would have you believe. It is complex, involves opinions and the changing perceptions of society. It cannot be studied in a 'closed-system' or with a closed mind. It is this aspect that each of us has found has given our own students excitement, pleasure and headaches over the years. We can do no less than wish you the same.

Acknowledgements

The authors would wish to recognize the enormous help and support they have received from many colleagues, friends and family. Particular thanks are due to Peter Booth (Griffiths University), George Harte (Edinburgh University), Bob Perks (Middlesex Polytechnic) and Linda Lewis and Brian Strudwick (Huddersfield Polytechnic) who read and commented on various drafts of the book and who, in their various ways, contributed greatly to the quality of the finished product. More general thanks are due to Charles Medawar (Social Audit Ltd), Harold Warburton (Lancashire Polytechnic), Desmond McComb (Southampton University) and David Wells (Nottingham University) for the diverse help they gave, in particular with material for the book.

A special acknowledgement is due to Giles Wright of Prentice-Hall International whose support and enthusiasm made this book a possibility. Similarly the help and encouragement of Maggie McDougall of PHI in the later stages of the project deserves special thanks.

Chapter 1

Social accountability – its meaning and context

Twenty or thirty years ago, one would have been hard pressed to find more than the occasional reference to anything which sounded like 'social accountability'. There appeared to be a fairly general, if implicit, view that business and non-business organizations alike were essentially beneficial and well-intentioned entities which, guided by a presumed 'enlightened self-interest', strove to fulfil an essential and desirable role in Western societies. Of course, problems did arise but these would usually be construed as narrow issues. Corruption scandals, fraud, examples of irresponsible management etc., were instances of 'financial' problems calling for greater financial control and accountability; strikes, lock-outs, sit-ins were 'labour' problems – specific issues of work-force management, which had wider implications only in so far as they generated concern over the viability of enterprises or over the power of political minorities; examples of unsuitable or dangerous products, similarly, would generally be treated in isolation.

By the early 1970s much of this had changed. Greater effort was exerted in attempting to understand systems as a whole, rather than as a series of unrelated parts (see, for example, Kempner *et al.*, 1976; Votaw, 1973). The interrelationships between groups, organizations and societies, were being recognized as exceptionally complex and of utmost importance. Pollution, resource depletion, waste, product quality and safety, the rights and status of labour, the power of large companies, were examples of issues which gained increasing attention and concern. Changing social attitudes were reflected in the increasing number and power of pressure groups and in a quantum leap in the amount of statute law (on employment conditions, product safety, pollution etc.) with which organizations were required to comply. Little emphasizes the change better than the new language which developed over

this period. Terms like social responsibility, social reporting, social accounting, social audit etc., gained a currency which implied a new and vigorous
area of study emerging to meet new needs.

The plethora of articles and books with these new phrases in the title which
emerged in the five or so years up to about 1975, while reflecting a lively
interest in the subject, on the whole tended to confuse the issues rather than
clarify them. Answers to questions like: 'What are a company's responsibilities?', 'What should a company's social report contain?', 'Who is it for?',
'Who should do the social audit?', appeared to be more elusive than ever.
Statisticians, sociologists, accountants, management personnel, lawyers *et al.*
battled over the terms, concepts and subject property rights with negligible
success.

This confusion plus the onset of the world recession from the mid-1970s
combined to slow the bandwagon. Gambling (1977a) suggests that generalized social concern over the environment, the Third World, the plight of
labour, etc., is really the froth on society's coffee. If you have your second car
then you will worry about whales becoming extinct; if a recession threatens
your way of life, whales take a back seat. Whatever the reasons, by 1976 most
champions of social responsibility and reporting had fled the bandwagon for
safer means of transport. With some of the impetus gone out of the subject, a
more thoughtful and steady approach has emerged. It is possible now to look
back over the last twenty years with a cooler mind and try and determine just
how far we *have* come – to sit back and try to provide an overview of the
subject, what it is, what it can and cannot do, and how it might progress.

ACCOUNTABILITY

The indiscriminate and sloppy use of terms was (and is) to a large extent
responsible for much of the confusion to be found in discussions of organizations and society. Social responsibility, reporting, accounting, and audit
are all terms which can be linked by the term 'accountability' and can thereby
be given fairly precise definitions.

The term 'accountability' means the onus, requirement, or responsibility to
provide an account (by no means necessarily a *financial* account) or reckon-
ing of the actions for which one is held responsible. What it means in practice
can be seen more clearly if we talk in terms of 'principals' and 'agents'. The
words 'principal' and 'agent' are used in their common, law of contract sense
to mean one party (the agent) acting on behalf of some other party (the
principal). There exists, between the principal and agent, a contract which
determines the rights and duties of the parties. The contract need be neither
written nor explicit. Under the (possibly implicit) contract, the principal
typically gives instructions to the agent on what actions are expected of him,
gives some consideration (typically remuneration) and some power over
resources with which to fulfil these actions. In so doing the principal places
two responsibilities upon the agent:

- responsibility for action
- responsibility to account for those actions, i.e. accountability. (For more detail see Gray, 1983a, 1983b.) This is summarized in Figure 1.1.

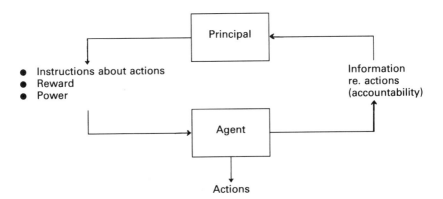

Figure 1.1 The principal–agent accountability contract

Figure 1.1 is, of course, an over-simplification of the issues but we can employ it to good effect to model the basic relationships and responsibilities of society and organizations. Consider the simplest of all cases – company directors (agents) and shareholders (principals). The shareholder passes power (control over his investment) to the directors and enters into a contract with them. The contract is largely implicit[1] but its general terms are governed by the Companies Acts. The directors draw a reward (their emoluments) and are effectively instructed to act to generate future cash wealth. The actions are to be expressed in financial terms (generation of cash, profit, etc.) and the directors are required to discharge their accountability through financial reports.

The point is that the contract between the shareholders and directors can be viewed as a financial one – the actions and the accountability are thus also similarly financial. Very few 'contracts' can be said to be strictly financial – the relationship between ratepayers and the local authority, taxpayers and health authorities, employee and employer, the local community and local organizations; all involve different degrees of non-financial or *social* accountability. That is because the principal (the ratepayer, taxpayer, employee, or community) has placed a responsibility on the agent to fulfil actions which are partly financial (e.g. payment of wages) and partly non-financial (e.g. provision of health care, emptying of dustbins, protection of the environment, maintenance of a safe workplace and the dignity of the employee). Hence the responsibility arising from such actions cannot be shown to be completely discharged through financial measures of performance.

We can therefore state that accountability exists when we have established a principal–agent contract. We can similarly identify the form that accountability must take when we have established the terms (i.e. the actions required) of the contract. Establishing the contract and its terms is not always that straightforward. Some contracts cause few problems, e.g. the shareholder *qua* shareholder and the company, and the majority of contracts in the bulk of not-for-profit organizations. In these cases, it is relatively easy to *see* the contracts, since they are either enshrined in law (e.g. Companies Acts) or are effectively established by statements from Government departments and/ or professional bodies. The requirements of accountability for health authorities and local authorities are of this type (CIPFA/AHST, 1982, HMSO, 1981). The same is true, to a large extent, for nationalized industries where a larger (i.e. beyond 'shareholder') accountability is enshrined in Government White Papers (Cmnd 3437; Cmnd 7131). The real problems occur when we attempt to establish the contracts for:

● private sector business organizations beyond those concerning the shareholder; or
● nearly all organizations with respect to, for example, the environment, labour, and the community.

Thus, do companies have a responsibility to protect the environment, to be responsive to the needs of employees, to consider the needs of the community?

These questions are at the very crux of the issue. As Benston (1982) has noted, if responsibilities do not exist, then there is little logical reason to concern oneself with accountability that derives from that non-responsibility. We will return shortly to these issues, as we are now in a position to clarify the other basic terminology.

Social responsibilities are the responsibilities for actions which do not have purely financial implications and which are demanded of an organization under some (implicit or explicit) identifiable contract. We thus exclude the shareholder *qua* shareholder's contract with a company (a financial responsibility) but include the employee/employer contract, since this usually covers conditions, as well as terms, of employment.

Social accountability is the responsibility to account for actions for which one has social responsibility under an established contract. The terms in which the accountability is discharged (or in which the account is rendered) must be appropriate to the actions. Thus, for example, a financial account is inadequate to discharge accountability about actions designed to improve health care or the environment.

Note that issues like the provision of financial information to employees (which has other than strictly financial implications and which we do not wish to exclude from our discussion) are subsumed in this definition of social accountability.

Social reporting (or corporate social reporting – CSR) is the process of providing information designed to discharge social accountability. Typically this act would (and should) be undertaken by the accountable organisation and thus might include information in the annual report, special publications or reports or even socially orientated advertising (see Exhibit 1.1). Frequently,

Invisible asset.

You can't actually see fresh air. Or peace and quiet, or water purity. But a decent environment is an asset which everyone values: an invisible asset.

And, like blank space in a newspaper, it comes at a price.

At Mobil's new refinery development on the Thames Estuary, that price will be around £12 million – the cost of equipment to curb air, water and noise pollution.

Is even £12 million enough? There'd be still less risk if we spent more. But as well as protecting the environment, companies have a responsibility to hold down the cost of their products. And no amount of investment would completely abolish pollution – or eliminate the possibility of human error.

So where do we draw the line?

In practice, we don't. Environmental standards for industry are set by government authorities. Companies can either stick scrupulously to those basic standards or, as many do, they can go a little further, to improve conditions for their employees or to leave a safety margin – a little extra insurance.

But, as with any insurance policy, the degree of risk must be weighed against the cost of the premium.

Environmental standards are a delicate compromise between what technology can achieve and what society can afford; and that's a balance which can only be struck for society through its elected representatives.

Industry's responsibility is to demonstrate a real concern for the environment; to meet government standards without cutting corners; and to use its imagination and skill to meet them at the lowest possible cost to the consumer.

Mobil's £12 million may seem a lot to pay for an invisible asset. But it meets public standards generously, at the lowest cost we can manage.

And that's money well spent.

Mobil

Exhibit 1.1 Mobil (UK) advertisement. Source: Mobil (UK), published in *Vole* 1979. Used with permission.

Social Accounts

Social Income

Statement

		(Rs. in Lakhs)	
I.	**Social Benefits & Cost to Staff**	**1980–81**	**1979–80**
	A. Social Benefits to Staff:		
	1. Medical and Hospital amenties	**32.14**	20.35
	2. Educational facilities	**4.10**	2.39
	3. Canteen facilities	**5.71**	3.46
	4. Recreation, entertainment & cultural activities	**3.07**	1.77
	5. Housing and Township facilities	**112.54**	84.33
	6. Water Supply, concessional electricity and transport	**18.15**	13.59
	7. Training & career development	**4.93**	3.85
	8. Other benefits to employees	**192.01**	149.97
	Total benefits to staff:	**372.65**	279.71
	B. Social Cost to Staff:		
	1. Lay off & involuntary terminations	**0.86**	—
	2. Extra hours put in by Executives voluntarily	**9.26**	7.75
	Total cost to staff:	**10.12**	7.75
	Net Social income to staff (A—B)	**362.53**	271.96
II.	**Social Benefits & Cost to Community**		
	A. Social Benefits to Community:		
	1. Local Taxes paid to Panchyat/ Municipality	**0.21**	0.08
	2. Environmental Improvements	**6.97**	7.01
	3. Generation of job potential	**550.69**	448.67
	4. Generation of business	**95.63**	75.90
	Total social benefits to community	**653.50**	531.66
	B. Social Cost to Community: Increase in cost of living in the vicinity on account of cement plants	**155.00**	127.40
	Net Social Income to community (A—B)	**498.50**	404.26
III.	**Social Benefits & Costs to General Public**		
	A. Total Benefits to General Public:		
	1. Taxes, duties, etc. paid to State Governments	**735.55**	496.80
	2. Taxes, duties, etc. paid to Central Government	**1499.61**	1284.77
	Total benefits to General Public	**2235.16**	1781.57
	B. Costs to General Public:		
	1. State Services Consumed: Electricity charges paid	**519.72**	325.20
	2. Central Services Consumed: Telephones, telegrams, postage & bank charges	**14.37**	11.96
	Total cost to General Public	**534.09**	337.16
	Net Social benefit to General Public (A—B)	**1701.07**	1444.41
	NET SOCIAL INCOME TO STAFF, COMMUNITY AND GENERAL PUBLIC (I + II + III)	**2562.10**	2120.63

Social Balance Sheet

LIABILITIES			ASSETS		
	(Rs. in Lakhs)			(Rs. in Lakhs)	
	As at 31.3.81	As at 31.3.80		As at 31.3.81	As at 31.3.80
I. Organisation Equity	720.48	546.54	I. Social Capital: Investment		
II. Social Equity			1. Township Land	15.74	15.73
Contribution by Staff	3584.15	2869.11	2. Buildings		
			(i) Township (Residential & Welfare Buildings)	581.51	444.23
			(ii) Canteen Buildings	9.36	5.49
			3. Township Water supply & Sewage	47.16	24.56
			4. Township—Roads	29.13	23.51
			5. Township—Electrification	17.33	15.07
			II. Other Social Assets:		
			1. Hospital Equipments	1.38	0.59
			2. Hospital Vehicle/ Ambulance	4.66	4.00
			3. School Equipments	0.76	0.71
			4. Club Equipments	0.80	0.74
			5. Play ground/Park	0.32	0.20
			6. School buses	12.33	11.71
			III. Human Assets:	3584.15	2869.11
	4304.63	3415.65		4304.63	3415.65

Exhibit 1.2 The Cement Corporation of India Ltd social accounts 1981.

however, the accountable agent is reluctant to provide such information, and so also under this heading comes information prepared by outside bodies, notably the press and institutions like (in the UK) Social Audit Ltd, and Counter Information Services.

Social accounting (or corporate social accounting – CSA) can have one of two meanings in the present context.[2] The most usual meaning is the presentation of financial information, usually in an income statement and balance sheet format, of the costs and benefit impact of an organizations' social behaviour (see Exhibit 1.2). As we shall see later (Chapter 6), enormous effort has been directed towards the production of these 'social accounts'. In the authors' view this is one of the major misguided developments in the subject. A second, less common meaning of social reporting refers to the regular presentation of a formal social report by the accountable organization. Typically, this would take the form of a 'social' statement in the organizations' annual report. It is usually obvious from the context which meaning is intended.

Social audit is the most misused of all the terms. An audit is generally defined as an independent attestation of the veracity of some information. We will use the term in this way to mean an independent opinion expressed on the reasonableness and validity ('truth and fairness') of a social report. However, many authors have used the term as synonymous with social reporting. This is wholly confusing and we will seek to avoid this use other than in proper names (such as Social Audit Ltd).

There is, however, a third use of the term 'social audit' to mean social reports produced by an outside organization. We will generally refer to this as an externally-prepared social report, but the confused use of the term 'social audit' is so pervasive in the literature that some of this confusion must spill over into our discussions (see Chapter 7).

Finally, the word 'audit', in common accounting parlance, is also used for 'internal audit' – the monitoring and assessment of procedures and performance by the management of an organization. Similar reference is also made in social reporting to 'internal social audits' although, again, carelessness in the use of terminology often leads to the omission of the word 'internal'. Internal social audits are not uncommon and have an objective very similar to traditional internal audit except that the emphasis is on the 'social' procedures and performance. These, also, will be touched upon throughout the book.

Before moving on, we should note that in CSR (corporate social reporting) there is often a distinction between reports for internal and external consumption. The distinction closely follows that usually made in accounting between management accounting (information for the managers, directors and other dominant hierarchy of the organization for the purposes of planning for and controlling the organization) and financial reporting (information intended for those 'external' to the organization – including employees outside the dominant hierarchy). While our concentration will be on the second of these, we will look at a number of the more interesting social management reports.

With some clarity of terminology now introduced we can return to the critical issue of 'responsibility' which we raised in the opening pages of the chapter to examine this in some detail.

RESPONSIBILITY – FOR WHAT AND TO WHOM?

In practice it is seldom hard to do one's duty when one knows what it is, but it is sometimes exceedingly difficult to find this out.
                              Samuel Butler, First Principles, *Note Books*, 1912

When we look around the organizations in society we find an inconsistent and erratic set of formally accepted responsibilities. Local Authorities are acknowledged as being responsible for (*inter alia*) caring for the aged and providing education; Water Authorities are responsible for providing a reliable supply of clean water; companies are legally responsible for the financial propriety of their actions and implicitly responsible for making best financial use of the shareholders' funds. The recent growth in legislation and quangos has extended the range of such responsibilities. So companies in the UK, for example, are now required to comply with (*inter alia*):

Responsibility focus

● *Health and Safety at Work Act 1974*   Employees
  Employment Act 1982
  Employment Protection Act 1975

● *Trade Descriptions Act 1968 and 1972*   Consumers
  Fair Trading Act 1973
  Weights and Measures Act 1963

● Scrutiny and Standards of the Water
  Board and the Industrial Air Pollution Inspectorate   Environment

There are problems with identifying the 'responsibility' of any organization because:

● responsibility changes over time and from place to place. It is dependent upon the societal environment of the organization. What might be an acknowledged responsibility now in the UK (for example) might not be acknowledged in the USA or may not have been acknowledged in the UK twenty years ago;
● who determines what responsibilities exist? Because Greenpeace insist that certain whales should be protected, does that automatically impose an immutable responsibility on the whaling nations? Is it necessary for both principal and agent to acknowledge the responsibility, for the said responsibility to exist?[3]

There is no way out of these dilemmas without making certain assumptions. For example, Milton Friedman (e.g. 1971) considers that companies do not have responsibilities beyond that of 'making as much money for their stake-holders as possible'. Kenneth Galbraith (e.g. 1974) believes that they do. Who is right? We could marshall supporters for either side until the cows come home but, in the end, with whom one agreed would depend entirely on one's own personal opinion, and opinions cannot be weighed, like marbles, to find out which are the heaviest. To see this more clearly we should consider the principal arguments which have been marshalled in favour of and in opposition to companies adopting wider social responsibilities.

The debate has been extensive (and at times quite heated) and we can do little more than skim the surface of many of the issues here.[4] Perhaps the simplest way of capturing the flavour of the arguments is for you to imagine you have just joined the audience of the debate (which has been going on for many years) in time for a few summing-up speeches from representatives of what we have identified as the main groups taking part in the debate:

1. The 'pristine-capitalists'. Those who deny the need for responsibility beyond efficient response to the market-place:

> In a free enterprise, private property system, a corporate executive is an employee of the owners of the business. He has a direct responsibility to his employers. That responsibility is to conduct the business in accordance with their desires, which generally will be to make as much money as possible while conforming to the basic rules of society, both those embodied in law, and those embodied in ethical custom.   Friedman, 1970

> There is no reason to think that shareholders are willing to tolerate an amount of corporate non-profit activity which appreciably reduces either dividends or the market performance of the stock.   Hetherington, 1973

2. The 'expedients'. Those who consider that long-term economic welfare and stability can only be achieved by acceptance of certain (usually minimal) wider social responsibilities:

> The important issues involve accommodation between different and often conflicting values. There are the values associated with the market economy – efficiency, freedom, innovation, decentralization, incentive, individual achievement. And there are the values associated with political and social rights – equality of opportunity, the right of an individual to participate in important decision affecting his or her life, the right to standards of health, education, personal privacy and personal dignity. What we are constantly faced with are the difficult choices and trade-offs needed to achieve balance among all these values.   J.G. Clarke, Exxon Corporation, 1981

> Business must learn to look upon its social responsibilities as inseparable from its economic function. If it fails to do so, it leaves a void that will quickly be filled by others – usually by the government.
> George Champion, Chase National Bank, 1966

3. Proponents of the 'social contract'. Those who consider that companies and other large organizations exist at society's will and therefore are beholden to society's wishes:

Any social institution – and business is no exception – operates in society via a social contract, expressed or implied, whereby its survival and growth are based on:
(1) The delivery of some socially desirable ends to society in general and
(2) The distribution of economic, social or political benefits to groups from which it derives its power.
In a dynamic society, neither the sources of institutional power nor the need for its services are permanent. Therefore an institution must constantly meet the twin tests of legitimacy and relevance by demonstrating that society requires its services and that the groups benefitting from its rewards have society's approval.　　　　　　　Shocker and Sethi, 1973, p. 97

... every large corporation should be thought of as a *social enterprise*; that is as an entity whose existence and decisions can be justified in so far as they serve public or social purposes.　　　　　　　R. Dahl, 1972

4. The 'social ecologists'. Those who are concerned for the environment (in the widest sense), see very serious problems developing if something is not done soon, and consider that large organizations have been influential in creating the problems and could be equally influential in helping eradicate them:

The principal defect of the industrial way of life with its ethos of expansion is that it is not sustainable. Its termination within the lifetime of someone born today is inevitable – unless it continues to be sustained for a while longer by an entrenched minority at the cost of imposing great suffering on the rest of mankind. We can be certain, however, that sooner or later it will end (only the precise time and circumstances are in doubt) and that it will do so in one of two ways: either against our will, in a succession of famines, epidemics, social crises and wars; or because we want it to – because we wish to create a society which will not impose hardship and cruelty upon our children – in a succession of thoughtful, humane and measured changes.　　　*The Ecologist*, 1972, p. 15

The rapid succession of crises which are currently engulfing the entire globe is the clearest indication that humanity is at a turning point in its historical evolution. The way to make doomsday prophecies self-fulfilling is to ignore the obvious signs of perils that lie ahead. Our scientifically conducted analysis of long term world development based on all available data points out quite clearly that such a passive course leads to disaster.
　　　　　Mesarovic and Pestel, 1975, as quoted in Robertson, 1978, pp. 22–23

5. The 'socialists'. Those who wish to see the economic and political dominance of capital broken in favour of economic as well as political socialism:

We shrink back from the truth if we believe that the destructive forces of the modern world can be 'brought under control' simply by mobilising more resources – of wealth, education, and research – to fight pollution, to preserve wildlife, to discover new sources of energy, and to arrive at more effective agreements on peaceful co-existence. Needless to say, wealth, education, research, and many other things are needed for any civilisation, but what is most needed today is a revision of the ends which these means are meant to serve. And this implies, above all else, the development of a life-style which accords to material things their proper, legitimate place, which is secondary and not primary.　　　　　　　Schumacher, 1973, p. 290

From the political point of view it is important to emphasize that the problems associated with advanced technology cannot be framed merely in terms of economic categories, concerning solely the ownership and control of the means of production, but challenge the political nature of our social and cultural institutions, that of the concept of the nature of man to which they have given rise, and the technological practices which have been based on them. Institutions that promote social hierarchies must be confronted with demands for the recognition of the equality and shared collective experience of *all* men. Not only must the division of society into oppressors and oppressed be broken down, but so too must the barriers that separate mental activity from manual labour, and abstract theory from concrete practice. Only through such changes can we create a situation that will enable us to reintegrate all aspects of social life and experience and to establish a situation in which man can be liberated to fulfil his full potential as a sensitive, creative and social being.   Dickson, 1974, p. 203

There is much that is persuasive in the arguments of each group. But the extent to which one is persuaded by them depends on one's individual preferences, personal concerns, frame of reference, and on the extent to which one either perceives these issues *as* issues and/or considers extrapolations foretelling social, economic or ecological doom to be accurate and/or important.

We see two possible ways forward. The first is to rely on evidence of *informal* establishment of responsibility. This would arise when an organization adopted some responsibility either voluntarily or as a result of a social pressure that it chose to acknowledge.[4] A considerable proportion of existing social reporting by organizations can be seen as falling into the second half of this category, much of this possibly being an attempt to either anticipate or forestall formal responsibility. The second way forward is to concentrate on the *formal* responsibilities which have been determined by the society as a whole. There can never be any completely accurate specifications of a society's preferences but in the law and (what we might call) 'quasi-law' we find our best (and only) approximation of the established responsibilities of any organization. Formal responsibility is imposed by society at large through government or, in rarer cases, by some body which has been given legitimate authority to impose standards (as, for example, in the case of District Health Authorities and CIPFA/AHST).

We can take these two elements together and thereby assume an empirical basis exists for identifying responsibilities. We also assume (if somewhat heroically) that the market-place and the democratic electoral and legal system function in a desirable manner. As society-as-a-whole would appear not to be overly concerned about such issues as resource depletion, the power of business and business marketing and the status of labour for example, these and other of the more potentially interesting and radical issues would be excluded from the identified set of responsibilities by this approach. Nevertheless, we will also consider the wider range of potential responsibilities where this seems appropriate (but see Tinker, 1985).

It follows that once we have determined the existence of responsibility, we must account for the extent to which that responsibility has been met. How the responsibility is expressed is crucial. If we state that a company has a responsibility to create wealth, we have to find a way of measuring the created wealth. If the responsibility of an organization is to generate improvements in the social welfare and well-being of a society, we will struggle to identify and measure these improvements. Expressions of responsibility couched in vague and general terms have created many of the problems of internal inconsistency and incompleteness revealed in social reports to date. In any event, as theorists have shown, we simply do not have any means of identifying and measuring social welfare or an organizations' contribution to it (see, for example, Arrow 1963). Thus, unless we can either be very specific about the responsibilities of an organization or else explicitly constrain reports in such a way as to ensure that no ambiguity results in the readers' mind, then social reports, no matter how genuinely intended, can always be accused of being biased, selective, partial, subjective and confusing (see Chapters 4 to 7). There is, therefore, a very practical reason for being so concerned with the concept of 'responsibility'. The more precisely it is defined the better the chance that a report will actually relate to it. Reports cannot effectively discharge accountability arising from responsibility if that responsibility is expressed in vague and woolly terms. The import of these questions of responsibility becomes clearer when we examine the objectives held for, and implicit in, CSR.

OBJECTIVES OF CSR

Given the rather contentious and disputed nature of the issues involved in social reporting, it comes as no surprise to find that there is a wide diversity of views on the purpose of the social-reporting process. Much of the failure to find common ground amongst those interested in CSR has arisen because of different (and usually implicit) objectives. If two interested parties, such as customers and employees, each produce a proposal on the sort of social report a particular organization should aim for, it is highly unlikely that the proposals will be fully reconcilable. No amount of argument about the pros and cons of the respective contents and methods will achieve reconciliation where it is the objectives that the proposal seeks to satisfy which are different. The objectives themselves will frequently be predicated upon very different political, social and ethical beliefs about society, organizations, accounting, and so on. Thus, in order to place any particular example of CSR discussion or practice in context, it is first necessary to identify the objectives of the writer(s) or preparer(s) as appropriate.

Perks and Gray (1978) provided a four-way categorization of objectives. This is summarized in Table 1.1.

The 'radical group' is typically (though not necessarily) associated with left wing politics and would generally be categorized by an emphasis on highlighting abuses brought about by the capitalist system. While there is a considerable amount of writing which falls into this category, little of it emerges in the management and accounting literature. Perhaps the best

Table 1.1 The different groups and their underlying objectives for CSR

Groups	Objectives
Radicals	To restructure society typically via attacking and discrediting corporate behaviour
Orthodox/defenders of the status quo	Legitimize, defend and enhance corporate behaviour
Partisan interest groups	Expansion of own 'territory'
The 'accountors'	Fulfilment of responsibility and discharge of accountability

Adapted from Perks and Gray, 1978, p. 4

known examples are the 'anti-reports' produced by Counter Information Services (see Chapter 7).

Perks and Gray suggest that the second category (the 'orthodox group') is the most densely populated. The majority of the company-produced reports could be seen as legitimizing devices, and a great proportion of the writing (for example, Humble, 1973; Hargreaves and Dauman, 1975; CBI, 1973; Jacoby 1973; Linowes, 1972b; Davis and Blomstrom, 1975) seems implicitly to adopt this stance. Other writers who have addressed the question of objectives have tended to concentrate on this group. Heard and Bolce (1981), for example, see CSR as a means whereby companies may seek to avoid increased government legislation. Preston (1981) also concentrated on this second group and identified three objectives:

(i) to improve public relations
(ii) as a response to the demands of specific constituencies
(iii) to increase managerial awareness and responsiveness.

Objectives (i) and (ii) here are clearly in the 'orthodox group'. Objective (iii) (that favoured by Preston) is also in this group because it ensures that power to decide what *is* a responsibility remains with the organization and thus emphasizes internal rather than external reporting, and is unconnected with external accountability and its discharge. A further important point is raised by Preston, namely that attitudes vary considerably from country to country. As Preston himself notes in an earlier piece of research (Preston *et al.*, 1978), the US and Canada (as opposed to, for example, Germany and France) tend to be more concerned with the social posture of organizations and their executives than with the actual reporting of activity. This raises the question of the validity of inter-country comparison. We leave this question for later consideration but raise it now as an important caveat and offer our own hostage to fortune by stating that the authors find the majority of US writing to be far more in the 'orthodox group' than is the case, say, with that from the UK and Europe.

The third category (the 'partisan interest groups') is a fairly heterogeneous category, but for present purposes the most important element of the group are accountants who see a potential for increased territory and employment in the development of CSR. Solomons (1974), Parker (1976), Renshall (1979), and Corbett (1980) are examples of accountants who have demonstrated territorial interest in the subject. Amongst the most obvious indicators to membership of this group are the insistence on the application of traditional financial accounting methods to CSR, the emphasis on income statement and balance sheet formats for reports and a tendency to consider the role of accountants alone in the process of discharging complex accountability despite the wide range of information that would be required. Medawar (1976, 1978c) and Perks and Gray (1979) give words of warning about such myopic and specialized approaches to the issues, not least for the reputation of accountants.

We believe, in contrast, that each society must, as a whole, find a way to uniquely identify the responsibilities that organizations must meet. Then some way must be found to report, as objectively, truthfully and fairly as possible, the extent to which those responsibilities have been met, i.e. to discharge the social accountability. It is our belief that *only* by focusing on responsibility and accountability can we establish any generally acceptable basis for the development of CSR.

Naturally enough, it is not a simple matter to identify the 'accountors'. In retrospect, much of the work of Social Audit Ltd appears to fall in this category. One or two reports produced in the USA, notably those by the Atlantic Richfield Company in 1974 and by Phillips Screw Company in 1973 (see Chapter 5), seem also to fall into this category as they convey a sense of balance and were independently audited – characteristics notably absent from most attempts in the area.

Finally, a brief word about the problems of simple categorization. In the first place, the categories are not discrete. Thus if, for example, the assumption that social reporting will alter the behaviour of the preparers (see, for example, Prakash and Rapapport, 1977) and the users (see, for example, Ramanathan, 1976) of such reports is correct, this will necessarily have some effect on the status quo. Thus any social reporting may partly satisfy the objectives of the radicals even though it was one of the other groups who implemented the report to satisfy their own objectives.

Secondly, one should beware of over-glib categorization. For example, Linowes (1972b), one of the major pioneers of the field, could be equally comfortable in either category (ii) or (iii) as he is both an influential US accountant and explicitly concerned to show the well-behaved company in a good light. Similarly, the work of Medawar and Social Audit Ltd, might be considered by some as better suited to category (i), in that they do state that they are concerned to show a balancing rather than balanced view.

WHOSE JOB IS IT?

Attempting any description of the social impact of organizations involves, however briefly, using the tools of sociology, politics, biology, chemistry, psychology, economics, communication theory, personnel management, statistics, etc. Experts from all these fields can each claim some comparative advantage in the area of CSR, but no one group could hope to cover all the expertise or seriously produce a report without the benefit of the experience of other groups.

As accountants, our focus and interest lies in the social report, as a means of communicating information, and yet much of the likely information to be contained in such a report (e.g. pollution data, health and safety at work data) involves concepts beyond our competence *qua* accountants. So as to avoid falling into the trap we noted in the earlier section on objectives, i.e. of indulging in partisan and myopic assumptions about the accountants' role, we should briefly examine the process of CSR and then establish what the accountant can and cannot do.

A social report may be produced by the organization itself or by an outside body (such as Social Audit Ltd). If the report is internally produced then the accountant is likely to have some involvement, if only because finance (budgeting for the costs of the report, preparing estimates of costs of performing certain social activities) will be involved. To date, those bodies which have produced the reports externally seem not to have found a need for accountants. However, internally-prepared reports, while hardly ubiquitous, are by far the most prevelant.

Unless social reports are to be considered as an extension of traditional reporting (as only a few would suggest, and we believe to be an unlikely and undesirable outcome) then, as we have already noted, much of the information is beyond the accountants' competence. Where however, the accountant *is* likely to be most able to contribute is in the communication and audit process and perhaps, most particularly, in the unique emphasis given by his training and socialization to the entity concept and the reporting of information about that entity. The annual report is an obvious (and not a presently uncommon) medium for the communication of social information. Whatever form the report takes the information will have to be collated, presented and (possibly) audited and the accountant has some skills of importance here.[5]

Nevertheless, three things are quite apparent: (a) social reports can be developed without accountants; (b) many ordinary practising accountants are convinced that CSR is none of their business, and yet (c) accounting academics and practitioners continue to exercise a commitment to the area as revealed by the astonishing plethora of CSR argument and research which is found in accounting literature.

This means, that some accountants are going to proceed with CSR whatever. There *is* no readily available alternative group who are the obvious champions of the cause. There seems no reason why accountants should not seek to develop what is undoubtedly a new, important and difficult area *as long as* they recognize:

● accountants *qua* accountants *are* limited in the requisite skills (but then so is everyone else); and
● as the area develops, new skills and training will become necessary (for more detail see, for example, Birnberg and Ghandi, 1976).

In the end, the simplest explanation for the phenomena of accountants concerning themselves with such a contentious and complex area, when there is no certainty of professional pay-off, is that accounting is about discharging accountability. Financial accounts discharge only a small proportion of an organization's accountability – some new form of accounting is necessary. Put in this way it should come as no surprise that accountants are seeking to develop such a new accounting (see, for example, Francis, 1973).

DIFFERENT APPROACHES TO CSR

Just as there are different approaches to financial reporting theory, so a number of different approaches can be taken to CSR.

The first and simplest basis of accounting is to attempt to describe 'reality', or at least those events which can be objectively captured (e.g. cash transactions). Any form of reporting must contain some correspondence with 'reality' if it is not to be incorrigible. The problems that arise, as much in financial accounting as CSR, are to do with:

● What parts of reality should we attempt to describe? (Cf. the allocation, aggregation and disclosure debates in financial accounting.)
● How should we describe it? (Cf. the HCA, CCA, realizable value etc., debate in financial accounting.)
● What *is* the reality we seek to describe? (E.g. what is profit outside the system used to measure?)

A simple requirement to 'describe reality' is insufficient to determine any accounting method. Some additional criteria are necessary. The most commonly employed in financial reporting is the relevance criterion. A report is supposed to provide information. If information is not to be worthless it must be useable and useful by those parties for whom it is intended. In the case of financial reporting the users are principally the shareholders and their advisors plus others, like bankers and creditors, who have a financial interest in the organization. In CSR the equivalent approach is known as the *stakeholder approach* whereby those with a 'social' interest or 'stake' in the organization should be provided with relevant information in social reports. It is normally assumed that there are four significant groups of stakeholders:

the community with respect to social concerns
the community with respect to environmental concerns
employees
the consumers.

Whilst it is definitionally necessary that information be useful, it is a notoriously difficult task to establish the needs of, and decision models used by, stakeholders. Even in the relatively straightforward case of financial information for shareholders, it is far from clear exactly what reports should contain. In the case of CSR there are additional problems arising from:

- the wide range of potential users;
- the complexities of the issues involved;
- the difficulties (or even near-impossibilities) of measurement;
- the fact that relatively few reports have been produced so that there are, to date, not many actual users.

A considerable amount of additional research must be done in this area before any empirical basis for user-relevant reports can emerge.

There is a further problem with the stakeholder approach, in that it is necessary first to establish that a user or stakeholder has a *right* to particular information for a particular decision. Having performed this difficult task it is then necessary to establish that the user-need overrides constraints of cost, confidentiality, etc.

Using the discharge of accountability as the principal criterion for determining reporting practices overcomes many of these problems without losing any of the essential elements of either the 'reality' approach or the requirement that information be useful. As we have already noted, to discharge accountability one first needs to establish the responsibility for actions of the accounting organization. If this can be done then the form of the report, rather than the content, is the remaining question of moment. In this, relative 'reality' and usefulness of the different forms can be used to choose how information should be presented.

SUMMARY AND CONCLUSIONS

CSR is a complex and wide-ranging subject within which few elements can be treated as uncontentious. In this chapter we have established a basic framework for CSR which we will employ and develop throughout the book. The cornerstone of the framework is the concept of 'accountability' which is a duty imposed upon organizations to provide information about the actions for which they are held responsible. The difficulty lies in identifying these responsibilities and, as we saw, views on this matter differ widely. As a means of bringing some order to this chaos, although it means formally excluding many of the more radical (and interesting) issues, we have decided that the only feasible approach is to deduce the responsibility from parameters of the status quo of the society under consideration. Social actions that lie outside the established responsibility, and radical interpretations of the status quo will be discussed, but we believe can be treated with more clarity when considered in a formal context such as the basic framework proposed here.

Other issues were also considered in the chapter. The objectives underlying a proposal or implicit in a report are closely related to the interpretation of responsibility that one adopts. To derive a generally acceptable basis of CSR, we believe the objective of a report must be the discharge of accountability.

We could debate for hours the propriety of the accountants' involvement in CSR. Recognition of the traditional accountants' limitations in this field is, we believe, essential but (and it is a big but) that need not prevent their involvement in, and successful development of, the subject.

Finally, we briefly considered the 'users' or stakeholders. Seeing accountability as a democratic ideal (Medawar, 1976) and democracy (however defined) as a desirable goal, then 'society-as-a-whole' is the audience for CSR. Although there is some danger in breaking down 'society' into seemingly discrete groups, our problems are more tractable if we think of the community, the employees and the consumers. Remember though, that such groups may be only artifacts and at the heart of CSR is (or perhaps should be) some overriding sense of society-as-a-whole.

NOTES

1. We should note that we have oversimplified this a little. The shareholders hold the implicit contract with the company which in turn holds an explicit contract with directors in the form of their service contracts. The company cannot act as agent, it is inanimate, a legal fiction. It is the directors who 'animate' the company and are thus the owners' agents.
2. 'Social accounting' has also been used by economists to refer to the preparation of National Income Accounts. This meaning is not employed in this book.
3. We should raise a further important distinction at this point between the actions of organizations which are directed towards that organization fulfilling its responsibilities properly and those actions which are proactive and over-and-above any responsibility imposed on the organization. For example, out-of-court settlements and donations to charities to compensate for the failure of an organization's products are part of the discharge of that organization's responsibilities (e.g. Distillers or Ford Motor Company). The donations of a chemical manufacturer (e.g. BP) to an orchestra, or an audit firm (e.g. Arthur Young) to a football club are clearly part of that organization's social actions but are over-and-above any responsibility imposed upon them.
4. A more extensive review of the social responsibility question can be found in Beesley and Evans (1978, Chapters 1 and 2), Strier (1980), and Kempner *et al.* (1976); and a simple overview of the pros and cons of social responsibility and reporting can be found in Gray and Perks (1982).
5. We should perhaps note that the reporting process of our preferred approach – The Compliance-with-Standard Report and Audit – could be almost exclusively under the control of accountants, whereas the data input to the report would be dependent on the acknowledged specialists in the appropriate areas. We believe this overcomes our problems of partisan bias.

Chapter 2

International developments

The purpose of this chapter is to begin the process of reviewing evidence on the practice of corporate social reporting to date. In a book which is both written and published in the UK, the major focus will, inevitably be on past, current and future developments in Britain. Even a xenophobe must, however, recognize that understanding of these is likely to be helped by consideration of overseas practice and policy. Not only are there the more obvious supranational legislative influences (e.g. the EEC) and the influence of cross-border transfers of accounting staff (e.g. by multinational accounting firms), but there are also implicit commonalities in the contexts of accounting which make it likely that there will be similar patterns of development in reporting between the UK and certain other countries. In so far as their accounting contexts are similar, therefore, we might expect to derive predictive lessons for the UK from countries with more 'developed' social reporting practices and vice versa. It is on international practice with special reference to countries with more developed reporting practices, particularly the USA, together with parts of western Europe and the Commonwealth, that this chapter will mainly focus.

SUPRANATIONAL INFLUENCES

There are, of course, institutional reasons why the UK should reflect practice in such countries. In particular the UK is a member of the UN, OECD and EEC whilst its accountants are associated with the International Accounting Standards Committee (IASC), the International Federation of Accountants (IFAC), the Union Européene des Experts Comptables, Economiques et

Financiers (UEC), amongst other bodies. Before considering individual country practices, therefore, some indication should be given of the 'infrastructure' provided for social reporting by these bodies.

As a general rule, CSR in Europe has emphasized the rights and needs of the employee group of stakeholders. This emphasis is also reflected in the UN publication of a *Draft Code of Conduct on Transnational Corporations* in 1982. Amongst other prescriptions for disclosure of information by such (multinational) companies, it includes 'employment information'. Perhaps more significantly, from an accountability point of view it also contains the following paragraph:

> With due regard to the relevant provisions of the ILO Tripartite Declaration of Principles concerning Multinational Enterprises and Social Policy and in accordance with national laws, regulations and practices in the field of labour relations, transnational corporations should/shall provide trade unions or other representatives of employees in their entities in each of the countries in which they operate, by appropriate means of communication, the necessary information on the activities dealt with in this code to enable them to obtain a true and fair view of the performance of the local entity and, where appropriate, the corporation as a whole. Such information should/shall include, where provided for by national law and practices *inter alia*, prospects or plans for future development having major economic and social effects on the employees concerned.   p. 13

These recommendations are not (yet) mandatory but their existence could clearly influence individual companies practice. The ILO Tripartite Declaration mentioned in the quotation has had a more tangible effect in the UK in leading to the Department of Industry publication *International Investment: guidelines for multinational enterprises* (1976, Cmnd. 6525) which requests multinational enterprises to give consideration, *inter alia*, to the aims and priorities of the countries within which they operate with respect to economic and social progress, protection of the environment and creation of employment opportunities. Cooperation with the local community and business interests is also to be encouraged and other aspects of fair business practices which should be followed are listed. Certain information relevant to these aims is recommended for publication at least annually.

Again, this represents a purely voluntary set of guidelines at present, transmitted to the UK as a result of its membership of the OECD. By the same route, but arising out of the membership of the UK in the EEC, has come a set of guidelines relating to companies with interests in South Africa. This 'Code of Conduct' (Cmnd. 7233, 1978) requests that the Annual Report or Chairman's Statement of such companies should contain a reference to the public availability of reports submitted to the Department of Trade in compliance with the code. These reports are intended to provide information about employment practices of subsidiaries and associated companies with respect to black workers in South Africa.

Whilst the UK's membership of these international bodies has not yet resulted in any significant imposition of mandatory social accounting or accountability requirements on UK-based companies, some slight extension of employment reporting has occurred as a result of EEC membership (via the *Companies Act 1981*).

In general, the accounting profession in Europe has shown little inclination towards assuming a leading role in the development of social reporting theory and practice, although one rare example is provided by a report of the social reporting working party of the UEC to its 1983 Congress in Strasbourg. The Working Party's report suggested a standardized structure for social reporting (see Figure 2.1).

1. **A summarized statement** An outline of the most significant aspects of the social performance of the enterprise over the year together with a statement of principal objectives and review of prospects for the following year.
2. **A social report** To be composed solely of quantitative indicators, the precise nature of which is not specified, in the following nine areas:
   - (a) Employment levels
   - (b) Working conditions
   - (c) Health and safety
   - (d) Education and training   The relationship between the
   - (e) Industrial relations   enterprise and the work-force
   - (f) Wages and other employee benefits
   - (g) Distribution of value added
   - (h) Impact on the environment
   - (i) The enterprise and external parties   The relationship between the
         (shareholders and other providers of   enterprise and society
         capital, local and national government,
         customers and suppliers)
3. **Notes to the accounts** Explaining where necessary the methods and principles used in calculating the figures appearing in the social report, giving full information on any changes of method and indicating the effect of the change on the results shown, and defining terminology used.

Figure 2.1 UEC's recommended form of social reporting

New ground was also broken in the report with the suggestion that social accounts should be subject to independent audit. In particular it is argued that the auditor should be able to ensure that a satisfactory system of internal control is in existence to safeguard the quality and reliability of social information produced, confirm that the definitions and methods of calculation used are acceptable, verify that figures used in the social report agree with those in financial and technical reports, and certify the truth and fairness of any financially quantified information.

The overriding theme of the UEC report is that to gain credibility, the production of social information must be tackled with the same degree of rigour as that applied to the more traditional financial statements. Hence the emphasis on formal structure and the audit function. Whether such a formalized approach to social reporting is practicable on a wide scale is of course very much open to doubt. However, given the enthusiasm for harmonization within the EEC, it is perhaps unwise to ignore European developments in social reporting of which the UEC report represents a rare supranational example.

As indicated earlier, it is not just to Europe that we should necessarily look for indicators as to how reporting practices could develop in the UK. In this century at least, advances in accounting theory and practice have often seemed to be a one-way transatlantic flow, out of the USA. Conversely, ideas which may have originated in the UK or USA have often been adopted and adapted in Commonwealth countries, generating lessons for both donors and recipients. To identify these, we now turn to social reporting experience in individual countries.

UNITED STATES OF AMERICA

As compared with the UK, corporate social reporting has had a much higher profile in the USA, especially in the last two decades. Evidence quoted below also suggests that such reporting has also achieved greater penetration of the business sector there. This is not to say, however, that the practice of social reporting in the USA has necessarily always been, in both depth and breadth, in advance of that in the UK, even in recent years.

To generalize, in terms of the stakeholder model, US practice has tended to be directed towards the interests of the general public and consumers rather than towards employees as in the UK and Europe. In part, this may be explained in terms of differing dominant social concerns – the impacts of consumerism, equal rights and the ecological movement in the US, compared with the impact of the trade union movement in the UK.

Whatever the initial stimuli may have been, institutional accounting involvement in social reporting in the USA has been notable. Both the American Institute of Certified Public Accountants (AICPA) and the National Association of Accountants, on the practising side of the profession have sponsored research and publications in the field, as has the American Accounting Association on the academic side. Such work has been based on both theoretical analysis and actual organizational reporting experience. To give a flavour of the breadth and depth of social reporting practice, we may refer to a survey of practice carried out on an annual basis by the accounting firm of Ernst and Ernst. Unfortunately, the last such survey was published in 1978 – the results of which are quoted in Table 2.1. In this survey, it was found that in the annual reports of the Fortune 500 Industrials, there were 446 (89.2%) companies making social responsibility disclosures. Relative to the 500 companies in the sample, the types of disclosure made and their frequencies are indicated in Table 2.1.

Identification and classification of social reporting information is notoriously subjective and difficult, for reasons indicated throughout this book, but the data quoted in Table 2.1 nevertheless appear to indicate a significant involvement on the part of large US industrial companies in social reporting.

It might be expected that the sample of large companies analyzed would not be representative of the corporate sector as a whole. Smaller companies may have a lesser range of experiences to report and are generally of lesser social significance, quite apart from any greater reluctance they may feel about making such disclosures. However, in another sense the Fortune 500

Table 2.1

CSR information	Number of companies disclosing
A Environment	
1. Pollution control	222
2. Prevention or repair of environmental damage	25
3. Conservation of natural resources	65
4. Other environmental disclosures	76
B Energy	
5. Conservation	210
6. Energy efficiency of products	75
7. Other energy related disclosures	48
C Fair business practices	
8. Employment of minorities	87
9. Advancement of minorities	78
10. Employment of women	81
11. Advancement of women	237
12. Employment of other special interest groups	30
13. Support for minority businesses	30
14. Socially responsible practices abroad	71
15. Other statements on fair business practices	173
D Human resources	
16. Employee health & safety	115
17. Employee training	133
18. Other human resource disclosures	54
E Community involvement	
19. Community activities	93
20. Health related activities	59
21. Education and the arts	116
22. Other community activity disclosures	93
F Products	
23. Safety	70
24. Reducing pollution from product use	37
25. Other product related disclosures	77
G Other social responsibility disclosures	
26. Other disclosures	94
27. Additional information	26

Source: Ernst & Ernst, 1978.

data are likely to be an under-representation of corporate social reporting in the USA. The provision of special-purpose information to specific stakeholder groups is, for instance, not covered. No recent evidence is available on the provision of information by companies to their individual employees (comparable to that on 'employee reporting' in the UK) although analysis of available literature indicates this practice has about as long a history in both countries.

In another respect, 'human resource'-related information (information about employees, classified here as part of social reporting) is potentially much more freely available in the US than in the UK, although again there is a lack of recent empirical evidence on the actual extent of such disclosures. This arises out of the 'Taft-Hartley Act' (the *Labor–Management Relations Act 1947*) and interpretations of that Act by the National Labor Relations Board and courts. The provision of certain information to unions by employers has been deemed to be part of the necessity for bargaining 'in good faith'. Whilst the scope of these interpretations is complex, it appears to have been generally accepted that 'Labour force data' are obtainable on demand by the union negotiators.

Thus, through the medium of both annual corporate reports and collective bargaining, information on corporate social performance appears to be more readily available in the USA than other comparable countries. In part this could be due to cultural characteristics – the notion of an 'open society' and 'freedom of information' can be traced back to the US Constitution. Another set of explanations, however, can be derived from the link between financial performance and social performance.

In one direction, the creation of economic wealth gives scope for greater alleviation of negative externalities (pollution control etc.) and positive social contributions (e.g. charitable donations, employee welfare).

An equally likely scenario, however, is that social performance may be viewed as a means of achieving better economic performance. This could occur either directly, where present 'social' expenditures create increased financial performance in the longer term (e.g. employee training), or indirectly where such expenditures postpone or alleviate the effects of externally imposed controls on corporate performance (e.g. tighter regulations on pollution). In either event, CSR can be justified from an organizational self-interest point of view.

Whether or not this self-interested as opposed to accountability-based motivation dominates amongst socially reporting companies in the US is an empirical question, to which a number of studies have been directly or indirectly addressed. For example, Williams (1980) in a laboratory-type study based on practising managers, found a majority in favour of companies adopting an active social role. Nevertheless, there is now a significant amount of evidence to indicate that even economic wealth maximizers should engage in (selective) social reporting in the USA.

Given the efficiency of stock markets in processing publicly available information, studies have found that corporate social reporting has information content, i.e. it affects share prices. For example, for companies in the same (systematic) risk class, Anderson and Frankle (1980) found socially disclosing portfolios to outperform (in terms of returns to investors) non-disclosing portfolios. Given also the prevalence of a link (either formal or informal) between managerial rewards and company share performance, this suggests that managers, on rational economic grounds, should be concerned with social reporting (and presumably with the activities which underlie it). Thus for the US in particular there are seemingly strong grounds for not rejecting the hypothesis that social reporting may be viewed as instrumental to self-interest rather than reflecting social concern *per se*.

COMMONWEALTH COUNTRIES

Historical analysis suggests that corporate reporting practices in the UK and Commonwealth countries should show strong similarities as a result of many shared influences (legislation, institutional traditions, immigration and emigration etc.), values and beliefs. Since the end of empire, however, other geographical and political relationships may have become dominant. For example, Canadian practice on CSR now broadly follows the American pattern, at least as far as external reporting is concerned (Maxwell and Mason, 1976).

More interestingly perhaps, recent Australian experience appears to reflect something of a mixture of UK and US approaches to CSR. Thus, some considerable interest seems to have been taken in employee reporting (Craig and Hussey, 1980), whilst the general level of corporate social reporting approaches that in the USA. Thus a survey of 1977 annual reports found that 69% of the one hundred largest Australian listed companies made social responsibility disclosures (Trotman, 1979).

One interesting 'outlier' which might be mentioned is the presence in the Indian public sector of an experiment in producing a full set of social accounts (on the lines of the Abt initiative in the US): the Cement Corporation of India, part of whose corporate report is reproduced in Chapter 1. Whilst such extensive social reporting practice is probably untypical both of India and other developing countries, it does draw attention to the possibilities as well as the potential for such reporting in a context where social performance may be both more divergent from (private) financial performance and of greater national significance than in developed countries.

Teoh and Thong (1984) draw attention to this significance of corporate social reporting for developing countries in a study of practices in Malaysia, although they report that 'predominantly foreign-owned companies were marginally ahead of Malaysian-owned companies in reporting social performance' (p. 204). In addition their finding that 'relatively greater corporate attention was directed to improving human resources and product/service to consumers compared to rendering community related services or alleviating environmental deterioration' (p. 205) suggests that a self-interest, investor–manager focus, rather than accountability motivation, dominates.

DEVELOPMENTS IN WESTERN EUROPE

Developments in CSR in Western Europe have been greatly influenced by a continuing debate concerning the status of labour and its position in the enterprise. This influence may be seen in the EEC Commission's adoption of the Fifth Directive on employee participation[1] and the Vredeling proposals for giving information rights to employees of 'large' companies. The latter proposals would impose upon multinational and national companies, with at

least 1,000 employees in the Community, an obligation to provide workers
with information, at least annually, on (a) the financial situation of their
employing enterprise; (b) probable business development; (c) production
and sales; (d) probable manpower trends; and (e) investment prospects.
Management would also be obliged to inform employee representatives of
any proposed action liable to have serious consequences for employees, and
to consult them at least thirty days before implementation of such decisions.

In Western Europe as a whole, concern with the enterprise–employee
relationship has tended to dominate the development of social reporting,
with much of the information produced on the social performance of companies focusing on the human resource. This does not mean to say, however,
that Europe has adopted a common, unified approach to social reporting,
and indeed there are major differences in approach between the states of
mainland Europe. This may be illustrated by considering developments taking place in France, the Federal Republic of Germany, and Sweden: three
countries which have been to the forefront in debate concerning issues of
corporate social accountability and reporting.

France: external reporting[2] – the legislative approach

The events of 1968, marked particularly by widespread strikes, plant occu-
pations and student riots, led to a major reappraisal of the role and social
responsibilities of business enterprises in French society. Thus, for example,
in 1970 the French Employers National Council (CNPF) officially acknowledged that the management of human resources could not be neglected to
the benefit of business and economy (Rey, 1978), and during the early 1970s
a growing number of companies began the practice of issuing voluntary
social reports, largely concerned with employment issues, on a regular basis.
In 1975 a further major development took place with the publication of the
Sudreau Report – the recommendations of a working party under the chairmanship of Pierre Sudreau which was set up by President Valery Giscard
d'Estaing to generate proposals for the reform of the enterprise. Although
the report's recommendations were extremely wide-ranging, covering matters such as shareholder protection, relations with consumers and the environment, inflation accounting, regional development and the promotion of
small businesses, the main thrust of the recommendations concerned the
relationship between the enterprise and employees. In particular much attention was directed towards improving working conditions together with
employee consultation and information rights. In the latter context it was
recommended that each enterprise produce an annual social balance sheet
based on indicators of its social and working conditions. This particular
recommendation was immediately taken up by the French government and a
bill was passed on 12 July 1977, requiring companies with more than seven
hundred and fifty employees to publish social balance sheets in 1979. This
requirement was extended to companies employing more than three hundred
people in 1982 so that now more than 7,000 French companies produce an
annual social balance sheet.

French social balance sheets are exclusively concerned with employment related issues. Information has to be provided under the following seven headings:

number employed
wages and fringe benefits
health and safety conditions
other working conditions
education and training
industrial relations
other matters relating to the quality of working life

to cover the current year and two preceding years.

A decree of 8 December 1977 lists the information to be included under the above headings, which varies according to the size of the company and the economic sector in which it operates.[3] It is common practice, for example, for the social balance sheets of larger companies to run to forty or fifty pages of statistical analysis relating solely to employment data. Much use also tends to be made of techniques such as pie charts and bar diagrams in order to present an intelligible outline of major developments to the less sophisticated reader. Recent social balance sheets published by the Société Lyonnaise des Eaux et de l'Eclairage, a public utilities concern, provide a good example of the level of detail presented by leading companies in the field.

The preparation of social balance sheets is a management responsibility, although an initial draft must be presented to the Works Council (Comité d'Enterprise) for comment and the expression of an opinion prior to subsequent publication. Whereas management may consider any such opinion expressed, they alone are responsible for the final draft which is, incidentally, not subject to an independent audit. Whilst much of the information contained in the social balance sheet concerns matters of particular interest to the work-force, and copies are made available to any employee requesting them, the document is also widely circulated amongst shareholders and other interested parties.

According to Rey (1978), publication of social balance sheets should encourage the spread of useful information to interested parties – not only employees but also shareholders. Furthermore:

> Because the social balance sheet meets the needs for information and provides quantitative unbiased data to each party, it will be easier for them to enter negotiations and reach a mutual agreement. ... As discussions occur within the Comité d'Enterprise, parties will finally be induced to analyze the actions to be taken and to perform social planning while examining the past.   p. 134

Whilst such statements deserve some scepticism (e.g. What is meant by unbiased?), publication of such indicators over a three-year period should presumably be helpful for appreciating changes occurring whilst also providing some possible insights for planning future courses of action.

Little empirical evidence is available yet to indicate whether publication of social balance sheets has had much practical impact along the lines indicated by Rey, although early work by Danziger and Scheid (1980) suggested that workers' committees made little use of information contained in social balance sheets, and appeared overwhelmed by the mass of data presented to them. However, as Danziger and Scheid point out, it is only in the years after 1980, when a full three years data are available, that workers' representatives will be able to fully appreciate the variations of the indicators and thus to formulate their own opinion upon the social policy of the firm.

One possible drawback to the French legalistic approach, indicated by Rey, is that it represents an early concentration on a relatively narrow range of indicators which could stifle and inhibit future experimentation in the production of relevant social information. However, the development of surplus accounting – a form of corporate reporting now utilized by several nationalized concerns in France as well as a few private firms, notably British Petroleum France – suggests this fear may prove unfounded. Surplus accounting seeks to show the effect on profit of price and quantity changes in inputs and outputs, analyzes the impact of price changes in terms of their effect on benefits or costs to different stakeholders (such as customers, suppliers and employees) and focuses on productivity increases during the year by analyzing the impact of increases in input and output quantities. The possible advantages of this method as a form of social reporting are discussed in Chapter 6.

The Federal Republic of Germany: external reporting – the voluntary approach[4]

Despite the absence of any statutory provisions, many German companies have a long tradition of social reporting in the sense of reporting on company-employee relations. A survey of 296 company annual reports, mostly published in 1973, conducted by Brockhoff (quoted in Schreuder, 1979) indicated that no fewer than 205 of them contained a clearly identifiable 'social' section (*sozialbericht*). However, new ground was broken in 1972 with the publication by STEAG AG, an energy company based in Essen, of a *sozialbilanz* which represented an attempt to present the firm's performance and results as they affected the total societal environment, rather than merely the employee group. Since that time, latest available figures (UEC, 1983) indicate that some forty, for the most part large German companies, have published such a *sozialbilanz*: the first major companies to do so being mainly those in the chemical and oil industries.

Three different approaches towards the production of social reports can be clearly identified:
1. A broadly-based and partially integrated social cost-benefit reporting system. Reports of this type, notable examples of which are those of STEAG and Saabergwerke AG, attempt to relate corporate expenditure to specific societal benefits (e.g. disclosing expenditure incurred on anti-pollution measures, etc.). Drawbacks to this approach are that whereas private

| Performances | Costs of STEAG | | | | Benefits for society in catchwords |
	1972/1973 MDm	1971/1972 MDm	Change MDm	%	
A Inner constituency					
– Performances for employees	49.37	52.80	−3.43	−6.5	Income rises
– Addition to the general reserves	9.50	8.11	1.39	17.1	Security of work through growth and reservation
	58.87	60.91	−2.04	−3.3	
B Outer constituency					
– Performances for research and development	9.20	8.25	0.95	11.5	Security of energy supply and abatement of pollution
– Anti-pollution measures at existing plants	11.02	10.34	0.68	6.6	Abatement of emissions
– Relations with the public	17.24	16.81	0.43	2.6	Fostering of public goals
C Total of the performances					These performances are set against an unchanged dividend of 10 million Dm (10%) to stockholders
Inner and outer constituency	96.33	96.31	0.02	0.02	The price of energy remained with an increase of 6.6% in 12 years almost constant

Exhibit 2.1 Summary of STEAG social report for 1972–1973. Source: Dierkes, M., Corporate social reporting in Germany: conceptual developments and practical experience, *Accounting, Organizations and Society*, Vol. 4, no. 1/2, 1979, p.93. Copyright Pergamon Press; reproduced by permission.

corporate costs incurred can be stated more or less exactly, societal benefits cannot be satisfactorily quantified, and are therefore stated verbally only, whilst societal costs themselves are completely omitted.

2. An extension of the traditional employee orientated *sozialbericht*, by including more information, largely verbal, on the wider societal aspects of the company's activities. Notable examples of reports employing this essentially incremental approach include those of Rank Xerox Gmbh and Bertelsmann AG.

3. Corporate goal accounting and reporting in which quantitative indicators are used wherever possible to describe the attainments of corporate objectives in areas of social performance (such as consumer and employee relations) and promotion of the general public welfare. This particular concept has been championed in particular by Deutsche Shell AG, extracts from whose 1975 report are given in Exhibit 2.2. The concept of goal accounting and reporting has attracted much attention in the academic literature with writers such as Jaggi (1980) and Dierkes (1979) in particular

THE GOALS OF SHELL'S CORPORATE POLICY

Every company in a free market must achieve a reasonable return on the capital that has been invested, to a large degree, at high risk. On the other hand, we are aware of our responsibility in a social market economy and, besides its purely economic activities, we see the company as a part of society, as the employer of those working for us, as a part of the whole. As long ago as 1974 we laid down in our principles of management the following five goals. Each carries the same weight, but they do not always operate in the same direction.

- Supplying the consumer on conditions determined by the market;
- Developing new applications of techniques and products;
- Achieving a reasonable return on investment;
- Taking into account our employees' interests;
- Paying regard to the general public welfare.

This overall objective explains why we have extended the Annual Report, which was in the main a report intended for the shareholders, to include a complete account of the degree to which all five of these corporate goals have been achieved.

Table of Contents

Social accounts

RELATIONS TO PERSONNEL

		Report page	P & L position	Cost (000 DM) 1975	Cost (000 DM) 1974
I	Wages	24	16	60,725	58,894
	Salaries		16	133,249	131,341
Total I				**193,974**	**190,235**
II	Benefits accruing directly to employees (excl. wages and salaries)				
	1. General				
	(a) Christmas bonus (13th month)		16	16,055	15,764
	(b) Holiday pay		17	5,750	4,590
	(c) State-sponsored saving scheme (employer contribution)		16	3,099	3,262
	(d) other (incl. rebate on Shell products)		1 and 26	1,821	1,753
	2. For special reasons				
	(a) Suggestion scheme	28	16	90	64
	(b) Long-service bonus		16	300	395
	(c) Birth grant		18	32	32
	(d) Marriage grant		18	173	131
	(e) Work safety competition	26/28	16	646	712
	(f) Rent subsidies		16	398	424
Total II				**28,364**	**27,127**
III	Benefits accruing indirectly to employees				
	(a) Employer contribution – pension insurance				
	(b) Employer contribution – health insurance		14,16,17	20,857	13,852
	(c) Employer contribution – unemployment insurance				
	(d) Employer's liability insurance		17	1,670	1,643
	(e) Work undertaken for company health scheme (salaries, rent etc.)		various	622	612
Total III				**23,149**	**16,107**
IV	Benefits accruing directly to personnel as a group				
	1. (a) Company medical service	28		806	799
	(b) Accident prevention	26–28	various	2,000	2,000
	(c) Holiday homes			130	112
	(d) Subsidies to sports associations	25		514	493
				3,450	3,404
	2. Education and training				
	(a) Training centre			523	546
	(b) Language courses	25	various	64	46
	(c) Other training			1,401	1,372
	(d) Trainees and apprentices			1,136	1,289
				3,124	3,253

					1975	1974
	3. Other					
	(a) Works clothes			26	624	538
	(b) Cost of canteen			26	4,023	4,400
					4,647	4,938
Total IV					**11,221**	**11,595**
V	Benefits to pensioners and dependants					
	(a) Pension payments				27,030	22,772
	(b) Transfer to pension reserves		24	18	77,329	74,107
	(c) Insolvency insurance				669	74,017
Total V					**105,028**	**96,789**
VI	Works councils			various	1,579	1,559
	Relations with Personnel					
Total I – VI					**363,315**	**343,412**
	Less double counting (especially personnel costs)				(6,507)	(7,012)
					356,808	336,400

ATTENTION TO PUBLIC CONCERNS

		Report page	P & L position	1975	1974
I	Relations to the consumer				
	(a) Research and development	18/19	various	35,717	32,578
	(b) Cost to secure supplies	11		NA	NA
Total I				**35,717**	**32,578**
II	Relations to environment				
	(a) Air purification				
	(b) Noise control				
	(c) Preservation of the countryside	33/34	various	62,000	NA
	(d) Waste-water control				
Total II				**62,000**	**NA**
III	Relations to the public				
	(a) Youth work	30/31	various	722	590
	(b) Donations and charitable contributions	32	26	390	363
	(c) Publications etc.	28/29	various	1,791	2,697
	(d) Taxation and rates (incl. capital gains tax)	35	24 a,b,c	138,870	209,782
	(e) Subscriptions to associations, institutes etc.		26	5,225	4,705
	(f) Other contributions		26	3,721	2,786
Total III				**150,719**	**220,923**
Total I – III				**248,436**	**253,501**
	Less double counting				(10,747)	(11,109)
				237,689	**242,392**

Exhibit 2.2 Some financial statements in the Deutsche Shell report for 1975 (translation by Van den Bergh, 1976). Source: Schreuder, H., Corporate social reporting in the Federal Republic of Germany: an overview, *Accounting, Organizations and Society*, Vol. 4, no 1/2, 1979, pp. 117–9. Copyright Pergamon Press; reproduced by permission.

identifying this approach as being the most fruitful for further experimentation and development. However, as Jaggi points out, the present state of development of goal accounting and reporting is not such as to permit it being described as a fully comprehensive form of social reporting. In common with other forms of reporting the overriding emphasis is still placed on the employee constituency, whilst physical and social environmental issues have attracted much less attention.[5]

In addition to the practical advances outlined above a number of theoretical developments in the area of social reporting are of German origin. Notable amongst these is the work of Eichhorn (reported in Schreuder, 1979)[6] who, employing concepts from the field of welfare economics, constructed models for a social profit and loss account, analogous to the traditional profit and loss account, and societal balance sheet, showing both human and public assets and liabilities. Much theoretical work has also been performed at institutions such as the 'Business and Society' Foundation in Frankfurt, an institution established by business leaders to study important social developments affecting the business community; the Social and Behavioural Science Division of the Battelle Institute in Frankfurt; and the government-sponsored International Institute for Environment and Society at the Science Centre in Berlin. It is also interesting to note that in Germany, unlike the United Kingdom, business enterprise itself has shown great interest in the development of the concept of social reporting. A particularly influential group were the Study Group on Practical Aspects of Social Reporting (*Arbeitskreis Sozialbilanzen Praxis*), established by seven leading companies in the field who, recognizing a need for consensus and standardization in social reporting, developed the following formal structure and content for such reports in 1977:

● A social report, providing primarily verbal descriptions of goals, actions taken and achievements in areas of social concern.
● A value added statement, indicating the company's contibution to GNP and its distribution amongst the various stakeholders.
● A social account, providing a quantitative presentation of all measurable societally orientated corporate expenditures and revenues.

Despite this initiative, available empirical evidence still points to a wide variety amongst published reports with respect to concepts employed, areas of concern considered and indicators used (Dierkes, 1979).

In view of the active involvement of business enterprise in the practical and theoretical development of corporate social accounting in Germany, it is perhaps surprising that there has been a marked lack of interest amongst accountants at institutional level in the field. A similar lack of interest has apparently been displayed by shareholders and citizen action groups (Ullmann, 1979), with only trade union organizations making their views known. Initial union reaction was hostile, the published opinion of the German Federation of Trade Unions (*Deutsche Gewerkschaftsbund*) in early

1977 being that social reports were merely corporate public relations exercises disclosing inadequate information whilst using pseudo-objective terminology. However, since this initially negative response the union side has shown some interest in entering into a dialogue with management concerning the objectives of social reporting. For example one trade union published an anti-report to the 1976 BASF report (Exhibit 2.3) which challenged the indicators used by management, calculations presented and results reported, whilst other labour union publications have questioned some methodological aspects of the preparation of value added statements (see Ullmann, 1979).

BASF	Anti-BASF
Environment: figures about pollution abatement control measures	No distinction is made between legally required measures taken and voluntary actions
Investments: 71% of the investments occurred in Germany, mainly in the BASF A.G.	When related to the size of the labor force, investments in BASF A.G. are below average (45% of total investments vs 47% total labor force) in contrast to foreign investments (29 vs 21%)
Foreign investments contribute positively to the domestic employment situation (figures 1971–1976)	Taking 1974 as the initial year, domestic employment has decreased whilst foreign employment has increased
Distribution of value added: employees received 72%, capital owners 14% of the net value added	The figures published do not reflect reality. Based on speculative calculations, only 16% of the profits are declared. Based on this, the distribution goes as follows: employees 50%, capital owners 40% and the state 10%

Exhibit 2.3 Some results of the BASF and anti-BASF social reports. Source: Ullmann, A.A., Corporate social reporting: political interests and conflicts in Germany, *Accounting, Organizations, and Society*, Vol. 4, no. 1⁄2, 1979, p.129. Copyright Pergamon Press; reproduced by permission.

A later publication by a social reporting working party of the *Deutsche Gewerkschaftsbund* in 1979 developed a set of indicators for inclusion in social reports, which whilst mainly concerned with employment issues also dealt with factors such as environmental pollution and corporate contribution to societal goals such as regional development (see Ullmann, 1979).

As may be seen from the above, all too brief, review of developments it is clear that Germany has contributed significantly to both the theory and practice of social reporting. Indeed, UK companies contemplating undertaking reporting initiatives would undoubtedly benefit from a closer study of German experiences in the area!

Sweden: internal social reporting

Developments in France and Germany have mainly centred on external corporate reporting, however writers such as Preston (1981) have argued that the value of corporate social reporting activity depends essentially on its usefulness to management for purposes of monitoring and, where appropriate, altering such performance. Thus,

> ... external reporting should be encouraged wherever possible, but such external reports should – precisely as in the case of financial data – constitute summaries drawn from more detailed and comprehensive information systems designed for use by internal management.   p. 258

The importance of social information for internal decision-making purposes has indeed been recognized in Sweden, where despite some experimentation with external reporting[7] the focus of interest has tended to be on the use of such information by management rather than external stakeholders. However, like in France and Germany, information produced has focused almost exclusively on the areas of industrial relations and employee welfare. Companies such as AB Volvo, Astra AB and ASSI, part of the state holding group Statsforetag AB, have been particularly active in developing administrative systems which attempt to integrate personnel reporting into the rest of the management information system (Burchell, 1980). Allied to this development has been the incorporation in co-determination agreements of provisions giving trade unions the right to use employee consultants (*arbeitstagarkonsulter*), accountants working on behalf of unions who have rights of access to corporate financial and economic information similar to those of the auditor in this country. Such agreements were entered into in the public sector, banks and insurance companies in the late 1970s (Kjellen, 1980).

A particularly interesting example of the use of social information for managerial decision-making purposes is provided by the Volvo Company, where a social accounting model has been developed which is capable of providing a preliminary account of the economic and social effects resulting from personnel turnover and absenteeism.[8] The work of Volvo was based on the premise that priorities for investment should take into account investments in a better physical and mental working environment.

Such a need became apparent after observing particularly high rates of personnel turnover in the most rapidly expanding production units. Recognizing the fact that high rates of personnel turnover resulted in increased costs for the company, efforts were made to financially quantify such effects and to similarly quantify savings that could be achieved if investment in preventative measures designed to improve working conditions and eliminate monotonous tasks was undertaken.

Initially, case studies were undertaken to broaden the information base for decision making and develop a model for future use. One such case study centred on the Skövde Plant, one department of which, the petrol engine block refinery, can be used for illustrative purposes. Prior to any change in the production process this department employed forty-four people in total on two shifts. Personnel turnover in 1973 was 77% and absenteeism 13.3% with resultant production losses. A decision was made in 1974 to mechanize the process, eliminating hard monotonous work whilst retaining more skilled tasks, such as quality inspection and rectification. Due to mechanization, employment fell by 36% whilst personnel turnover fell to 44% and absenteeism to 8.5%. An attitude survey conducted after the change indicated that employees perceived their status to have increased and job position, together with noise levels and air pollution, to have improved, although there was some evidence of mechanization causing more stress. An economic calculation of gains stemming from lower turnover and absenteeism, particularly in the areas of quality control and production, indicated a total saving of Skr 329,100 together with gains from direct rationalization of employment amounting to Skr 850,000 (see Exhibit 2.4). The social accounting calculations of Exhibit 2.4 were extended to include the consequences for the community and the state of the reductions in personnel turnover and absenteeism in terms of savings in governmental and community spending to alleviate resultant social problems, and additional tax revenue (Exhibit 2.5).

	Cost reduction (Skr.)	
	Lower personnel turnover	Lower absenteeism
Recruitment	24,000	—
Training	16,500	—
Overtime	10,300	10,300
Quality	216,000	—
Production losses	26,000	26,000
Total	292,800	36,300

Exhibit 2.4   Economic calculation of the gains due to lower turnover and absenteeism. Source: Jonson, L.C., Jonsson, B., and Svennson, G., The application of social accounting to absenteeism and personnel turnover, *Accounting, Organizations, and Society*, Vol. 3, no. 3⁄4, 1978, p.265. Copyright Pergamon Press; reproduced by permission

As Jonson *et al.* (1978) point out, this extension of the model may prove to be an effective vehicle for opening up communication between the company and its stakeholders. For example, it may provide a suitable basis for discussing manpower problems and labour market policies with external organizations, including public authorities. As such it indicates a possible external

	Summary of decreased demand on financial resources (Skr.)
	Refinery department
STATE	
Decreased sickness pay	15,500
Increased taxes due to:	
– higher income	345
– productivity increase	314,700
Total	330,545
MUNICIPALITY	
Increased taxes due to:	
– higher income	580
– productivity increase	217,900
Total	218,480
Total societal effects in terms of reduction of financial resources	549,025
SAVINGS IN REAL PRODUCTION COSTS	
Lower absenteeism and turnover	329,100
Rationalization	850,000
Total	1,179,100

Exhibit 2.5 Social accounting of societal consequences. Source: Jonson *et al.*, *op. cit.*, p.266.

role for social accounting techniques originally developed for management decision-making purposes.

As well as these examples of France, Germany and Sweden, developments in social reporting have taken place in other European countries, notably the Netherlands. Social reporting there has a long tradition, the first report being that of the Gist-Brocades company in 1959, with latest estimates putting the number of companies producing an annual report at over two hundred. Again, these reports, which are produced voluntarily, concentrate on relations between the company and its employees and are, as in France, mainly directed to the employee constituency.[9] Additionally, Dutch companies are required by law to disclose a wide range of financial and manpower information to works councils. A further interesting development in the Netherlands is provided by the inclusion of trade union representatives on the Dutch equivalent of the Accounting Standards Committee; the government backed Council for Annual Reporting.

Developments in Belgium have largely followed the Dutch pattern in that companies are obliged to provide a wide range of corporate information to works councils. Surveys by Theunisse (1979) and Delmot (1983) also indicate that many Belgian companies provide some social data in their annual published reports, mostly non-financially quantified and dealing with employment issues. In addition, Delmot's survey suggests that a growing number of companies are providing a separate social report for their work-forces, which again concentrates on employment information.

Elsewhere in Europe corporate social reports tend to be more isolated phenomena, depending solely on individual initiatives. Notable examples here are a report produced in 1978 by Migros (the largest conglomerate in the Swiss service industry) which dealt with the firm's relations with em-ployees, customers and the environment in some detail, and the 216-page report produced in 1978 by the Spanish Banco de Bilbao, *Balance Social del Banco de Bilbao*. The latter document included details of revenue generated and its distribution, personnel, shareholders and the relations of the bank with its clients and society in general including a breakdown of the data by region.

SUMMARY AND CONCLUSIONS

In looking at practice in corporate social reporting in the US, some Commonwealth countries and Western Europe excluding Britain, what has become apparent is the diversity of aims, target audiences, and practices which have been shown to be feasible for such reporting. The task in the next chapter will be to examine developments in the UK in the light of the availability of these alternatives, from both a predictive and prescriptive perspective.

NOTES

1. The Fifth Directive calls for employee representation in all companies with over 1,000 employees. Such representation may be achieved through employees elect-ing representatives to the Board of directors, via enhanced information and consul-tation rights for works councils or by means of employee representation regulated by collective agreements.
2. In using the term 'external' reporting we are following the terminology introduced in Chapter 1 and therefore consider employees outside the dominant hierarchy as being external users of information.
3. The major sectors identified are:
   industrial and agricultural
   service and trading
   construction
   transportation
   For an example of requirements as they affect the industrial and agricultural sector see Rey (1978).
4. The German approach to social reporting has attracted much attention in the academic literature. In writing this section we have drawn particularly on the work of Dierkes (1979), Jaggi (1980), Schreuder (1979) and Ullmann (1979) as well as that of the UEC group (1983).

5. A content analysis of fourteen German social reports, including a number adopting the goal accounting and reporting approach, revealed that the main emphasis was on the company–employee relationship, second was the physical environment, third the social environment, whilst other areas of concern such as customer relations, supplier relations and the societal dimension of research and development were largely ignored (see Dierkes, 1979).

6. The work of Eichhorn is discussed further in Chapter 6. Also see Schreuder (1979) for a fuller discussion of theoretical developments in Germany.

7. See Grojer and Stark (1977) for a detailed description of an external reporting exercise undertaken by the Fortia Group which was based on goal orientated model giving explicit consideration to the differing interests of various organizational participants such as employees, shareholders, local and national government and the community at large.

8. For a fuller account of work carried out in AB Volvo see the article by Jonson *et al.* (1978) which we have drawn on extensively here.

9. At their most comprehensive the reports resemble the French *bilan socials*. For a contents survey of Dutch social reports see Schreuder (1981).

Chapter 3

Developments in the United Kingdom

The purpose of this chapter is to complete a review of the 'infrastructure' of corporate social reporting in the UK and thereafter to provide a general impression of its impact to date. On the former point, we have already seen in Chapter 2 that certain guidelines on CSR have been laid down by international bodies, so the intention here is to concentrate on the major features of specifically UK legislation and regulative influences.[1] In addition we include a brief review of the special considerations which may apply in the case of public sector and non-commercial organizations. Following this, summary evidence is presented on the incidence of CSR in company reporting practice in the UK. No attempt is made to illustrate or evaluate this in depth at this stage, since this is the purpose of much of the rest of the book.

We begin with a brief outline of some of the major pieces of UK legislation which may be considered relevant to social reporting.

A BRIEF REVIEW OF SOCIAL LEGISLATION

Employees
1. *The Health and Safety at Work Act 1974* requires employers and factory inspectors to keep workers informed about the hazards they face through handling substances used in the place of work. Much of the information is generally obtained from suppliers' data sheets (detailing potential dangers and hazards), which have been found to vary considerably in terms of quality of information provided (Frankel, 1981).

    Interestingly, the Act also provides for regulations to be made requiring companies to disclose information in their Directors' Report (within the statutory annual accounts) concerning arrangements in force for securing the health, safety and welfare at work of employees of the company and its subsidiaries and for protecting other persons against risks to health or safety arising out of, or in connection with, the activities at work of these employees. No such regulations have yet been made, although the reporting requirements have been reiterated in the *Companies Act 1985*.

2. *The Employment Protection Act 1975* gives trade unions certain rights to obtain corporate financial information for the purposes of collective bargaining.[2]

3. *The Employment Act 1982* places an obligation on companies employing more than 250 people to disclose in the Directors' Report steps taken during the year to encourage employee involvement in company affairs through, for example, information provision, development of consultative arrangements and participation in share schemes or similar arrangements. This requirement is repeated in the *Companies Act 1985*, Schedule 7.

4. *The Companies Act 1985* consolidates a series of disclosure requirements in the Directors' Report which, apart from those noted under (1) and (3) above, also includes statistical data on employee numbers, earnings and costs, and for companies employing over 250:

> a statement describing such policy as the company has applied during the financial year –
>
> (a) for giving full and fair consideration to applications for employment by the company made by disabled persons, having regard to their particular aptitude and abilities,
>
> (b) for continuing the employment of, and for arranging appropriate training for, employees of the company who have become disabled persons during the period when they were employed by the company and,
>
> (c) otherwise for the training, career development and promotion of disabled persons employed by the company.   Schedule 7

Consumers

The consumer legislation referred to in Chapter 1 regulates matters such as conditions and terms of sale, product quality and safety, price regulation and marking, competition and provision of credit. There are no reporting requirements as such, for example relating to number of customer complaints received, or repair and rectification work carried out under warranty. More detailed discussion of the particular legislation is therefore considered beyond the scope of this text.[3]

Charities

It is something of an idiosyncracy of UK legislation that companies are required to disclose gifts exceeding £200 made for charitable purposes (*Companies Act 1985*). This can clearly be regarded as an element of CSR which has been (exceptionally) part of UK company law since 1967 (see Chapter 5).

Environment
The major piece of legislation covering information on pollution levels in air and water caused by corporate activities is the *Control of Pollution Act 1974*. Under this Act local authorities have the right, but not the duty, to obtain and publish information about air pollution emissions from industrial enterprises in their areas, including those registered works under the control of the Industrial Air Pollution Inspectorate, a body well known for its unwillingness to release information itself (Frankel, 1978). In the case of water pollution, the Act requires water authorities to keep a register, open to public inspection, containing details both of firms' effluent discharges and consequent action taken by the authority.

Legislative progress
As may be seen from the above (sketchy) analysis, a major problem in using legislative provisions in order to build up a picture of a company's social performance centres on the lack of uniformity under current statutes, with rights to information being dealt with in different ways. Imberg and MacMahon (1973) have argued that there is an urgent need to correlate and reconcile the various branches of labour, consumer and environmental law in order to enable a composite picture of a company's performance to be arrived at. One way in which this might be achieved is by means of a 'compliance with statute' audit and report (Gray, 1981).[4]

A further difficulty encountered in trying to obtain information on a company's social performance, referred to by Imberg and MacMahon, is that of the climate of secrecy fostered by government, not only in the all-embracing provisions of the *Official Secrets Act*, but also under specific requirements for secrecy in over sixty different statutes (Medawar, 1978c). This philosophy permeates the work of quasi-government bodies and government agencies charged with ensuring compliance by industry with social legislation, notably the Factory and Industrial Air Pollution Inspectorates.

A step towards remedying the above situation was taken in the 1973 White Paper on Company Law Reform (Cmnd. 5391) which placed an overriding emphasis on openness in company affairs as the first principle to be adopted in securing responsible behaviour, and articulated the need for corporate reports which enabled shareholders and public to pass judgement on companies' behaviour by social as well as financial criteria. In the latter context, part 2 of the White Paper raised a number of issues related to the social responsibilities of companies and invited public discussion of them. For example it was suggested that:

> The Directors may be required to report on the performance of the company in regard to the safety and health of the company's employees, on the number of consumer complaints and how they were dealt with and on the conduct of industrial relations.   para. 12

Furthermore, whilst reference to individual aspects of environmental concern was omitted the idea was put forward that:

> A useful step forward would be to impose a duty on directors to report to the shareholders on specific parts of the company's response to the social environment ... these are matters of legitimate public concern. There is no lack of informed and interested people (including employees of the company) to mark what is said.   para. 58

The Companies Bill which followed the White Paper, whilst possibly falling short of the promise of the latter document particularly with regard to establishing the overriding principle advanced (that of openness) nevertheless identified four main social areas for information disclosure:

- labour turnover
- personnel and employment policies
- arrangements for protecting the health and safety of employees and public
- compliance with consumer protection legislation.

However, following the fall of the Conservative government, the bill lapsed in March 1974, and with it disappeared the impetus to bring aspects of corporate social performance under the umbrella of Companies Acts reporting requirements.

Despite such lack of progress in the legislative field the thinking behind the 1973 White Paper's tentative proposals without doubt reflected the prevailing climate of opinion at the time. For example in the same year the CBI published their views on *The Responsibilities of the British Public Company* which included a suggestion that:

> ... the Government might consider, as part of their doctrine of wider disclosure, a general legislative encouragement for companies: 'to recognise duties and obligations (within the context of the objectives for which the company was established) arising from the company's relationships with creditors, suppliers, customers, employees and society at large; and in so doing to exercise their best judgement to strike a balance between the interests of the aforementioned groups and between the interests of those groups and the interests of the proprietors of the company   para. 23

Such views inevitably influenced the accounting profession itself and in October 1974 the Accounting Standards Steering Committee set up a working party, under the chairmanship of Derek Boothman, charged with undertaking a complete re-examination of the scope and aims of published financial reports in the light of modern needs and conditions. The working party was to concern itself with the public accountability of economic entities of all kinds, but especially business enterprises, and to seek to establish a set of concepts for financial reporting. A particular aim of the study was to identify persons or groups for whom published financial reports should be prepared, and the information appropriate to their interests.

The working party completed their allotted task in July 1975 and presented their results to the ASSC in the form of a discussion paper: *The Corporate Report*. It is to a consideration of the recommendations contained in this document that we now turn our attention.

THE CORPORATE REPORT

The basic philosophy underpinning the recommendations of *The Corporate Report* is one of 'public accountability'. It was considered that to report publicly is an implicit responsibility incumbent upon every economic entity regarded as significant in terms of the scale of its command over human and material resources being such that the results of its activities have significant economic implications for the community as a whole.

The responsibility to report publicly was regarded as being separate from, and broader than, the legal obligation to report and arises from the custodial role played in the community by economic entities. In this context it was noted that:

> economic entities compete for resources of manpower, management and organ-
> isational skills, materials and energy, and they utilise community owned assets
> and facilities. They have a responsibility for the present and future livelihoods
> of employees, and because of the interdependence of all social groups, they are
> involved in the maintenance of standards of life and the creation of wealth for
> and on behalf of the community.   para. 1.3

The term economic entity was taken to embrace not only limited companies, listed and unlisted, but also partnerships together with a wide range of non-commercial and public sector organizations, including nationalized industries. However, *The Corporate Report* did not attempt to consider in detail how non-commercial and public sector entities might fulfil their responsibilities to report, and indeed the main thrust of its recommendations were largely concerned with private sector limited companies, upon which the emphasis of this part of the chapter is accordingly placed.

In reporting publicly it was stressed that enterprises should seek to satisfy as far as possible the information needs of those considered to have reasonable rights to information concerning the reporting entity. Such 'user groups' were indentified as being:

- the equity investor group
- the loan creditor group
- the employee group
- the analyst–advisor group
- the business contact group
- the government (including local government)
- the public (including taxpayers, ratepayers, consumers, and community or special interest groups such as political parties, consumer and environmental protection societies and regional pressure groups).

In order to meet the fundamental objective of corporate reports, i.e. to communicate economic measurements of, and information about, the resources and performance of the reporting entity useful to the above categories of user, it was suggested that such reports should possess certain characteristics, namely those of relevance, understandability, reliability, completeness, objectivity, timeliness, and comparability.

Following a review of user information needs, it was argued that current reporting practices, with their emphasis on short-term profitability and proprietorial interests, do not fully meet the needs of user groups other than shareholders and creditors. Furthermore, a survey of corporate objectives conducted amongst the chairmen of the three hundred largest UK listed companies led the working party to conclude that there was a trend towards their acceptance of multiple responsibilities towards groups affected by corporate decision-making, and that distributable profit could no longer be regarded as the sole or premier indicator of company performance. The Boothman Committee went on to suggest that wider disclosure, particularly in the form of additional indicators of performance, within the corporate reports of significant entities, would go some way towards satisfying the information needs of users, in so far as this can be achieved within the confines of an annual general purpose report, as well as meeting the general social objective of providing:

> an insight into the reporting entity's employment policies, use of human resources and contribution to national efficiency.   para. 4.34

Additional published statements
It was recommended that corporate reports should contain the following additional statements to assist understanding of corporate financial statements and reveal more fully how resources have been utilized:

- a value added statement
- an employment report
- a statement of money exchanges with government
- a statement of transactions in foreign currency
- a statement of future prospects
- a statement of corporate objectives.

A brief discussion of each of these follows.

Value added statement
The Corporate Report suggested:

> The simplest and most immediate way of putting profit into proper perspective *vis-à-vis* the whole enterprise as a collective effort by capital, management and employees is by presentation of a statement of value added (that is, sales income less materials and services purchased). Value added is the wealth the reporting entity has been able to create by its own and its employees' effort. This statement would show how value added has been used to pay those contributing to its creation.   para 6.7

Such a statement, it was argued, provides a useful measure to help not only in gauging performance and activity, in particular providing a pointer to the net output of the firm and hence its contribution to national income, but also making apparent the interdependence of profit, wages, dividends and interest, taxes and funds for new investment.

An example of a published value added statement, that of the BBA Group for 1984, is shown in Exhibit 3.1.

BBA GROUP PLC AND GROUP COMPANIES

Statement of value added for the year ended 31st December 1984

A main business objective of the group is the creation and distribution of wealth. Value added is the wealth the company has been able to create by its own and its employees' efforts. This statement shows how it has been created and how it has been used to pay those contributing to its creation

			1984			**1983**
	£'000	**£'000**	**%**	£'000	£'000	%
Turnover	176,110			156,112		
Bought in materials and services	101,550			86,604		
		74,560	96·6		69,508	96·9
Other income		2,653	3·4		2,190	3·1
Value added		77,213	100·0		71,698	100·0
APPLIED AS FOLLOWS:						
To pay employees						
Wages and salaries including associated labour charges		64,008	82·9		57,771	80·6
To providers of capital						
Net interest payable	3,339			3,130		
Dividends to BBA GROUP PLC shareholders	1,014			1,014		
Profit attributable to outside shareholders in group companies	678			368		
		5,031	6·5		4,512	6·3
To governments						
Taxation		4,192	5·4		3,382	4·7
To provide for additional fixed assets and working capital						
Depreciation of tangible fixed assets	5,915			5,574		
Retained profit/(loss) for the financial year	(1,933)			459		
		3,982	5·2		6,033	8·4
		77,213	100·0		71,698	100·0

Exhibit 3.1   BBA Group plc and group companies statement of value added for the year ended 31 December 1984.

Employment report

The Boothman Committee suggested:

> Nothing illustrates more vividly the nineteenth century origin of British Company Law than the way in which employees are almost totally ignored in the present Companies Acts and in corporate reports.   para. 6.12

It was argued that employers are essentially in a position of trust in respect of employees who depend on the enterprise for employment security and prospects. Also employment prospects affect whole communities therefore the community looks to employers to maintain certain standards of conduct. Thus it follows that the enterprise has a responsibility to report to and about employees, and to report employment information to the community at large. Whilst rejecting human asset accounting (which attempts to quantify in financial terms an enterprise's investment in human resources), as its present state of development does not permit its use as a generalized method of reporting employment information,[5] it was suggested that significant information about the work-force could be readily given by other means. Basically this entails the publication of statistical information about time worked and numbers employed, together with information on employment costs. It was recommended (para. 6.19) that employment reports contain the following information:

(a) Numbers employed, average for the financial year and actual on the first and last day.
(b) Broad reasons for changes in the numbers employed.
(c) The age distribution and sex of employees.
(d) The functions of employees.
(e) The geographical location of major employment centres.
(f) Major plant and site closures, disposals and acquisitions during the past year.
(g) The hours scheduled and worked by employees giving as much detail as possible concerning differences between groups of employees.
(h) Employment costs including fringe benefits.
(i) The costs and benefits associated with pension schemes and ability of such schemes to meet future commitments.
(j) The cost and time spent on training.
(k) The names of unions recognized by the entity for the purpose of collective bargaining and membership figures where available or the fact that this information has not been made available by the unions concerned.
(l) Information concerning safety and health including the frequency and severity of accidents and occupational diseases.
(m) Selected ratios relating to employment.

Such information, it was suggested, would be of use not only in judging efficiency and productivity but would also provide significant information concerning the personnel policies and industrial relations record of the enterprise.

An example of a published employment report is included as Appendix I to Chapter 8.

Statement of money exchanges with government
All businesses have economic relationships with government both in terms of direct financial dealings, paying and collecting taxes and receiving grants and subsidies, as well as indirectly in, for example, making use of government-provided community facilities and services. Furthermore, a company's ultimate performance in inextricably linked with government policies and actions, a fact amply demonstrated in the years of the Thatcher government. It was argued that the extent of these relationships is not revealed by current reporting practices and it was recommended that a statement of money

receipts from, and payments to, national and local government would add a valuable dimension to corporate financial reporting. The objective of the statement is to demonstrate the degree of interdependence between the enterprise and the state, although it would not, of course, reflect the full extent of direct and indirect benefits derived by the enterprise from government-provided social services and public facilities (see Chapter 4).

Statement of transactions in foreign currency
The economy as a whole is dependent upon the ability of business enterprises to earn net funds from abroad. Therefore the extent to which economic entities contribute to the balance of payments is an important aspect of their economic function and performance in relation to society and the national interest. Pointing out that this aspect of performance is inadequately dealt with in corporate reports, the Boothman Committee recommended that enterprises present a statement of cash transactions in foreign currency during the reporting period, which should contain information on export and import activity together with investment and loan transactions.

As well as indicating an enterprise's contribution to national welfare, it was further suggested that as the degree of risk attached to overseas trading may be significantly greater than that attached to UK operations, due to factors such as fluctuating exchange rates and international political developments, such a statement might assist users in assessing the stability and vulnerability of an enterprise's earnings.

Statement of future prospects
Users of company information, whether they be investors, creditors, suppliers or employees are primarily concerned to assess the future prospects and stability of the enterprise. However, although projections are commonly made for internal management use, these would normally only be published in prospectuses or take-over circulars. Of course, there are valid objections on the part of corporate management against providing financially quantified projections of future performance, due to factors such as users not appreciating the inherent uncertainty of such estimates and hence judging management unfairly on subsequent performance. Furthermore, the provision of forecasts by enterprises suffering financial difficulties may well precipitate a crisis of confidence and, possibly, an otherwise avoidable collapse.

Whilst therefore recognizing that it would be unrealistic to expect enterprises to publish precisely quantified forecasts as a standard part of corporate reports, nevertheless the Boothman Committee envisaged that it would be possible, and desirable, to publish a statement including information concerning:

future profit levels
future employment levels and prospects
future investment levels

together with a note of the major assumptions on which the statement has been based.

In the case of quantified forecasts it was suggested that differences between such forecasts and eventual results be subsequently explained.

Statement of corporate objectives
It was argued that users need to be able to assess the effectiveness of the enterprise in achieving managerially-established objectives and indeed to compare such objectives, particularly those relating to social factors such as employment practice, consumer affairs and environmental matters, with their own. The Boothman Committee therefore called for a statement of corporate objectives to be published, comprising:

● A statement of general philosophy or policy
● Information concerning medium term strategic targets, as steps towards implementing management philosophy or policy, in areas such as sales, profitability, investment, and employment together with consumer and environmental issues.

It was further suggested that strategic targets should be quantified wherever possible.

Reactions to *The Corporate Report*
For almost a year following its publication there was a distinct absence of reaction on the part of the accounting profession and the business community generally towards the Boothman Committee's proposals. Such a situation was probably due in part to the appearance of the Sandilands report on inflation accounting in the month following publication of *The Corporate Report* and the subsequent turmoil into which the UK accounting profession was thrown. However, *The Corporate Report* proposals were firmly put back on the agenda for consideration when the Department of Trade stepped in with publication in May 1976 of its discussion document *Aims and scope of company reports* which broadly endorsed much of *The Corporate Report*'s message, particularly its call for publication of additional indicators of performance.

At this stage it quickly became apparent that the previous silence on the part of the business community had in fact masked latent hostility. In reaction to the Department of Trade document both the Stock Exchange and CBI expressed their profound disapproval of any move away from the traditional stewardship concept, with its narrowly acknowledged obligations towards shareholders, in favour of a more public form of accountability. For example, the CBI expressed the view that whereas user groups other than shareholders had a right to ask for information, they had no general right to expect it to be provided, and it would certainly be wrong to impose such a legal duty upon companies (CBI, September 1976). Clearly, their previously expressed support for more openness in company affairs (CBI, 1973) fell far short of actually taking any meaningful steps towards achieving such an objective!

Whereas the reaction of the accounting profession, as registered by the Consultative Committee of Accounting Bodies (CCAB), was not so openly hostile towards the Department of Trade discussion document, neither could it be regarded as wildly enthusiastic. The general tone of their comments was that legislation on *The Corporate Report*'s suggestions for publication of additional performance statements would certainly be premature, and that any further developments should await the findings of the research studies into their feasibility which had just been initiated. Unfortunately the profession injected little urgency into the research process and although studies were eventually published, notably on the value added statement (Morley, 1978; Renshall *et al.*, 1979; Gray and Maunders, 1980) and the employment report (Thompson and Knell, 1979; Maunders, 1984), they have had little apparent impact on accounting practice. Interestingly Tweedie (1981) has criticized the profession for merely concentrating on the detail of the additional disclosure provisions suggested by *The Corporate Report* rather than tackling the more conceptual problems of substance, notably the fundamental study of users and their needs. However Jeuda (1980) has gone further in suggesting that such an approach was adopted precisely because there never was any support from the accounting profession for the conceptual arguments put forward in *The Corporate Report*, and that the approach was nothing more than a very effective delaying tactic! We shall return to this point later.

Despite the general lack of encouraging response to *The Corporate Report*'s first sortie, the then Labour government followed up the Department of Trade discussion document with publication of a Green Paper on *The Future of Company Reports* (Cmnd. 6888) in July 1977. This document clearly signalled their intention to push ahead with reforms in corporate reporting practice along the lines suggested by the Boothman Committee. In particular it was envisaged that there would be a legislative requirement to publish a value added statement in the annual report and accounts and that an employment statement would be included in the directors' report. It was further suggested that an amended version of *The Corporate Report*'s statement of transactions in foreign currency also be included in the directors' report. This would focus on disclosure of material assets and liabilities held overseas or denominated in foreign currencies, indentifying any predominant currencies, together with any material amounts in blocked currencies which the directors considered not transferable to the UK. In addition, it was proposed that companies be required to disclose the total amount of direct exports and direct imports in a separate statement of international trade. A call was also made for further study to be undertaken into the possibility of issuing detailed guidelines concerning a formal requirement for publication of a statement of future prospects.

The Green Paper unequivocally made out the case for the development of a coherent structure for company reports and accounts reflecting the wider public responsibilities and concerns of companies, and the performance of the directors in meeting these, toward which the formal proposals in the document were merely a first step. Lack of parliamentary time prevented any further action on the proposals during the remainder of the Labour Government's period of office. With the election of the Thatcher Government in 1979, supposedly committed to improving the climate within which the 'wealth creators' be allowed to operate freely, not surprisingly a reaction set in. The Green Paper on *Company Accounting and Disclosure* (Cmnd. 7654) published in July 1979, signalled a strong lurch to the right and return to the more traditional stewardship concept of financial reporting. There was to be no legislative requirement for a statement of value added, nor would an employment statement appear in the directors' report. The Labour Government's proposals for statements of transactions in foreign currency and international trade were also dropped. Although some backing was given for inclusion of a statement of future prospects in company reports, this apparently owed more to the requirements of the EEC Fourth Directive than to any commitment to meaningful disclosure. In addition, as Jeuda (1980) points out, the framing of such proposals leaves so much discretion to directors that its value to shareholders, employees and other user groups is likely to be minimal.

Apparently, then, the wheel has turned full circle and UK reporting practice, has remained largely undisturbed by the radical proposals contained in *The Corporate Report*. Nevertheless, as was pointed out in the previous chapter, developments are taking place in Western Europe which our membership of the EEC will hardly allow us to ignore indefinitely. Perhaps the time is not too distant when *The Corporate Report* will be taken from the shelf and dusted down as attention is again paid to a company's social responsibilities and performance. Therefore, it appears useful to take a brief critical look at the conceptual problems raised by that document.

The Corporate Report: a discussion
In seeking to specify new performance indicators for business the Boothman Committee was attempting to reflect what it saw as the multiple responsibilities of modern business, based on the premises that enterprises can only survive with the approval of the community in which they operate, and hence have an interest in revealing information which displays how differing interests are being balanced for the benefit of the whole community. As Renshall (1976) puts it.

> The Corporate Report takes a global, ecological and pluralistic view of economic organisations and that, at least for accountants, is a major new departure
>   p. 105

Picking up on this point Cooper and Sherer (1984) express the view that:

> One of the strengths of the Corporate Report was that it saw the need to change legal definitions of accountability if accounting reports are to have value in improving stewardship and thereby social welfare.   p. 219

Two of the suggested additional statements to be included in published company reports in particular reflect a pluralistic, extended view of corporate accountability. These are the employment statement, focusing on how the company meets it social obligations towards the work-force (which we shall discuss further in Chapter 8), and the value added statement which purports to show how the wealth created by the company is distributed to those contributing to that wealth. The value added statement has both attracted far more attention amongst researchers and achieved a far higher degree of acceptance in practice than any of the other suggested additional statements.

Although much discussion of the value added statement has centred on technical matters relating to classification and definition problems, together with issues of presentation (e.g. Morley, 1978; Renshall *et al.*, 1979; Rutherford, 1977, 1980) some attention has also been paid to its role in evaluating social performance. Thus Morley sees the value added statement as reflecting a social change, in that shareholders are no longer regarded as the sole beneficiaries of a company's income: they have been joined by other suppliers of finance, the work-force and government, and a wider more complete accountability relationship between the company and its larger 'team' of contributors.[6] Gray and Maunders (1980) suggest that as the value added statement reveals the comparative shares of each of the stakeholder groups in the firm's net output for a given period, it presents a potentially useful means of evaluating 'relative equity' amongst the groups. Furthermore, in treating the workforce as members of the wealth creating team, an improvement in industrial relations may be brought about (Morley, 1978).[7]

Despite the above arguments it should be pointed out that the role of value added statements in evaluating social performance is somewhat problematical. For example, showing the comparative share received by each stakeholder group may merely succeed in highlighting the antagonistic nature of such relationships, as an increased share for one group is associated with a corresponding reduction for others. Furthermore, there are problems in defining who the team members should be. As Morley argues, why should government, which is uninvited, plays no part in decision making and whose benefits are proportional to profits rather than to contribution made, be regarded as a member, whilst suppliers of specialized components, whose entire commercial picture may be bound up with their (possibly) sole customer's fortunes, are excluded?

Perhaps these problems concerning the value added statement are symptomatic of a more fundamental flaw in the general approach adopted in *The Corporate Report*. As Hussey (1978) puts it:

> ... throughout the Corporate Report one is confronted with problems, often posed in terms of measuring economic performance, but which are based upon assumptions which pay regard to possible changes in our society, and which are not explored.   p. 111

Steeds (1976) compares the approach adopted by *The Corporate Report* which:

> dealt solely with the disclosure of information in corporate reports, albeit in an
> enlightened fashion, without adequately considering the corporation's social
> and political environment

with that of the Sudreau Report, considered in the previous chapter, which:

> examined in detail the dynamic interactions between corporations and their
> host society ... [and was] centrally concerned with reconciling industrial
> efficiency and the quality of life.   p. 76 ·

In other words, what *The Corporate Report* tantalizingly omits to discuss is the
rationale of disclosure (Renshall, 1976). The Boothman Committee did indeed express the view that:

> It is tempting to propose that entities disclose information which will show
> their impact on, and their endeavours to protect society, its amenities and
> environment ...   para. 6.45

but abandoned such a concept as impractical due to a lack of generally agreed
measurement techniques, and merely called for further study to be conducted
into methods of social accounting. Having therefore been unable to endorse
fully the need for accounting reports to be developed in accordance with the
philosophy that an organization is an integral part of the total society entity, and
hence accounting disclosures should focus on its contribution to society, the
Boothman Committee's proposals, although radical in terms of traditional accounting procedures and knowledge, may be viewed merely as, in effect, a de-
fence against the threat of an even more radical social and political philosophy.

Whether viewed as radical or not, the Boothman Committee proposals
appear to have had little impact on an essentially conservative accounting
profession. Renshall (1976) predicted that the proposals would find 'an
increasing response in practice', while Hammill's (1979) view was that companies' increasing awareness of their widened social accountability would
mean that the trend towards more socially orientated disclosure would continue. However, recent work looking into the possibilities for developing an
agreed structure or 'conceptual framework' for financial accounting and
reporting carried out by Macve (1981) on behalf of the Accounting Standards
Committee has once again placed a firm emphasis on financial accounting and
cash flow information:

> users of accounting reports have a common interest in 'predicting the amount,
> timing and uncertainty of future cash flows'.   p. 35

As Burchell *et al.* (1982) point out this represents a step backward from the
broader approach adopted in *The Corporate Report* which at least recognized
the need for the development of non-financial performance indicators and the
potential utility of social accounting. They argue strongly that a conceptual
framework should enable consideration to be given to alternative proxies for
the welfare of individuals and society – for example, the impact on employment levels, measures of health, safety and job satisfaction and the effects on
the balance of payments.

There can be little doubt that the reaction of the UK accounting profession, which has traditionally focused its concern on the interests of capital in

matters of corporate reporting practice, goes a long way towards explaining the overall lack of success the Boothman Committee experienced in achieving acceptance of their recommendations. However, a further problem centred on the conceptual approach towards accountability adopted in *The Corporate Report*. As Tricker (1983) has pointed out,

> Global concepts of general or public accountability to a wide amorphous set of 'stakeholders' become a mirage of responsiveness to meet pseudo demands.   p. 35

Tricker argues that accountability involves a more precise relationship that is specific and bounded, with the right to demand accountability resting on the potential to exercise power. Thus, rather than the company being held accountable to all external stakeholders concerning the performance of the business as a whole, rights to seek accountability should be pursued in terms of the specific relationship between a particular stakeholder group and the company. This approach has, as we have seen, been adopted with some success in France, where social reporting and related notions of social accountability have centred on the employee group on the basis of a coalition of interests between capital and labour, with employee rights to information and participation in decision making arising from their provision of labour. The approach adopted in *The Corporate Report* tends to confuse issues of accountability with those of disclosure and socially responsible behaviour in general which involves merely discretion and *ex gratia* action on the part of management.

Despite such reservations concerning the conceptual approach adopted in *The Corporate Report*, and its failure to present a rigorous analysis of the interrelationships between modern business enterprises and the social and political environment within which they operate, the thrust of the Boothman Committee's proposal was, and still is, in tune with much modern day progressive thinking. We would tend to concur with Bedford's (1976) viewpoint that whereas, historically, accounting has adjusted to changes in the social environment, causing the accounting function to expand and grow significantly as society has changed, there is still a need for further change. It is to a consideration of such possible changes that much of the remainder of this book is devoted.

Before proceeding to this, however, we first need to examine, in the light of their social significance, the degree to which particular issues in CSR arise for public sector and non-commercial organizations. Then, we will look briefly at some evidence on the extent and type of CSR which has been practised in the UK, although examples of this also pervade the book as a whole.

NON-COMMERCIAL ORGANIZATIONS AND THE PUBLIC SECTOR

The Corporate Report, and indeed most CSR, focuses on industrial companies. Non-commercial organizations (e.g. charities, clubs, trade unions) and the public sector in the UK (e.g. local and central government, health authorities and nationalized industries) are too important to ignore, however. The emphasis on, and pursuit of (social) accountability has evolved differently between private sector commercial organizations and the rest, and this is a useful point at which to explore these differences in order to highlight to what extent the general discussion of CSR can be applied equally to the public and private sectors, to commercial and non-commercial organizations.

There is, in principle, no reason why our earlier discussion (and the book as a whole) cannot apply equally to all organizations. For example, national-ized industries are not only subject to the laws reviewed earlier in this chapter, but are also governed by regulatory documents *requiring* them to be socially responsible (Cmnd. 7131, 1978; Pryke, 1981). They are something of a hybrid of commercial and non-commercial organizations and, subject as they are to changes in government policy, on occasion something of a political football. Thus, the CEGB, the Coal Board, the Passenger Transport Authorities, British Rail, etc. can face explicit conflict between commercial (e.g. profit) goals and social (e.g. quality of service) goals. The emphasis placed on each from time to time is a matter of government policy. This brings out one crucial difference between private sector commercial organ-izations and other types of organization. While in a private sector company there is no *conceptual* connection between the requirements of the 'owners' (e.g. for dividends) and those of the customers (e.g. quality), these two are (presumably) linked through profit (no sales, no profit, no dividend). In a non-commercial organization the 'owners' (ratepayers, taxpayers, electorate, government) and the 'customers' (society) have conceptually similar goals (quality of 'product' – or service delivery) but these are *not* linked by anything like profit (see e.g. Anthony and Young, 1984).

The implication of this is that financial accounting needs to take second place to a more general 'social accounting'. The financial performance of Nationalised industries is constrained by social performance criteria in a far more explicit way than is the case with private sector companies. Similarly, the performance of all non-commercial organizations (whether private or public) needs to be measured by reference to social criteria. In fact, some-thing approaching social reporting is occasionally practised in non-commercial organizations and the public sector. In illustration of this, Exhibit 3.2 is an excerpt from the annual report of a health authority.

Such reporting is, however, relatively recent and probably prompted by a dawning realization that public sector bodies *do* owe an accountability to society. The initiative for these developments has come from both the government (e.g. Department of the Environment, 1980) and from profes-sional bodies (e.g. Chartered Institute of Finance and Accountancy/ Association of Health Service Treasurers, 1981). A number of organizations, such as water authorities, building societies, and charities, for example, still lag these developments (Barnes, 1984; Bird and Morgan-Jones, 1981; Gray, 1984a) and, hence, compliance with this new form of accountability is distinctly patchy (Likierman, 1979; Gray 1984b; 1985).

Chairman's Report

It gives me great pleasure to introduce this report of the activities of the Isle of Wight Health Authority during the year 1983 – 1984.

The main feature of the year has been the establishment and consolidation of the five Unit Management Teams. These were introduced as part of the 1982 "Patients First" Reorganisation with the intention of delegating responsibility for the management service to those nearest the patient. Generally the new arrangements have worked well.

The main activities durinn the year have been: –

ACUTE SERVICES UNIT MANAGEMENT TEAM: The continuation of planning for the new St. Mary's Development (Phase III). Considerable concern has arisen about the delay in starting this project. The foundations are completed and it is now intended that a start should be made on the main building in early 1985, giving completion in 1988.

MENTAL ILLNESS UNIT MANAGEMENT TEAM: Planning the run-down of Whitecroft Hospital and the provision of new, locally-based, units for the Elderly Mentally Ill. Two of these Units will be ready in 1986. The other major step forward is that the Regional Health Authority has agreed to go ahead with the provision of an Acute Unit for the Mentally Ill. This should be ready in 1988/89 and, with the Units for the Elderly Mentally Ill, will enable Whitecroft to be closed.

MENTAL HANDICAP UNIT MANAGEMENT TEAM: The acquisition of houses in the community. This is part of the agreed policy of caring for the Mentally Handicapped in the Community and as near to their own homes as possible. Progress has not been as swift as hoped because of the difficulty in finding suitable houses. Nevertheless, by the end of the next financial year, four homes should be in operation.

PRIMARY CARE UNIT MANAGEMENT TEAM: The opening of the East Cowes Health Centre. This achieved a design Award from the Island Society. Building of the Health Centre at Freshwater, to be known as Brookside Health Centre has continued and the building should be ready for use in the Autumn.

ELDERLY UNIT MANAGEMENT TEAM: The Unit Management Team for Service for the Elderly has been undertaking innovative and much needed planning work with the King Edward's Fund. Care of the Elderly remains one of the biggest problems on the Island and continued management effort will be devoted to planning Services for the Elderly during the forthcoming years.

One of the significant steps forward which the Health Authority took during the year was to agree to appoint a Health Promotion Officer. Wessex Regional Health Authority has taken the lead in the Country in the development of health promotion and the Isle of Wight Health Authority considered it important that there should be an officer on the Island with specific responsibility for Health Promotion. This decision could be one of the biggest steps forward in improving the health of the population of the Island.

Finally, I should like to mention the role of the Isle of Wight Community Health Council in helping the Authority during the past year. The Council was set up to represent the views of the Public to the Health Authority and, on the Island, this is done extremely well. The Community Health Council has produced useful and helpful reports, for example, on the provision of Services for the Elderly. Where necessary, it does not hesitate to criticise the Authority and this is a most important part of its function. At the same time, Members of the Community Health Council and its Secretary play a most constructive role in helping to improve services for the Island and I am most grateful to them.

D.A.R. Naylor
Chairman, IWHA   June, 1984

What we do . . .

1982/3	In-Patients Treated	1983/4
3263	GENERAL SURGICAL	3395
3180	GENERAL MEDICAL	3235
1538	ORTHOPAEDIC	1692
1587	OBSTETRICS	1612
1388	GYNAECOLOGY	1447
736	PAEDIATRICS (Children)	938
752	EAR, NOSE & THROAT/DENTAL	701
570	GERIATRIC	631
553	MENTALLY ILL	525
120	MENTALLY HANDICAPPED	131
13687		14307

1982/3	Other Hospital Patients	1983/4
71242	Out-Patients	71165
29834	Accident & Emergency	28390
24697	Day-Patients	29064

	Community and Ambulance Services	
21832	Health Visitor Calls	31573
101150	District Nurse Calls	101039
4337	School Dental Courses	4451
4667	Family Planning Cases	4705
2915	Emergency Ambulance Calls	2846
33457	Total Patients Moved by Ambulance Service	36135

	Family Practitioner Services	
524810	G.P. Prescriptions Dispensed	542491
94170	Dental Courses	95765

Award Winning East Cowes Clinic.

. . . and who does it

✦✦✦✦✦✦✦✦✦✦✦✦	Hospital Nurses	640
✦✦✦✦✦✦✦▲	Ancillary — Cook, Cleaner, Porters, etc.	366
✦✦✦✦	Health Visitors & District Nurses	193
✦✦✦	Hospital & Family Doctors	184
✦✦✦	Professional & Technical — X-Ray, Pathology, etc.	152
✦✦✦	Student & Pupil Nurses	137
✦✦▲	Hospital Clerks & Secretaries	123
✦▲	Other Admin.	72
✦	Maintenance	64
✦	Ambulance	55

Exhibit 3.2 Isle of Wight Health Authority. Extract from the *Report and Accounts 1983/4.* **Used with permission.**

Encouraging though such developments may be, they still represent only a partial discharge of accountability. Most such initiatives have concentrated on the stakeholder groups (Chapter 1) of 'customers' and 'community with respect to social concerns'. There is no evidence to suggest that, for example, employees receive any better accountability in non-commercial and public sector organizations than in private sector companies. In addition, environmental CSR is a remarkably rare phenomenon in the public sector. As public sector organizations are ostensibly an expression of the will and wishes of society, one might expect a higher level of accountability from them. This is rarely the case. Although they act as society's agents over such matters as pollution and planning for example, these organizations do not lead the way in informing society about how well either they or the organizations they monitor perform in the general social arena.

In summary, the differences in potential accountability between private commercial sector organizations on the one hand and non-commercial and public sector organizations on the other, should not be overemphasized. With a few exceptions, all discussion of CSR can be treated as taking in all organizations whatever their goals, ownership, and control structures. The major differences lie, normatively, in the social goals which govern the so-called not-for-profit organizations and in the position and role they take as purported agents of the society. Certain of these organizations *have* pioneered reporting practices in the field of 'customer' accountability (through performance indicators and other measures of service and product quality) but in other areas their performance with respect to accountability has not been sufficient to distinguish them empirically from private sector, commercial organizations.

THE INCIDENCE OF CSR IN THE UK

In this section we shall examine the broad pattern of CSR in the UK in so far as it is reflected in corporate annual (or more frequent) reports. *Ad hoc* publications (for example, social audit reports) are not covered here since they are illustrated elsewhere in the book. They represent, in any event, comparatively rare observations in relation to the general population of corporate social communications since, as we will see below, the inclusion of at least some social information in annual corporate reports (of large organizations) has become a relatively regular phenomenon.

In terms of systematic publications, CSR can be grouped under four headings:

Value added statements
Employment reports
Employee reports
'Other' social reporting.

Each of the above, with the exception of employee reports which are considered in Chapter 8, will be dealt with separately, although it is clearly their combination which best indicates the incidence of CSR.

Value added statements
Although value added statements have achieved a higher degree of acceptance in practice than other additional performance indicators suggested in *The Corporate Report*, there is some evidence (Table 3.1) that their popularity may be declining. It will also be noted from the table that value added reporting has been identified as a large-firm phenomenon.

No systematic survey of value added reporting in the UK appears to have been carried out since 1983, but the above figures form part of an apparent trend of rapid growth immediately after the publication of *The Corporate Report*, rising to a peak in 1979/80 and followed by steady decline since then (Table 3.2).

Table 3.1 Companies providing value added statements

	1982/83				1981/82	1980/81
	Large listed	Medium listed	Large unlisted	Total	Total	Total
No. of companies	100	150	50	300	300	300
	%	%	%	%	%	%
Statements provided	38	16	1	21	26	29
Statements not provided	62	84	99	79	74	71

Source: Bougen, P.D, 1983, Table 1.

Table 3.2 Percentage of companies providing value added statements

1975/76	76/77	77/78	78/79	79/80	80/81	81/82	82/83
5	14	22	28	30	29	26	21

Sources: *Survey of Published Accounts 1978–82; Financial Reporting 1982–84.* Based on all 300 companies in respective samples.

Nevertheless, it is also apparent that a substantial minority of (large) companies still engage in value added reporting – whatever the reason for its origins, it seems to have a continuing rationale for some companies.

Employment reporting

In *The Corporate Report* it was envisaged that information about the workforce be gathered together within the annual report. In this form, employment statements have never apparently been as widespread a phenomenon as value added reports, even amongst large companies (Table 3.3).

Table 3.3 Percentage of companies providing employment statements

1975/76	76/77	77/78	78/79	79/80	80/81	81/82	82/83*
2	5	6	4	5	6	5	3

*Own analysis of *Financial Reporting 1983–84* sample of company reports, not previously published.
Sources: *Surveys of Published Accounts 1978–82; Financial Reporting 1982–83.*

For the purposes of Table 3.3 employment statements were defined as information about employees collected together in one part of the annual report which is one page or more in length. This mirrors the relatively extensive and compacted illustrative employment statement included as an appendix in *The Corporate Report* and discussed in Maunders (1984).

As such, Table 3.3 considerably understates the degree of disclosure of human resource information in company annual reports (see Table 3.6). Of course, certain statutory information about the work-force (e.g. average number of employees and aggregate remuneration) has to be reported under

Company Law and in this sense all of the (larger) companies disclose information about their human resources. To derive a more interesting statistic, therefore, the degree of voluntary disclosure of employment information in excess of Companies Act requirements was examined and this is the basis for the 'human resource' figure in Table 3.7. An impression of the specific information covered by this is given in Table 3.4.

Table 3.4 Disclosure of employment information in excess of
Companies Act requirements

	Number of companies 1981/82 (total 300)
Total employees (UK and overseas)	135
Total remuneration (UK and overseas)	32
Analysis of numbers employed	98
Number of disabled employed	3
Expatriate workers	3
Employee turnover	1
Analysis of days/hours worked/lost	3
Accident and sickness details	7
Welfare details or costs	1
Employee education and training details	14
Recognized trade unions	4
Employment ratios	35

Notes   1. The above includes only those companies providing quantitative or specific information on the subject indicated even though this may have been incomplete (e.g. a geographic analysis may not cover all employees).
            2. The number of companies disclosing at least one item was 186 (out of 300).
Source: Maunders, 1982a, p. 182.

No analysis of this type has been performed for 1982/83 or later, but it should be noted, in any event, that the incidence of such disclosure is dependent upon legislative requirements, which have since been expanded in the *Companies Acts 1981* and *1985* to cover the most popular of the items in Table 3.4 (total employee numbers and analysis by 'category' of numbers employed). When we take into account narrative as well as quantitative information on human resources, however, there is still evidence of relatively substantial inclusion of such information in the annual reports of (large) companies. Further analysis of the *Financial Reporting 1983–84* sample of 300 companies in relation to human resource information is given in Table 3.5.

Again, it may be noticed that the most popular item (consultation, etc.) is anticipatory of statutory requirements later embodied in the *Companies Act 1985* whilst, conversely, the disclosure of health and safety policies could be interpreted as the residual effects of requirements presaged in the *Health and Safety at Work Act 1974* which have never been implemented. Even after removing these legislation influenced or associated effects, however, we are left, as with value added statements, with a substantial minority of companies apparently still concerned with the voluntary provision of information about their work-forces in annual reports.

Table 3.5 Human resource information disclosure in excess of
Companies Act requirements

Type of information	Number of companies 1982/83 (total 300)
Health and safety	46
Training	53
Employee communication/participation/policy etc.	65
Pensioners	16

The number of companies disclosing at least one item was 120 (out of 300).

'Other' social reporting

Although value added and employment information are the major categories of 'hard' (quantified or specific) social disclosures regularly published by companies, a significant proportion of corporate reports include 'soft' (narrative or non-specific) social information and this section is intended to provide an overview which is inclusive of both hard and soft disclosures. Typically, 'soft' social information takes the form of policy statements or anecdotal illustrations in the Chairmans' Statement or Directors' Report.

It will be recalled, from Chapter 2, that a systematic survey of social responsibility disclosures amongst large companies in the USA was carried out for some years by Ernst & Ernst (e.g. 1978) and that we summarized the results of their 1978 Survey in Table 2.1. A similar exercise was carried out for the UK on the annual reports included in the survey for *Financial Reporting 1983–84* and the results, not previously published, are shown in the first column of data in Table 3.6.

As will be seen from the notes to Table 3.6. the second column of figures are essentially those from Table 2.1 multiplied by 0.6 and rounded, in order to provide a direct numerical comparison with the UK data.

Comparisons of this kind are fraught with danger. Firstly, we are comparing observations in different time periods and, as already noted, social reporting seems to have experienced different temporal patterns in different countries (Lewis *et al.*, 1984a). Secondly, cross-cultural comparisons are likely to be equally odious. We can see this, perhaps, by examining the only two elements in Table 3.6 in which the UK exceeds the US figure. For D18 – other human resource disclosures – the major constituent for the UK was statements on communication/participation/consultation arrangements which are now required under the *Companies Act 1985*, although they were strictly voluntary (and therefore counted) at the time of the sample. No such 'anticipation of legislation' effect presumably influenced the US figure.

Similarly, item G.27 – additional information – has been used for the UK data to capture information about the availability of statements prepared for the Department of Trade about black employment in South Africa. Since this is in accordance with a voluntary Code of Conduct it is counted, although no such statistic presumably affected the US data.

Table 3.6 Frequency of publication of CSR information

		UK 1982/83	USA 1978
A.	**Environment**		
	1. Pollution control	10	133
	2. Prevention or repair of environmental damage	7	15
	3. Conservation of natural resources	–	39
	4. Other environmental disclosures	–	46
B.	**Energy**		
	5. Conservation	16	126
	6. Energy efficiency of products	10	45
	7. Other energy related disclosures	2	29
C.	**Fair Business Practices**		
	8. Employment of minorities	1	52
	9. Advancement of minorities	26	47
	10. Employment of women	6	49
	11. Advancement of women	–	142
	12. Employment of other special interest groups	11	18
	13. Support for minority businesses	–	18
	14. Socially responsible practices abroad	15	43
	15. Other statements on fair business practices	1	104
D.	**Human resources**		
	16. Employee health and safety	46	69
	17. Employee training	53	80
	18. Other human resource disclosures	75	32
E.	**Community involvement**		
	19. Community activities	13	56
	20. Health and related activities	5	35
	21. Education and the arts	11	70
	22. Other community activity disclosures	7	56
F.	**Products**		
	23. Safety	11	42
	24. Reducing pollution from product use	–	22
	25. Other product related disclosures	14	46
G.	**Other social responsibilities disclosed**		
	26. Other disclosures	11	56
	27. Additional information	49	16

Sources: *UK data* – analysis of sample of 300 reports used for *Financial Reporting 1983–84*.
USA data – Ernst & Ernst (1978) adjusted from sample size of 500 *pro rata* to 300 to provide comparison with UK.

Given these reservations and exceptions, it nevertheless appears that there was (in 1978) more CSR in the USA than in the UK (in 1983/84). But this conclusion is subject to a more general qualification. Much of the data on which the table is based is 'soft', i.e. narrative and descriptive. A single policy statement could, for example, be subdivided according to contents so as to count under a number of the headings given. Alternatively, it could be classified under its main content. This is a matter of interpretation by the recorder and, whilst subjectivity can be controlled for a single sample, it is impossible to determine its relative effects where studies are separated in time and space.

In contrast, because a single researcher was involved, it is possible more confidently to look at the trend of CSR in the UK from 1980/81 to 1982/83, although even this comparison is bedevilled by changes in the sample of companies involved. This trend is shown in Table 3.7.

Table 3.7 Social reporting

Category of information	Number of companies		
	1980/81	1981/82	1982/83
Human resources	115	119	120
Other social responsibility disclosures	65	65	55
Fair business practices	48	58	47
Energy	29	46	27
Community involvement	28	37	25
Product related	18	30	21
Environmental	23	27	16
Total companies disclosing at least one item	134	183	160

Three hundred companies were sampled in each year.

Sources: *Financial Reporting 1982–83*. Analysis of sample used in *Financial Reporting 1983–84*.

From the above, for all but one item (human resources) there appears to have been a peak of disclosure in 1981/82. This is confirmed in the figures for companies disclosing at least one social item.

SUMMARY AND CONCLUSIONS

The picture emerging from consideration of both legislative developments and practice in relation to CSR in the UK is one of a gradual build up to what appears to have been a peak of activity and influence at the beginning of the 1980s, followed by some decline more recently. This, of course, mirrors the path of events in the economy generally and on the political scene. In so far as the disclosure of social performance reflects corporate 'social' activities it also provides some support for the hypothesis that it is financial performance which 'causes' social performance and not vice versa. That is, when companies are making profits they are willing and able to use some of them in ways which improve their social image. If, however, 'social' expenditures (e.g. on training) affect future financial performance, then there is clearly an in-built danger of such myopic behaviour reinforcing the trade cycle effect for a company.

But maybe things are not as bleak as this reasoning might suggest. A minority of organizations *are* still engaging in CSR (albeit perhaps on a largely 'defensive' basis) and could form the springboard from which, given a

more receptive political and economic climate future progression in social
activities and the associated CSR takes place. For the sake of these and, we
hope, an increased number of practitioners in the future, the next chapters
will be concerned with the question of what directions future CSR might
'best' take.

NOTES

1. For a fuller discussion of such legislation see Frankel (1978, 1981), and Medawar
    (1978b).
2. Further discussion of this issue can be found in Chapter 9.
3. See Medawar (1978b) for a critical analysis of such legislation.
4. See Chapter 5 for further discussions on this topic.
5. Human asset accounting is discussed further in Chapter 8.
6. According to Morley, this offers practising accountants a useful enlargement of
    their potential client group. In particular, if the auditor was to report on the value
    added statement he would be taking a first step away from the traditional exclusive
    accountability to shareholders towards a new role, that of impartial auditor ensur-
    ing a true and fair view is given to all members of the company team.
7. Gray and Maunders express some reservations concerning this potential develop-
    ment pointing out that in larger enterprizes an individual working in one constitu-
    ent plant will see little direct relationship between his or her own performance and
    the overall group performance.

Chapter 4

Corporate social reporting and accounting theory

Discussion of CSR is, on the whole, steeped in the concepts, terminology and conventions of financial accounting. There is a common, although usually implicit, assumption that the framework of accounting theory is appropriate to the analysis of CSR issues and that the ideas and conventions of accounting can be usefully and appropriately employed to illuminate and settle CSR problems. While we do not, generally speaking, disagree with the principle of applying traditional accounting thought to a study of CSR (and have done so extensively in the earlier chapters) we nevertheless would point out that this must be done with care. In this chapter, therefore, we first critically examine mainstream accounting theory. This will enable us to assess the extent to which it is compatible with CSR and thus determine to what extent we can employ established accounting thought in an analysis of CSR. There are seven sections:

A Review of Accounting Theories
Lessons from Financial Accounting Theory
Another Look at Objectives
The Context of CSR
A Framework for CSR
Constituencies and Issues
Summary and Conclusions

A REVIEW OF ACCOUNTING THEORIES

Figure 4.1 provides a useful (if rather oversimplified) categorization of accounting theories.[1] The *Statement of Accounting Theory and Theory Acceptance*

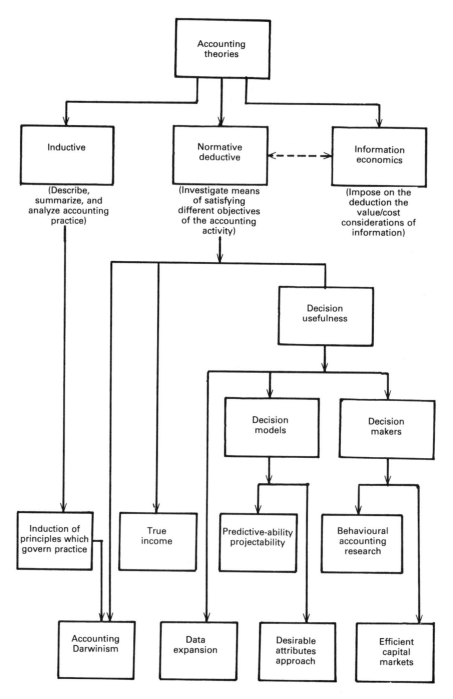

Figure 4.1 A categorization of accounting theories (adapted from SOATATA, AAA, 1977).

(SOATATA, AAA, 1977) from which it is largely derived, identifies two broad groups of theories: what it calls the *inductive* theories and the *normative–deductive* theories.

In broad terms, the inductive theories arise from attempts to:

● codify and explain actual accounting practice;
● discover and describe their determinants; and
● identify illogical gaps in that practice.

That is, they describe practice and try to answer the question: 'What does accounting practice do?' and, from this, attempt to establish both the principles that appear to govern practice and the forces that have resulted in practice being what it is.

The normative–deductive theories attempt to answer the questions: 'How well does accounting practice satisfy objective X? (e.g. users' needs), or 'How might accounting practice be improved in order to satisfy objective X?' They are thus more evaluative and are deduced from both our empirical knowledge of accounting practice and from some objective *held for* the accounting activity. As a result of being goal/objective-orientated, the normative–deductive theories are claimed to be more value-laden than the inductive theories in that they start from a value-judgement such as 'accounting activity *should* satisfy users' needs'.

Turning back to CSR we can use the framework in Figure 4.1 to analyze the applicability of accounting thought to CSR and categorize some of the approaches which have been adopted to the issues of social reporting.

The inductive approach

Inductive theories have not been the main focus of modern accounting research. Whilst the early pioneers of the subject (e.g. Paton, 1922; Hatfield, 1927; Paton and Littleton, 1940; Ijiri, 1975) largely emphasized this approach, it later tended to lose popularity in favour of the normative–deductive approach (with occasional exceptions such as Imke, 1966; Popoff, 1972) – that is, until fairly recently. Influential work by, for example, Burchell *et al.* (1980), and Tomkins and Groves (1983) has re-emphasized the need for the inductive approach and more recent analyses of CSR practice (by writers such as Lessem, 1977; Preston *et al.*, 1978; Schreuder, 1979; Teoh and Thong, 1984) are the first tentative steps in this direction. These latter studies have identified one major broad principle governing current CSR practice, namely the effect of culture. Attitudes to, experiments with, and focuses on, CSR vary noticeably from country to country and thus simply translating ideas from, say, the USA to the UK, or Canada to Sweden is not to be recommended. Trevor Gambling, for example, has argued this point for many years (1974, 1977a, 1977b, 1978a, 1978b) and it is the one basic idea that has emerged from comparative research.

The only other major point that appears to be emerging from the principally inductive study of CSR practice is its essentially political nature

(Medawar, 1976; Ullman, 1979; Heard and Bolce, 1981). That is, CSR is generally speaking used by organizations to strengthen or defend their position with respect to government and pressure groups within society. However, on occasions, a development in practice reflects a change in the political power of some constituency group. Ullman (1979) argues that the increase in employee reporting in Europe is just such a case as this.

Hopefully from this, you may begin to see how the inductive approach works and its obvious strengths (and less obvious weaknesses) begin to emerge. There is, however, a general problem with this approach that becomes critical in the area of CSR. Studying extant practice is a study of 'what is' and, by definition does not study 'what is not' or 'what should be'. It therefore concentrates on the status quo, is reactionary in attitude, and cannot provide a basis upon which current practice may be evaluated or from which future improvements may be deduced. This is especially critical in CSR. As we saw in the earlier chapters, CSR is currently still a relatively rare phenomenon and trying to study 'what is not' is notoriously difficult.

We may still use the inductive approach to study *why* CSR is so little practised but, given the present state of knowledge, we must necessarily rely on some degree of speculation. For instance, it might be that CSR is simply not in the interests of those with power over information (e.g. managers), who may thus seek to mobilize the issue out of the debate. Arguably this has been achieved in part at least, by insistence on 'acceptable, objective, verifiable measurement techniques' (*The Corporate Report*, ASSC, 1975, p. 58) which has effectively constrained the 'official view' of CSR to a probably impossible method while maintaining apparent support for the concept.

The inductive approach is nevertheless applicable to CSR if we remember the caveats:

● It studies only 'what is' and cannot study 'what is not'.
● It cannot provide an evaluative framework by which current practice and future developments might be judged.

In addition, in common with all forms of empirical investigation we must recognize that all perception is theory-laden. That is, our preconceptions about the world significantly colour what we observe and which aspects of particular events we focus upon. Thus accountants are more likely to view the world through accounting frameworks and conventions – for example, none of the CSR papers to which we referred earlier as 'inductive' mention socially-orientated advertising which clearly falls into the area of CSR but is outside the *accountants'* normal focus of interest. It is therefore generally ignored, probably incorrectly. Our interests as accountants *will* influence what we see and how we interpret it.

The first two problems are overcome by studying CSR in the 'normative–deductive' framework. The last problem is more difficult and we will attempt to deal with it in later sections of this chapter when we look in more detail at the objectives and context of CSR.

The normative–deductive approaches

The normative–deductive approach has been both more generally applied in CSR and has provided the greater number of categories of theory in mainstream accounting thought. We now look at each of its subgroups, as given in Figure 4.1.

'Accounting Darwinism'

This approach maintains that those practices which evolve and survive are likely to be 'fitter' practices, better adapted for the context in which they operate. In so far as this approach involves understanding how current practice 'evolved', it is inductive; in so far as such evolution and survival is considered desirable it is normative–deductive. There are few accounting theorists (and, to date, no CSR writers) who subscribe to this position (other than by implication). The danger of it is that one is led to assume that 'what is' is what 'should be' (a logically doubtful proposition). When stripped of this normative element, this evolutionary analysis is, as we noted, fundamentally of the 'inductive' approach and therefore shares the same advantages and disadvantages that we briefly outlined in the previous section.

True income

Much of accounting theory is concerned with the seeking of a single perfect profit measure (see, for example, Lee, 1974; 1985; Alexander, 1978), predicated upon the assumption that this is the objective of the accounting activity. We see elements of this idea in action in some writing on CSR. Linowes (1972b) and Abt (1972, 1973) for example, have sought to value the benefits and detriments arising from an organization's activities and thereby produce a 'bottom line' figure which represents 'net social profit or loss'. This is a difficult and potentially rocky road for CSR, and while there is clearly some absolute net benefit/detriment from an organization's activities, it equally clearly depends upon:

● the views and perceptions of the observer; and
● the ability to identify and measure enormously complex reactions and ifluences arising from organizational activity.

As we suggested in Chapter 1, CSR is an area in which opinions and individual value-systems become much more apparent than is usually perceived to be the case with conventional accounting. Thus, unless we can find:

(a) some means of restricting the area of influence which a CS report tries to cover;
(b) some means of uniquely identifying what constitutes cost and benefit; and
(c) some unarguable method of measuring these costs and benefits,

then the search for 'true social income' will provide no useful basis for CSR evaluation and development.

We will return to these matters later in this chapter and in later chapters.

Decision usefulness

Decision usefulness (DU) is probably the most popular general objective held for the accounting activity in recent years. The general argument is:

- as accountants, we prepare information,
- information is of no importance unless it is used,
- information is used to make decisions,
- therefore accounting must provide information that is useful for decisions.

The DU approach is now so engrained in accounting thinking that it is not surprising to find it underlying a great deal of the discussion on CSR. In particular we find that the 'decision models' subgroup – 'desirable attributes approach' – has held the most sway and so we will leave this to last and briefly survey the other theory subgroups.

Data expansion

At its simplest, the data expansion view (e.g. Sorter, 1969) argues that as we cannot know all users and all needs, and as we as accountants have no particular right either to aggregate data (thus losing the richness of it) or to undertake data transformations which are truly the province of the user; our duty as accountants is to communicate enough data to enable users to make their own selections and transformations. At the extreme this implies that we simply allow users access to our databanks (accounting records) and let them 'get on with it' (Lieberman and Whinston, 1975). The principal criticisms of the approach relate to the costs, confusion and loss of confidentiality that may result. No one (outside the field of employee reporting – see Cuthbert and Whitaker, 1977) has yet suggested this as a way forward for CSR despite the approach's theoretical applicability. As we shall see, identifying users and their needs in the CSR context verges on the impossible and the attractions of CSR based simply on raw data (accidents, pollution, complaints, etc.) are that it avoids both this and the crucial measurement/identification problem.

Behavioural accounting research

Behavioural accounting research (BAR) focuses on the individual and how he makes decisions, particularly in response to financial information (see, for example, Libby, 1981; Snowball, 1980). The difficulties of the approach have been well discussed (Ashton, 1982; Hofstedt, 1976) but the approach has been seen as a practical means of determining how to choose between alternative accounting elements and methods, and, in its simplest form, is being employed widely in financial reporting research (see, for example, Benjamin and Stanga, 1977; Chenhall and Juchau, 1977; Chandra, 1974; Lee and Tweedie, 1981; Arnold and Moizer, 1984). There has been an element of this approach in CSR in attitude surveys undertaken by (for example) First National Bank of Minneapolis in 1973 (reported in Jensen, 1976). But the comprehensive study necessary to develop reliable theory in this way, for general application, is some distance off. In addition there are three important differences between financial reporting and CSR which affect the applicability of this approach:

● In financial reporting we can identify the users. As we shall see, this is not necessarily the case in CSR.
● The general types of information used by (say) an investor are relatively easy to specify. Those used by (say) an environmental interest group are not.
● There is an implicit assumption that the nature of the actions taken by the user on the basis of financial information are relatively restricted: e.g. to buy, hold, or sell shares. No such assumption can be made about CSR.

A small number of CSR-related BAR studies have been carried out, *not* on the reactions of society to CSR but on the reactions of *investors*. Belkaoui (1980), for example, found that bankers (and to a lesser extent, accountants) were influenced in their decisions by pollution data about the company, and Buzby and Falk (1978) found that while social information was considered by mutual fund managers (particularly information on illegal dealings, pollution and hazardous products), all social items were weighted lower than the financial ones.

An indication of the weakness of the investor preference for CSR is given in a later study by Buzby and Falk (1979) who found that universities are unaffected in their investment decisions by the social posture of the company. (See also Social Audit, 1974.)

While such research might allow a tentative suggestion that CSR has some relevance to investors, it is arguable whether investor reactions are of much direct relevance to the study of CSR. Investors *qua* investors must see CSR in much the same way as they see all environmental changes which can influence their returns (such as labour unrest, new competitors, change in government policy, altering tastes amongst consumers, and so forth). But whilst having investor groups supporting the call for increased social disclosure may well hasten a more systematic practice of CSR, its rationale lies in providing information for groups who are not presently the information receiving participants of an organization. CSR is based on the idea that groups *other than shareholders* also have rights to information about things which affect their lives, and so to develop CSR solely on the basis of investor needs would be to miss the whole point of developing a wider social accountability.

Efficient capital markets

Many of the points about BAR apply equally to the efficient capital markets approach (ECM). ECM examines decision makers' behaviour in the aggregate by focusing on the reactions of stock markets to accounting information (Dyckman *et al.*, 1975). Despite the limitations of the approach (AAA, 1977, pp. 15–16; Bierman, 1974; Chapman-Findlay, 1977; Downes and Dyckman, 1973; Hines, 1984), and subject to the relevance of the question, ECM studies can cast light on market reactions to social information. That is, how is CSR perceived by the market as being related to profitability? For example, do investors view CSR as a detraction from managers' primary role of 'making money for stockholders', and what social events are perceived by the market as having significant financial and profit impacts?

Although still in its early stages there has been a fair amount of systematic study of these questions. Bowman (1973) argued that it may often be in the shareholders' interests for a company to be seen to be socially responsible. In effect, management must be seen to be working to avoid any future bad publicity from 'socially irresponsible' acts (i.e. being 'found out') and should work to anticipate any future legislation changes that will have cost implications for the company (e.g. pollution abatement costs). However, the evidence is mixed and rather weak on whether investors do react to social disclosures. Spicer (1978a) and Ingram (1978) found weak but noticeable reaction in the market to social disclosure while Fogler and Nutt (1975) found no reaction to the release of pollution data about companies. To the extent that such evidence is seen as relevant there is clearly a need for further research but, as we noted in the previous section, it is unlikely that investor studies at the micro or macro level have much bearing on the development of CSR.

Predictive ability/projectability
This criterion for selecting the more desirable accounting methods is well established in traditional accounting research (see, for example, Beaver *et al.*, 1968). At its simplest, it is suggested that the ideal accounting system is one which allows the observer either to predict future earnings from past earnings (projectability), or to predict other items of relevance to the investor (earnings, dividends etc.) from a whole set of accounts (predictive ability). Such a characteristic is clearly desirable in relation to any (relevant) information, at least from the recipients' point of view. However, as a criterion it has met problems such as determining how investors *do* predict and whether in fact prediction from historic data is feasible.

In CSR these problems are exacerbated and the criterion becomes largely inoperative when we consider what society might wish to predict. Prediction of an organization's pollution or accident rate would clearly be useful but is difficult (see, for example, Maunders, 1984). The thing we most wish to predict – the full impact of an organization's activity on society takes us into the realm of fantasy. This subgroup of accounting theory has, therefore, had little impact on CSR writing as yet.

Desirable attributes approach
Finally we can turn to the subgroup of approaches to accounting theory which has perhaps had the greatest influence on CSR. The approach of

employing qualitative criteria to evaluate financial accounting methods has influenced the accounting professions in the USA and the UK (AAA, 1966; APB, 1970; AICPA, 1973; ASSC, 1975) and has often been the cornerstone of many of the more developed theses on CSR. We find Estes (1976), AICPA (1977) and Johnson (1979), for example, all building their ideas of CSR upon concepts such as relevance, completeness, freedom from bias, understandability, and so on. Similar principles run through much other influential material on the subject (e.g. Churchill, 1974; Ramanathan, 1976; Anderson, 1978). The extent to which such theorists have sought to directly apply this essentially financial accounting model can be seen in Figure 4.2 where we compare the qualities that the writers of *The Corporate Report* (who were talking principally about financial reports) and the AICPA and Estes (who were talking exclusively about CSR) would hope to find in their respective ideal systems of reporting.

	ASSC	AICPA	Estes
Characteristics	Relevant	Useful for decisions	Relevance
	Understandable	–	Understandable
	Reliable/directness	Directness	Verifiable
	Complete	Complete	Completeness
	Objective/unbiased	Neutral	Freedom from bias
	Timely	–	Timely
	Comparable	–	Comparable
	–	Cost effective	–
Conventions/concepts	Money measurement	Money measurement	Monetary expression
	Going concern	–	–
	Entity	Entity	Localized
	Accrual	–	Matching
	Prudence	–	Conservatism
	Consistency	Consistency	Consistency

Figure 4.2 The qualities of suggested ideal reporting systems

Qualitative criteria, such as those contained in Figure 4.2, are common in accounting discussion and represent useful 'mental furniture' for considering some of the issues involved in setting accounting policy. There are, however, a number of obvious differences between CSR and mainstream financial accounting – including the extent to which each is practised, the range of uses and users of the information, and the range and extent of information that might be included in appropriate reports. To that extent we must be cautious in transferring ideas from one to the other. More specifically we must assess:

● Is decision usefulness (DU) the 'best' criterion, and can it be applied to CSR?
● Can the qualitative criteria be applied to CSR?

How to determine the 'best' criteria for a reporting method is obviously a crucial point – if one which is wholly value-laden. It deserves very careful attention and so we examine the question in some detail later in this chapter when we re-examine objectives. Accepting for the moment that DU is a generally appropriate criterion, we run into serious problems applying it to CSR. In particular, how should we identify users and the decisions they wish to take? Researchers have normally addressed this problem by listing groups of potential users. As may be recalled from Chapter 3, *The Corporate Report*, for example, listed seven 'user groups' whom it was suggested have 'reasonable rights to information and whose information needs should be recognized by corporate reports' (p. 17). However, if we accept the propriety of the DU criterion and the legitimacy of the selected user groups we must then establish their information needs – and these in turn must be *legitimate* information needs. That is, for example, while trade unions may have a very real need for information about redundancies and plant closures, and a local community's need for information about a local plant's effluent may be based on a very genuine concern, not all would necessarily agree that these groups had a legitimate right to the information. The absence of public information on these sorts of issue demonstrates that those with the power over information do not necessarily recognize (or choose to acknowledge) these information needs.

Thus despite the genuine contribution that research into users' needs could probably make to our general knowledge it is not at all clear that it would advance the development of CSR in any practical sense. For all these reasons, the DU criterion, and calls for research into it (see, for example, Dierkes and Antal, 1985) do not appear to us to be the best way forward.

If we turn back to an analysis of the qualitative criteria in Figure 4.2 even a cursory analysis will show:

● Such criteria are probably impossible to operationalize.[2]
● Many of the criteria are simply inappropriate to CSR in their present form.

Consider first the conventions/concepts (i.e. money measurement, accruals, etc.). There is no *a priori* reason why any of them need be applicable to anything other than financial information. That accountants are used to the concepts is irrelevant – relevant information need not be in money terms and much social information rarely is. Similarly 'going concern', 'accrual', and 'prudence' have no necessary relevance for CSR. 'Consistency' is only relevant to the extent that changing bases of calculation might not be identified by the recipient of the information and thus this 'concept' may be effectively subsumed within the characteristic of 'reliability' (and perhaps freedom from bias). The entity concept, may have some relevance in CSR. For example, social information related to a multinational company's global activities (e.g. twenty-two employee fatalities worldwide) may be less appropriate than information relating to specific plants or operations in that, while the broad social impact of organizational activity is affecting (and maybe even creating) societies-as-a-whole, the immediate, obvious, and acute impacts are likely to be local.

Turning to the 'characteristics' (i.e. relevance, etc.) it is likely that each is desirable for *any* information. Therefore, despite the problems of oper-ationalizing them we must give attention to the extent to which they are present in CSR.

Completeness is a characteristic that CSR is unlikely to be able to fulfil. In the sense of describing fully all interactions of an organization and its en-vironment, completeness can only be realistically applied when:

- the information completely covers some restricted objective (e.g. the ex-tent to which pollution control regulation has been complied with); or
- there is complete information for a decision or a set of decisions.

The first sense has something to recommend it – information is clearly less misleading to the extent that we know to what it does and does not relate. As we shall see later in this chapter and subsequent chapters, much CSR infor-mation tends to confuse rather than clarify, as it is rarely clear which aspects of organizational activity it is intended to cover and therefore what is ex-plicitly excluded. The second sense is only appropriate to the extent that the DU criterion is appropriate and can be operationalized successfully.

The relevance criterion is the principal means of imposing selectivity onto the whole set of possible data that underlies financial accounting. But it can only be applied if it is known to what the information is relevant. As we do not know the CSR users and their information needs, we cannot apply the criterion in the strict financial reporting sense. Thus some other selectivity criterion must be found, or else relevance must be applied in some context other than directly to decisions. As the range of potential information is so much greater in CSR than in financial reporting this issue is all the more critical for it.

Timeliness poses similar problems in that it implies that information is received in sufficient time for the receiver to act upon it. In the case of investors the act is assumed to be the buying, holding or selling of shares. No such clear alternatives can necessarily be assumed for the recipients of CSR.

Thus completeness, relevance and timeliness are not characteristics that can necessarily be directly transferred from financial accounting, yet along with 'freedom from bias' and 'understandability' they are clearly very desirable characteristics of any information. How we might operationalize them for CSR is altogether another question.

LESSONS FROM FINANCIAL ACCOUNTING THEORY

While, as we said in the introduction to this chapter, it appears self-evident to us that there is no *a priori* reason why financial accounting concepts and intellectual frameworks need be applicable to CSR, it is nevertheless salutary to realize just how fragile is the accountants' conceptual framework and how ill-equipped it is to cope with the broader social dimension. We find that the inductive approach is as appropriate to CSR as it is to the study of any phenomenon. The inductive approach, however, cannot serve directly any needs for evaluation, prescription and suggestions for improvement.

The normative–deductive approach can meet these needs. It requires, however, that the objectives, axioms, and values from which deductions are to be made be identified. But those which underlie traditional financial accounting travel uncomfortably to CSR. Much of the problem apparently lies in overcoming the prejudices of accountants. Emphasis on measurement and the true income approaches are probable symptoms of this and are dealt with in detail in Chapter 6. The decision usefulness criterion, the backbone of much of financial accounting, likewise transposes badly. When applied to CSR it is a poor and rather flaccid framework that raises the problem of identifying users and their needs – a critical problem as the potential number of groups and the potential range of data are largely unconstrained. In addition, those with power who *could* legitimize the user groups appear content not to do so. The DU criterion thus gets us nowhere very quickly. It does, however, draw attention to the qualitative characteristics desirable in any information. These cannot be operationalized as yet but are clearly potentially important factors in evaluating proposals.

But we are not simply back to square one. One major thread has run through this analysis of financial accounting and its relevance to CSR; namely the *raison d'être* of the two subjects is crucially different in two ways:

● In the choice of objectives for financial accounting or CSR
● In the context in which each is studied.

We therefore need to undertake a more careful analysis of these two aspects before going on to try to deduce our own evaluative and prescriptive framework.

ANOTHER LOOK AT OBJECTIVES

No activity (like accounting) or document (such as a financial or social report) can have an objective. The objective is held *for* the activity by those who either perform and/or direct the activity. It would not be too cynical to observe that the dominant objectives of CSR, as evidenced by practice, are to legitimize organizations and to improve their public image. As CSR is largely under the control of management, whom one would reasonably expect to fall into what we referred to as the pro-capitalist group, this should not be surprising. However, it makes nonsense of the suggestion that the objective of the current practice of CSR is to satisfy users' needs or to discharge accountability. That is, broadly speaking, the *real* influence on the development of reporting in general and CSR in particular lies with those who perform or directly control the reporting process – management, auditors, accountants, to a greater or lesser extent.[3] Developments will tend to occur to the extent that these groups see it as being in their interests. Thus, for example, the Bank of America's social reporting might appear to be a response to pressure from anti-apartheid groups, and the report by Atlantic Richfield (see Chapter 5) may have been a response to their significant nuclear waste leak and subsequent scare (see Patterson, 1976). In each case it was in the interests of the management to respond with social reporting and so their objectives – survival, public relations etc. – predominate.

Of course there are other influences, but arguably their effects have tended to be less important. For example, proposals in *The Corporate Report* have, as we saw in Chapters 2 and 3, succeeded in 'putting CSR on the agenda' but had little effect (if any) on practice.

The least effectual of all influences are the 'functional claims and pretensions' (Burchell *et al.*, 1980) – objectives that an activity such as financial reporting or CSR is *supposed* to fulfil. While it might be accepted that financial reporting of companies is supposed to satisfy users' needs, and that CSR is supposed to discharge accountability, it is clear that these objectives are *not* satisfied and that the pursuit of these objectives is *not*, on the whole, what prompts developments in practice.[4]

This does not, of course, remove the validity or importance from studying and pursuing what 'should be', it simply means that agreement on what 'should be' is rarely sufficient, on its own, to translate it into what 'will be'. For the following reasons therefore, we remain with the 'functional claims and pretensions' justification as the normative thread of the book:

● We believe that CSR is a fundamentally radical concept. As long as it remains within the control of the reporters (the pro-capitalist group) it will remain 'safe' and its interesting and challenging consequences will be ignored.
● We believe that as accountants our aim should be to aid the discharge of accountability. To achieve this: (i) we need to know how this might be achieved; and (ii) we require some model against which to judge our own efforts and the efforts of others.
● Studying simply 'what is' – the status quo – provides little development of new ideas and improvement. As Sterling (1970) points out, this can become a sterile and arid exercise (see, for example, Baxter, 1982; Brilloff, 1984).

Thus we come full circle. Studying CSR practice will increase knowledge but limits analysis. Seeking to explain why practice is as it is also adds to knowledge – not least about the perceived nature of CSR by those who hold power in society and who are thus able to legitimize activities. To evaluate, develop and understand practice, however, we need a normative framework – the first element of which is the identification of a justifiable and acceptable (legitimate?) objective. We believe the discharge of accountability is such an objective and will seek to justify this later in the chapter. Before doing this, we begin our construction of a theoretical edifice for CSR by analyzing the context of CSR and the influences it seeks to report upon.

THE CONTEXT OF CSR

We began the book by stating that social reporting is the process of communicating the social and environmental effects of organizations' actions to particular groups within society and to society at large. Let us put this into some sort of context by first trying to recognize the enormously complex nature of the interactions and interconnections between organizations and groups, both within and between societies. In Britain, for example, just the range of organizational forms gives some indication of this diversity of interaction and interdependence. Public sector organizations such as the nationalized industries, local government, and health authorities, provide many of the services – the 'social infrastructure' as it is sometimes known – which, while required in a mixed economy society, are not provided by the market-place. In the private sector, a myriad of diverse organizations interact, providing the commercial life of the economy and filling gaps left by the interpersonal market-place or by the public sector organizations. All these organizational forms are simultaneously competing and complementary, each determining and dependent upon the activities of each other.

Each of these groups or organizations is itself a complex system influencing and influenced by the environment, the society, other societies and other organizations. If we wish to communicate the effects of this complex of activity, we must be able first to identify these effects. By way of an example consider the hypothetical case of a medium-sized manufacturing company. Figure 4.3 indicates some of the immediate economic influences of that company's activities. The figure is, of course, oversimplified, but it indicates the extent to which organizations are mutually dependent. All of the transactions shown in Figure 4.3. are presently captured and described by the traditional accounting systems of the organizations concerned. From their financial accounts it is possible to glean some indication of the entity's importance as a provider of goods and services, as a provider of funds to the public sector, and as a source of income to other groups including employees. No description of an organizations' impact would be complete without capturing these 'primary level' influences, but there are other immediate impacts of the activities that do not reflect directly in the accounting systems. These are the immediate impacts on the social and physical environment, many of them known as 'externalities', i.e. impacts external to the organization. Some of these immediate social and environmental effects (the 'secondary level' influences) are shown in Figure 4.4. These effects have beneficial as well as detrimental aspects. Generally speaking, it is an individual's perceptions and values which will determine the relative weight given to the 'goods' and 'ills' arising from the organization's activities.

It is worth introducing at this point an argument which has run for some time about the extent to which these social and environmental effects are already reflected in the economic, pricing and legal system of a society. It is argued that it is in fact inappropriate to consider these 'secondary level'

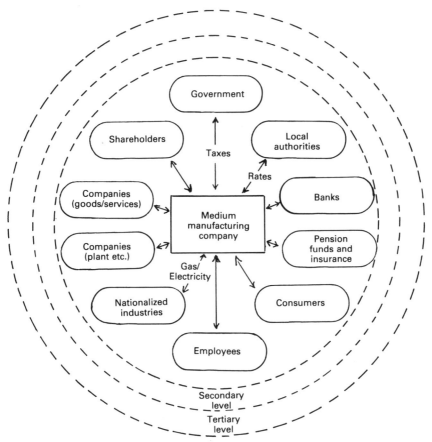

Figure 4.3 Primary level influences of organizational activity

influences separately and thus in effect duplicate attention and overemphasize them. This is an argument which hinges principally on the neo-classical economic view of the world. Thus in Figure 4.4, we can see that 'use of infrastructure' (e.g. roads, postal system, water system, waste disposal systems, etc.) is loosely linked to payment of rates, corporation taxes, road fund licenses and petrol tax for example. In addition, however, it is argued that 'resource depletion' (or 'scarcity' as the economist calls it) will reflect in higher prices; that the opportunity cost of capital will be reflected in the market-place; that the costs arising from disposable packaging and products and the demand for new technology and resources will all be reflected in prices. As well as this, it can be argued that society (through its laws), consumers (through their demand) and employees (through their choice to work and choice of work) express their preferences about the relative balance of these 'externalities' which result from organizational activity.

Such arguments depend upon the extent to which one believes that markets and society are 'efficient' and 'rational'.[5] That is, on the extent to

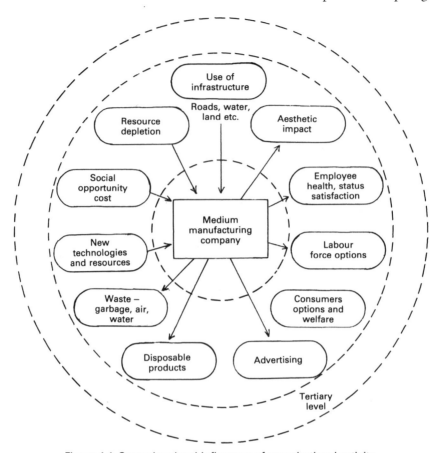

Figure 4.4 Secondary level influences of organizational activity.

which an economist's view of the world is a complete view. So, to the extent that all individuals:

have choice,
have an equal call over resources,
exercise choice through access to complete information, and,
exercise equal control over our government and laws,

then such arguments probably have some merit. They fail, however, to the extent that:

(i)   some group(s) have more power over economic resources and more power over the legal and government machinery;
(ii) individuals do not have (complete or even, at times partial) information about all choices and would be unable to assimilate all information even were it available to them (see, for example, Tinker, 1984a, 1985).

We would strongly suggest that markets and governments do not necessarily 'know best' and certainly cannot continuously allocate resources in the most

socially beneficial way if democratic control cannot be exercised over them.
CSR, as Medawar (1976) says, is essentially a democratic tool. Control
cannot be sensibly exercised without information and CSR seeks to provide
that, at least in part. Such a role is seen more clearly when one looks at, what
we might call, the tertiary level of organizational influences. This is crudely
shown in Figure 4.5. It is now less realistic to look just at our medium-sized
manufacturing company, as the influences arise from a wide variety of sources
of which our company is only one and identifying specific influences is
particularly difficult.

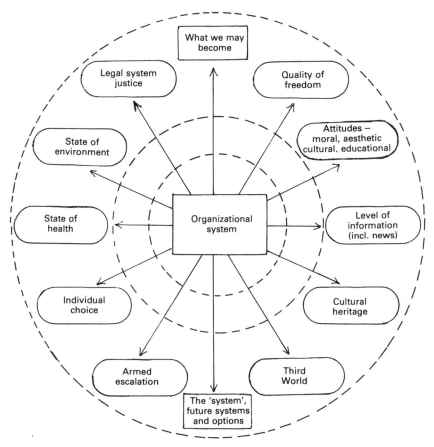

Figure 4.5   Tertiary level influence on organizational activity.

The tertiary level of influence starts fairly simply but then by a series of ever
more complex knock-on effects, like ripples in an enormous pond, becomes
increasingly interrelated and subtle. For illustration, consider again our
manufacturing company and a specific event. Let us say that an important
raw material used by the company is paper and the company decides to move
from their present supplier and transfer their custom to a company in the Far

East. Their profits rise as the cost of raw materials has dropped (otherwise why change?). This profit leads to new investment, greater dividends and higher taxes to the government. Their previous supplier, of course, all things being equal, will suffer the corollary – reduced business, redundancy, etc. A relatively minor decision has more or less immediately influenced, in the one country, the public purse (taxes and redundancies) the labour market, shareholders' wealth, employees' wealth, etc. Immediate knock-on effects may relate to hauliers and suppliers of the two companies, their customers and their respective local governments (through the rates). Further influences occur – the use of paper affects deforestation, infrastructure is changed in the Third World, changes occur in waste disposal, pollution, carbon deposits in the atmosphere, etc. Every decision has some, however tenuous, link with thousands of impacts felt throughout the world.

Three important points arise from this brief illustration. The first is that the effects of any action are so extensive and impossible to trace that a goal of reporting 'social and environmental effects' such as we stated for CSR is clearly not achievable. Secondly, pointing at (say) paper milling companies and blaming them for deforestation and its potentially horrendous consequences is too simple. Those organizations may be simply trying to survive – is that necessarily wrong? Perhaps the finger should be pointed at all users of paper. It comes down to, in effect, a collective influence from all parts of the 'system' with responsibility shared according to individual power within the system.

This leads to the third point, namely, those of a more radical disposition would see the system itself as fundamentally at fault. The sheer complexity of interaction is so vast and so inexorably tied up with (predominantly) capitalist culture that nobody within the system can possibly act without causing inevitable detrimental effects. Such a view therefore sees CSR, even in its more radical forms, as effectively legitimizing the system (if not the individual organization) and thus as an activity to be eschewed (Puxty, 1986).

Thus we see that the context in which CSR operates and the range of influences and impacts it might try to capture are extremely complex and thus there must be some selectivity in the events that the information seeks to describe.

A FRAMEWORK FOR CSR

There are many bases upon which any artifact or activity may be evaluated or judged. For an activity like accounting or an artifact such as a financial or social report, many of these bases are peripheral or even irrelevant. While an example of CSR might be aesthetically pleasing, cunningly constructed or technically innovative, such characteristics, although interesting and possibly desirable, do not directly relate to the *purpose* of the activity. Evaluation must focus on the objectives of the activity; it must consider four elements:

- *Objectives.* The propriety of the objectives.
- *The internal logic.* The extent to which the (proposed) activity is in harmony with its stated objectives.
- *Qualitative characteristics.* The extent to which certain chosen desirable characteristics of the information and its communication are met.
- *Impact.* The (actual or potential) impact of the activity.

We will deal first with the identification and evaluation of *impact*.

As we saw earlier in this chapter, total impact of organizational activity is virtually impossible to identify. Similar problems arise in attempting to assess the impact of information. Certain approaches to financial accounting could, as we saw, isolate the information and the area in which its impact was to be observed (the efficient capital markets and – to a lesser extent – the behavioural accounting research approaches). But even here, while the *response* of decision makers to information could be separately identified, the *effect* of those decisions (on, for example, economic efficiency, distribution of wealth, changes in corporate behaviour, etc.) was not analyzed. We know (or rather strongly suspect) that reporting information not only influences decision makers – the receivers of the information – but also the information providers, through something called the information inductance effect (Prakash and Rappaport, 1977). This effect arises when an information provider, concerned with how his information may look, be interpreted or reacted upon, either alters his behaviour so that his acts will produce information which will be better received, or else manipulates information to present a 'better' picture. The information inductance effect represents one side of what is known as the economic consequences debate. The other side consists of reactions by the receivers of the information – investors, competitors, regulatory bodies (including the Inland Revenue and Government) and so on (see, for example, Beaver, 1983, p. 155).

Thus by piecing together elements of the economic consequences debate research and knowledge acquired through behavioural accounting research, some indication of (mainly) primary level effects from information can be gleaned. It is clear, however, that the broader and more profound effects elude us. For example, it is by no means unlikely that certain reporting practices required by multinational corporations (say, with respect to currency translation, taxation, or plant closures and redundancies) may directly encourage an economic response from the company that could have quite drastic effects on local and national (typically Third World) economies.

If such complex impacts can result from financial accounting information and despite their widespread incidence, we still know little about them, how much more difficult will it be to identify (and subsequently evaluate) the impacts from CSR information?

We conclude that evaluation based on the impact of the information is virtually impossible in that these impacts cannot be systematically identified. Nevertheless, impact must ultimately be the *raison d'être* of CSR and despite this impossibility we must not lose sight of this. We can overcome this difficulty (at least partially) by focusing on objectives.

The objectives of CSR have cropped up regularly in both this chapter and in Chapter 1. The objective of a report is the aim which is held for it; thus a statement of the objective(s) of a social report indicates what it is hoped will be the impact of the information. Such a statement is therefore probably the most important element in any social report in that it allows the reader the opportunity to assess why the information has been made available in this particular way and to thus accept, discount, or reject the contents in the light of his own value-system.

This then constitutes our first prescription for our framework for CSR – our first characteristic of an ideal system of corporate social reporting.

Required characteristics of a social report – 1

The report must be accompanied by a full statement of the intended general objectives of the report. The statement should also allow the reader to assess: (a) what selectivity of data has been made and why; and (b) why that particular presentation has been chosen.

Such a characteristic is very general but is, to our minds, a prerequisite for both systematic CSR and the evaluation of CSR attempts. That is, we must know, in the first place, why the preparer produced a social report. However, while Required Characteristic 1 may encompass any of the objectives held for CSR, in our 'ideal world' we would not be satisfied with a report whose objectives were other than the discharge of accountability. You may remember that in Chapter 1 we, following Perks and Gray (1978), identified four broad classifications of the objectives held for CSR by groups we called: radicals, orthodox, partisan interest groups, and accountors. You may also remember that we unequivocally favoured the accountors group, whose objective we identified as 'fulfilment of responsibility and discharge of accountability'.

The choice of the fourth group is based on the beliefs that:

● Democracy is an ideal shared (in principle at least) by all western countries and by many peoples in the non-democratic countries and (again in principle) is the foundation of social and political life in the UK.
● Democracy implies that: (a) power and responsibility are equated, and (b) information about the equation (i.e. accountability) is the right of a society,
● CSR represents (and must represent) an essentially democratic activity.

This is essentially Medawar's (1976) thesis:

> Full social accountability is self-evident as a democratic ideal, and one which may be considered an end in itself.   p. 393

Thus this choice of accountability as the basis of CSR derives from the values of present society-as-a-whole. Of course, should society-as-a-whole choose to either ignore the information or use it to develop the objectives of one of the other groups (radicals, special interest groups), that is society's prerogative. The accountability/democracy basis of CSR requires only that CSR be available – not that society-as-a-whole use it in any particular way or to any predetermined purpose.[6]

Thus we can state formally our second prescription for CSR:

Required characteristics of a social report – 2

The objective of a social report should be to inform society about the extent to which actions for which an organization is held responsible have been fulfilled.

Characteristic 1 requires that the objectives – whatever they are – be stated. Characteristic 2 requires that these objectives relate specifically to accountability rather than to any other 'held' objectives. Although these two may be in conflict the reason for specifying both is that, as we shall see in subsequent chapters, few examples of CSR presently meet the 'ideal' characteristic of discharging accountability. To simply dismiss all such CSR on this basis may thus be a little too sweeping and therefore we have attempted to enable evaluation in relation to objectives to be made at two levels:

External. To what extent do we agree with the objectives?
Internal. To what extent does the report meet its own objectives and other more general qualitative criteria?

The extent to which a report meets its own objectives is largely a matter of logical analysis (although interpretation and opinion will come into it). It is first necessary to deduce what are the essential requirements of a stated objective and then assess the extent to which they are met. These essential requirements will include not only the selection and presentation elements we noted in Characteristic 1, but also the groups to whom the report is available. This can be stated formally as our third prescription for CSR.

Required characteristics of a social report – 3

The report, in its choice of data, emphasis, method of presentation, and availability, should provide information directly relevant to its objectives and in particular to the objectives it holds for the interest groups to whom it is directed.

This leads us into the final element – the required qualitative character-istics. As we saw earlier, qualitative characteristics can be split between those which relate to information *per se* and those which are deduced from either financial accounting conventions generally or the decision useful-ness criterion in particular. It is the first of these with which we are concerned here.

● *Relevance and completeness*. To the extent that these are appropriate characteristics they are dealt with by reference to the statement of objectives.
● *Comparability*. This characteristic is appropriate only to the extent that two or more organizations are subject to the same responsibilities and share the same objectives. There is no fixed guide on what might be comparable – banks and engineering companies are probably not comparable in any general sense. The accounting basis for the criterion arises from comparing profitability and related issues. There is less need in CSR as there *are* absolute yardsticks which can be applied – *no* accidents, *no* complaints, *no* strikes, *no* sackings, etc. (We should note that our ultimately proposed model – compliance with standard – would allow comparison as to the extent to which different organizations complied with law and other standards applicable *to that organization*.)
● *Timeliness*. It seems that although timeliness is a generally desirable charac-teristic it cannot be definitively operationalized at the moment. An arbit-rary requirement that all information must be made public in less than one year of the event to which it relates seems the best provisional way to operationalize it for the present time.
● *Understandability*. This is probably the least possible to fully operational-ize. We can only provide one guideline here, that is that the report should not assume that the reader is any sort of expert. If a report requires careful and intelligent reading but the reader is neither careful nor intelligent then information intermediaries (e.g. journalists – careful and intelligent?) could step in. If the report is misleading and obfuscatory, on the other hand, then it may not satisfy its objectives.
● *Reliability/directness/freedom from bias*. Although usually separated, it is convenient to take these characteristics together. There is a basic require-ment of information that it corresponds reasonably with the events it purports to describe. This is 'directness' and is a *sine qua non* of informa-tion. Information must also be free from bias but this is a more difficult aim. We believe that 'directness' and 'freedom from bias' are best achieved by reporting raw data. That is, information is not costed, valued, netted off, aggregated and reinterpreted unless any of these actions can be per-formed objectively. The reliability characteristic is also a *sine qua non* of information and can only be achieved, we believe, by audit. Who should be the auditor depends on the case in question.

We may thus state our fourth desirable characteristic(s) of CSR.

Required characteristics of a social report – 4

The report should present direct raw (unmanipulated) data that can be understood by a non-expert undertaking a careful and intelligent reading of the report. The report should be audited.

Characteristics 1–4 together give us an evaluative framework from which acceptable practices may be deduced. Although this largely completes our basic framework we need to look in more detail at the areas to be reported upon (the issues) and those to whom the report will be available (the constituencies).

CONSTITUENCIES AND ISSUES

If one starts from the objective that CSR is intended to discharge accountability then the report should:

(a) be available to all members of society; and
(b) relate to the whole spread of activities for which that organization is held responsible.

Instead of the phrase 'all members of society', it is more usual to talk in terms of stakeholders, participants, or constituencies. These are groups, within society, whose relationship with the organization tends to be centred upon a more specific set of issues. The groups are thus similar, *in principle*, to the concept of 'user groups' in financial accounting. For CSR the major constituencies are usually identified as:

the local community
employees
consumers/clients

There are problems and limitations with this approach but it, nevertheless makes a 'first approximation' framework for analyzing issues and constituencies which we shall follow below.

The local community
This group consists of all the people who, by reason of their physical proximity to an organization are socially and environmentally affected by its activities. With particular geographically discreet organizations (notably district health authorities, and district and county councils) what constitutes the

local community is relatively clear. For other organizations with a greater geographic spread of activity (typically large and multinational companies, but also central governments, banks, building societies, partnerships, unions, etc.) the concept of 'local effects' implies the need for organizations to report by locale of activity (as well as by type of activity) as global or macro information cannot inform local affected parties. (For example, X plc may have a quite 'acceptable' level of air pollution when measured across all their sites worldwide, but the community around one or two specific plants may be dropping like flies – deathbed reassurances that X plc is 'within acceptable standards' hardly seems apposite in these circumstances.)

The 'local community' is, however, typically a diverse aggregation of (*inter alia*), the rich and poor, the intelligent and stupid, local businesses, taxpayers, the unemployed, schools, group homes for the mentally handicapped, churches, and so on. Each segment of the community will be interested in, and perhaps demand, different responsibility (and thus accountability) from the organization in question. It is neither realistic nor reasonable to expect the organization to respond to all these groups. The issues on which responsibility is required must therefore be spelt out. Here the law (and other authoritative regulation) comes, however imperfectly, to our aid. All demands for information which relates to extant law can be justified (even if such justification is presently ignored by the organization).[7] Demands relating to issues which fall outside the law may be a matter of conflict, protest and political muscle. Rightly or wrongly, under capitalism, the owner of property can dispose of that property (usually) as he sees fit and thus gains the right to affect the lives of others to his own ends (MacPherson, 1973). Thus matters such as unsightly factories, the non-use of local suppliers or the use of heavy wagons for deliveries and so on, being outside the law, would be matters for 'local action' from which demands for additional CSR information and the acceptance of wider 'responsibility' might emerge.

Employees

Being, on the whole, members of the local community, employees' interests *qua* employees need to be distinguished from the general social and environmental issues of broader local community concern. Employee interests will probably be broadly of two types: working conditions and the security of employment. These issues and the role of the employee constituency will be dealt with in much more detail in Chapters 8 and 9. There are, however, a number of points that should be made at this stage.

It is usual to treat employees as a homogeneous group. This is probably incorrect in that, at very least, the 'career' employee (typically 'white collar', professional and management) and the 'workers' (typically 'blue collar') may face different pressures, problems, attitudes, and mobility opportunities. Whilst focus on employees usually concentrates on the blue collar sector, any complete CSR should also report on such white collar concerns as socializing effects, stress, and pressure on social and ethical (as opposed to work/

business) morality as factors in the influence of organizations on society. In addition, analysis usually assumes a commonality of beliefs and objectives for unions and employees. This need not necessarily be the case and thus the needs of these parties should be analyzed separately.

Secondly, although law governs much of the physical work environment (through, for example, the *Office and Factory* and *Health and Safety at Work* Acts), many of the more critical issues such as the 'white collar socialization' and the decisions on plant closures are outside the concern of the law and may fall into the 'local action' demand for information.

Unions and employees have not always been as successful at obtaining information as they might have hoped. Their political muscle is much weaker than the numbers involved might indicate. Therefore it is apposite to make a third, and extremely important, point. Accountability is principally discharged to shareholders (rather than employees) under current law and social convention. The majority of the equity in British (and US) companies is held by institutions, investment trusts, insurance companies, public sector bodies, pension funds, and so on. Estimates vary, but these account for over 50% of equity holdings by most calculations (Briston and Dobbins, 1978). But, as Drucker (1980) points out, employees, through pension funds alone, own approximately *one third* of all equity capital in the UK and USA. Employees are therefore, in effect, the major shareholder who, their rights as employees notwithstanding, are due an accountability and corresponding power over companies. At present this is clearly not forthcoming as pension funds (*inter alia*) do not discharge an accountability to *their* owners. (See, for example, Fanning, 1981.)

This critical point means that employees should be able to justify accountability beyond the legal statutes governing working conditions and should find themselves as the most powerful of groups within *the framework of shareholder law governing our society.*

Consumers

Consumers are the major constituency who are not geographically defined. Their lives are affected through:

- advertising, marketing and salesmanship (the stimulation of, perhaps unnecessary and improper, demand)
- available choice
- quality, price and life of the product.

Law (and quasi-law) governs (through, for example, the *Sale of Goods Acts*, the Office of Fair Trading, and the Advertising Standards Board) a number of the above aspects of the consumers' affected lives. As with other groups, many of the more subtle (beneficial as well as detrimental) effects are outside the direct concerns of the law and thus less easy to justify as responsibility and as requiring accountability. The influence of advertising and product availability upon our lives is virtually impossible to ascertain, although from

Vance Packard (1962, 1963) onward the 'case to answer' has been placed in the public domain. As with other groups, it once again probably requires local action to achieve extended responsibility in these respects. The work of Ralph Nader in the USA and, to a lesser extent, the Consumers' Association and Social Audit in the UK (see Chapter 7) have pushed for (and achieved) acknowledgement of responsibility beyond existing law, sometimes through having the law changed.

Other constituencies

While the three previous groups cover between them most of the effects with which CSR is concerned, in being specific and local in focus there is a danger that more general issues may be forgotten. We must not overlook, for example, the fact that 'consumers' include overseas countries (with occasionally critical effects; see, for example, Medawar, 1979) and that 'local community' also includes Third World communities and governments with production facilities there, and so on. But further, and most importantly, we must not overlook social and global effects as a whole – the conception of society or the human race as constituent. These matters lie beyond the law and thus do not involve legally enforceable responsibility, but to ignore them is to look at only half the story. We are talking here of the secondary and particularly the tertiary levels of influence we mentioned earlier. These include such matters as resource depletion, deforestation, social infrastructure destruction, transference and manipulation of values, exporting of arms, nuclear waste dumping at sea, extinction of species, and so on. If we are all stewards of our planet for future generations, then a discussion of social responsibility and thus CSR is incomplete without some recognition of these larger and potentially final consequences of organizational actions. The job of Government? – Of the UN? – The World Bank? But these are organizations too: probably the most influntial but least accountable. Nothing we have said should exclude these organizations, along with charities and multinational conglomerates, from the implications of our analysis.

SUMMARY AND CONCLUSIONS

We have seen that although accounting is also about information, in its 'traditional' form it cannot provide a complete framework for CSR. In particular, financial reporting and CSR differ in:

● their assumed purpose
● the groups to whom the information is addressed
● the range of events they seek to describe
● the focus of, and selectivity imposed upon, the information.

Nevertheless accounting theory provided a starting point from which four 'required characteristics of a social report' were derived. These are summarized in Figure 4.6.

---

1 Each report should include a statement of its objectives which allows (*inter alia*) the assessment of the:
- grounds for data selection
- reasons for form of presentation chosen,

2 The objective of a social report should be to discharge accountability in the spirit of improved democracy.

3 The information should be directly related to the objectives held for the particular groups to whom it is addressed.

4 The information should be unmanipulated and readable by a non-expert. It must be audited.

Figure 4.6 – Required characteristics of a social report

There will be occasions where Requirements 1 and 2 are in conflict. This was explicitly recognized. The scheme allows reports to be examined for their *internal* validity even when the reader disagrees with their perceived *external* validity (i.e. the reports' objectives). In addition, reports will normally be addressed to three major groups of constituents:

the local community,

employees,

consumers/clients.

Although this will usually imply a localized reporting emphasis, given that organizational impact is ultimately the point of interest, the more subtle but more important global and societal influences should also be covered.

Of course, there may be conflict between constituents. A typical example is where a call for pollution control might close a plant or reduce profitability, with an attendant impact on employment. These are matters outside the model itself. We seek information to discharge accountability, what society does with that information has to be society's concern. The information must, however, not only be available but be known to be available. This, of course, involves publicizing the information. This point is made colourfully by Douglas Adams, who can have the last word for this chapter:

> Mr Prosser said: 'You were quite entitled to make any suggestions or protests at the appropriate time you know.' 'Appropriate time?' hooted Arthur. 'Appropriate time? The first I knew about it was when a workman arrived at my home yesterday. I asked him if he'd come to clean the windows and he said no he'd come to demolish the house. He didn't tell me straight away of course. Oh no. First he wiped a couple of windows and charged me a fiver. Then he told me.'
> 'But Mr Dent, the plans have been available in the local planning office for the last nine months.'
> 'Oh yes, well as soon as I heard I went straight round to see them, yesterday afternoon. You hadn't exactly gone out of your way to call attention to them had you? I mean like actually telling anybody or anything.'
> 'But the plans were on display ... '
> 'On display? I eventually had to go down to the cellar to find them.'
> 'That's the display department.'

'With a torch.'
'Ah, well the lights had probably gone.'
'So had the stairs.'
'But look, you found the notice didn't you?'
'Yes', said Arthur, 'yes I did. It was on display in the bottom of a locked filing cabinet stuck in a disused lavatory with a sign on the door saying *Beware of the Leopard.*'

A few minutes later a voice is heard from the sky 'People of Earth, your attention please. . . . As you will no doubt be aware, the plans for developement of the outlying regions of the Galaxy require the building of a hyperspatial express route through your star system, and regrettably your planet is one of those scheduled for demolition. The process will take slightly less than two of your Earth minutes. Thank you.' . . . 'There's no point in acting all surprised about it. All the planning charts and demolition orders have been on display in your local planning department in Alpha Centauri for fifty of your Earth years, so you've had plenty of time to lodge any formal complaint and it's far too late to start making a fuss about it now.'

'What do you mean you've never been to Alpha Centauri? For heaven's sake mankind, it's only four light years away you know. I'm sorry, but if you can't be bothered to take an interest in local affairs that's your own lookout.'
'Energize the demolition beams.' . . . 'I don't know, . . . apathetic bloody planet, I've no sympathy at all.' Douglas Adams, *The Hitch Hikers Guide to The Galaxy*, Pan Books, London, 1979, pp. 12, 30–31

NOTES

1. Acknowledgement is due to Dr Paul Barnes and Dr Richard Laughlin for laying the groundwork upon which this analysis is built.
2. These contentions can be easily demonstrated. Consider 'understandability'. How are we to measure understandable? Understandable to whom? The most popular newspapers in the UK have an estimated reading age of between seven and nine years. Is this to be the criterion? If so, information will have to be dangerously simple. This is essentially a problem with all qualitative criteria. It applies to current financial reporting practice, although to a lesser degree because of convention and the (assumed) greater homogeneity within user groups. Thus, any evaluation based on qualitative criteria will itself be subjective.
3. Much of this section was stimulated by the seminal analysis of Burchell *et al.* (1980), wherein they examine the development and roles of accounting within the context of organizations and society.
4. There are myriad examples of accounting developments either failing to respond to these 'functional claims and pretensions' and/or being prompted by influences where the information recipients were not represented. Examples include the Sandilands report (Cmnd. 6225, p. 158) in which cash flow accounting is recognized as the most appropriate method but rejected as 'such a fundamental change would not be acceptable to British *companies* at the present time' (emphasis added). Hope and Gray (1982) demonstrate how it was the influence of a small group of companies which determined the outcome of the R&D standard, SSAP13. Gray and Hope (1982) and Gray (1983) show that there is some doubt over the rigour with which auditors enforce the disclosure requirements of accounting standards. Examples are also found in the non-commercial sector. Despite very widespread acceptance that (for example) charities and district health authorities should report

in order to discharge their accountability, developments either remain locked in inappropriate traditional accounting thinking (Gray, 1984a) or are implemented slowly and patchily (CIPFA/AHST, 1982; Gray, 1984b).

5. We should note that there are further assumptions implied here, principally that economies tend towards general equilibrium (see Tinker, 1984b).

6. We thus assume a high degree of 'consumer sovereignty' in information. That is, we believe that a reader must be allowed to identify and determine all assumptions and uncertainties underlying the information he receives. Information deliberately intended to mislead (see, for example, Bougen, 1984) we find distasteful. See Hird (1983) in this context with respect to financial accounting.

7. In a democratic society (sic) this information would be forthcoming. It is clear therefore that we do not live in a democratic society!

Chapter 5
Social reporting I – non-financial information

Chapters 1 to 4 have examined what we mean by corporate social reporting and have reviewed the theory and the general patterns of development of CSR. We now turn to examine proposed and applied approaches to CSR in some detail. This chapter covers disclosures of mainly non-financial information, Chapter 6 looks at financial social reporting with an emphasis on the social income statement and social balance sheet, Chapter 7 covers the so-called social audits, and Chapters 8 and 9 concentrate on reporting to and about employees.

This division of the chapters is an attempt to codify CSR theory and practice but it must be noted that the division is somewhat arbitrary. That is, much CSR involves financial, statistical *and* narrative disclosure and a number of the more interesting reports involve information prepared internally by the organization and then commented upon ('audited') by an outside body. Thus, the division of the chapters should be treated as a general categorization rather than as indicating a formal separation of reporting typologies.

In addition there are a number of other general points that must be borne in mind when considering methods of CSR. Firstly, the range of events and impacts with significant potential social effects is enormous. McAdam (1973) lists over one hundred and fifty areas upon which a company might consider disclosing information. These include product quality and safety, pricing practice, pollution, corporate sponsorship and donations, equal opportunities, etc. (See also Hargreaves and Dauman, 1975, p. 70.)

Secondly, CSR practice is immensely diverse, *ad hoc* and intermittent. We have already remarked that much CSR is a public relations or 'firefighting' exercise, and this goes some way to explaining why CSR is usually on an intermittent basis (see, for example, the ICI plc reports from the late 1970s through to the mid 1980s). Mathews (1984), developing Gambling's (1977a) point, has also argued that support for and practice of CSR bears a strong inverse relationship with economic climate. The recession which started to bite in the late 1970s appears to have been accompanied by a decrease in the amount of CSR. The optimists suggest we may see economic recovery in the late 1980s when, if the hypothesis holds, CSR may re-emerge. Those points should be borne in mind when considering the examples in the next few chapters and partly explain why 1970s references are at least as common as those of more recent vintage.

Finally, remember that we are looking at reported information. Whilst 'correspondence with reality' is a prerequisite of information (see Chapter 4) there is no way available to the average reader of CSR information to assess its accuracy and fairness. In fact, two studies by Wiseman (1982) and Rockness (1985) on environmental disclosures in the USA have shown that such disclosures are more likely *not* to correspond accurately with either the 'true facts' (whatever they are) or the perceptions of independent bodies.

With these points in mind, we can turn to an analysis of examples of non-financial social reporting. We have organized these examples into five categories:

● Narrative disclosure
● Statistical summaries
● Social indicators
● Compliance with standards
● Other (including advertising)

NARRATIVE DISCLOSURE

If an organization is considering experimenting with CSR then narrative disclosure is the easiest (and probably the quickest and cheapest) method. Narrative disclosures vary from general statements of good intention in the annual report and accounts through to relatively thorough analyses of specific issues produced as separate documents.

The American Accounting Association (AAA) in 1973 were perhaps the first to formally recommend this approach to CSR. As part of fuller disclosure of environmental costs the AAA committee suggested that a verbal statement be made by organizations of their environmental problems, goals and plans, and progress towards reducing the environmental impact of business activity. The most radical element of the proposal was the recommendation that the statement be audited as part of the annual financial audit (Belkaoui, 1984, pp. 151 and 152, gives examples of hypothetical audit reports). Needless to say the latter suggestion has not been widely implemented. Four years later the AICPA (1977) also recommended narrative disclosure as an important element in their extensive social report proposal. This similarly appears to have had little effect on practice.

Nevertheless, if one is willing to be fairly liberal in one's interpretation of what constitutes CSR narrative disclosure, CSR at this sort of level is relatively widespread. The Ernst & Ernst surveys of social disclosures amongst the Fortune 500 companies (USA) show that by the late 1970s, 90% had some explicit social disclosure, although this covered, on average, only about half a page of the full accounts. Brockoff (1979) reports that in 1973, 70% of German companies surveyed had some explicit social statement although the bulk were general and in the form of descriptive narrative. Singh and Ahuja (1983) imply that some level of CSR can be expected in virtually all Indian companies of any size. Even in the UK over one-third of the larger companies would appear to have *some* disclosure (see Chapter 3). Exhibit 5.1 provides two home-based examples.

Pilkington Bros. Ltd
Chairman's statement to shareholders: (*extract*)
Pilkington and the Community
We have continued to play a very active part in the communities where we manufacture. In St Helens, we are deeply involved in the creation of new jobs through three separate but complementary organisations.
The Community of St Helens Trust continues to make a real contribution to the foundation and growth of small business enterprises.
Rainford Venture Capital Ltd, a Pilkington subsidiary formed to identify opportunities which require more capital than would normally be available to a private individual, has made its first investments in a word processing company and in a specialist building products company.
Through Industrial Experience Projects Ltd Pilkington seeks to provide work experience and training facilities to enable school leavers to acquire and develop the necessary skills for future employment.
In these three organisations, Pilkington is committing management time, expertise, and finance, to encourage the creation of new job opportunities from within the community.
In Birmingham, following the closure of Chance Brothers, we are carrying out a rapid redevelopment of the site, including the building of small factory units, to provide for new employment in the area.
In all these initiatives, we have received the ready co-operation of the local authorities concerned, and of all who have been asked to help.

Source: *Pilkington Brothers Annual Report and Accounts 1981.* Used with permission.

The Rio Tinto-Zinc Corporation PLC
Directors Report (*extract*)
Environmental expenditure
The Group's environmental expenditure in 1982 was some £33 million. This figure includes grants to universities and other learned institutions undertaking research on subjects of importance to Group companies. Over the last ten years the Group spent some £258 million on environmental controls, an average of £26 million a year.
Emphasis continued to be given to all aspects of environmental protection and health and safety matters.

Source: *Rio Tinto-Zinc Corporation Annual Report and Accounts 1982.* Used with permission.

Exhibit 5.1 Examples of narrative disclosure.

While companies such as ICI, BP and Rio Tinto-Zinc have fairly consistently produced some acknowledgement of social responsibility, one more
commonly finds a spasmodic reporting rather than a consistent and developing approach to disclosure. For example, British Leyland produced a statement on their view of social responsibility in 1972. This disappeared in 1973
to be replaced by a statement on industrial relations. Courtaulds produced a
statement on energy conservation (including amount expended) in their
1975 and 1976 accounts. This statement disappeared in 1977 but reappeared
in 1979 and 1980. That company also produced statements on Health and
Safety and the Environment throughout the late 1970s and early 1980s.
A statement on conservation of the environment appeared in Unilever's
accounts in 1972 and 1973. It has since disappeared. 1976 (only) saw a note
on Health and Safety in Lucas' annual accounts.

Such statements really contain very little information and even a very
conventional text like Estes (1976) refers to examples of such disclosure in
the USA as 'incomplete, defensive and sprinkled with propaganda' and
'blatantly self-serving' (p. 55). Such accusations may be equally appropriate
to some of the more developed examples of narrative disclosure. As might
also be expected, the more developed the form of disclosure, the less common
the examples.[2]

One extensive example is that given by the Bank of America; however, the
report is still *ad hoc*, partial and unaudited. As with most reports there is no
statement of objectives and the reader can only guess at what is missing.
(Note the coy statement in the last sentence of the extract.) The report
neither discharges accountability nor informs the reader of the totality of the
organization's social performance. The experiment by the bank was continued through the 1970s but with no substantial change of emphasis (see
Heard and Bolce, 1981).

In the UK, we might be glad of even such 'inadequate' CSR. The nearest
UK example is provided by Rio Tinto-Zinc plc. RTZ have since 1974
published 'Fact Sheets'. These are 'advertised' in the annual accounts and
provide a description and analysis of aspects of the company's activities. For
example, between 1977 and 1984 various reports were produced on RTZ's
activities with respect to:

Mining in the environment
Employee conditions in South Africa, Zimbabwe and Namibia
Company attitude toward Australian Aborigines
Uranium: energy, safety and the environment.

The RTZ 'Fact Sheets' are probably Britain's most advanced form of CSR
produced by a company, and other companies, notably BP, have more
recently began producing similar publications. Despite RTZ's and BP's
efforts being highly developed by British company standards they are still
open to the earlier criticisms.

Two of the most sophisticated examples of narrative disclosure CSR come,

Urban Affairs

Urban Affairs assigned new officers, called regional urban development officers, to major metropolitan areas in seven of the bank's eleven California regions. These officers, all specialists in minority business lending, work closely with community offices and minority businesses to encourage and expand minority customer relations.

Two new programs were developed in Los Angeles to provide better career information for junior and senior high school students. One program includes a slide presentation on banking careers and trips to Bank of America facilities. The other acquaints students with a variety of career alternatives and provides visits to various industries.

Affirmative Action

Significant strides were made in the continuing efforts to identify, develop and upgrade minority and women employees as the chart below illustrates. Through intensive recruitment, training and development efforts, further Affirmative Action progress was made in 1974.

Overall, minorities represent the same proportion in Bank of America's staff as in the State of California.

The Equal Opportunity Section in Personnel Administration monitors all employment activities to insure equal opportunity for all persons.

The following chart shows the gains Bank of America has made since 1971 in its continuing commitment for equal opportunity in hiring and advancement for women and minorities:

	March 1971	March 1972	March 1973	March 1974	Dec. 31 1974
Women					
Total Bank Staff	72.4%	72.9%	73.4%	73.8%	74.3%
Officers	23.1%	25.3%	29.9%	32.4%	34.0%
Minorities					
Total Bank Staff	20.8%	22.5%	23.7%	25.3%	26.6%*
Officers	6.6%	7.4%	9.0%	10.4%	11.6%

* Minorities constitute 26.5% of California's population, according to the 1970 Census.

Investments

Bank of America's Trust Department in 1974 gained the services of an analyst whose full-time duty is to advise on the social responsibility of businesses as their conduct affects investment decisions. The corporate responsibility analyst was appointed by BA Investment Management Corporation, wholly-owned subsidiary of BankAmerica Corporation, which serves as investment advisor to the Trust Department.

Contributions and Grants

Bank of America made charitable contributions of $2.7 million to Bank of America Foundation and to other deserving organizations. These funds were distributed in the following approximate proportions: Health, 48 percent; Education, 31 percent; Community Involvement, 18 percent; other, 3 percent.

Public Broadcasting Service: Bank of America made two gifts to PBS television stations. It gave $57,000 to KQED, Inc., and the Pacific Film Archive of the University of California at Berkeley, to partially fund the showing of a series of 13 Japanese film masterpieces on the 240-station network.

The bank also made a $104,000 grant to seven California PBS stations for three series of programs: "Evening at Symphony," "Romagnoli's Table," and "Animated Film Festival."

Poppy Park: Bank of America Foundation supported a statewide effort by school children to preserve the best-known stand of the state flower, the California poppy. The pupils raised $18,000 and the foundation matched that amount to save a 1,000-acre area in Lancaster, California. The children have named the wildflower preserve "Poppy Park." It will be officially established as a state park in 1976.

Multicultural Resources: The Foundation also gave $30,000 to support a library of 5,000 books and other publications for and about various ethnic cultures. The library, a one-of-its-kind collection called "Multicultural Resources," is also receiving administrative and staff assistance from San Francisco State University and the San Francisco School District.

Paper Recycling

The corporation continued its program of using recycled paper and recycling waste paper wherever practical. More than 2,650 tons of used paper – principally old records, used corrugated cartons, and obsolete forms – were turned over to secondary fiber companies in 1974.

On the other side of the cycle, many bank forms and almost all bank envelopes use stock containing at least 75 percent recycled paper. All general bank letterhead stationery is 100 percent recycled paper.

However, scarcity and cost of recycled paper for production of the 1974 Annual Report forced the corporation to forego its use this year.

Exhibit 5.2 Extract from the *BankAmerica Corporation Annual Report 1974*. Used with permission.

ASSETS

Minority Affairs
Atlantic Richfield has worked hard to provide job opportunities for minorities. Minority group members account for 13 percent of the total work force, a ratio that ranks Atlantic Richfield at the top of the petroleum industry.

Jobs formerly restricted to men – such as refinery work – have been opened up to women.

The number of minorities and women in professional, managerial and sales positions has nearly doubled since 1970.

To aid minority economic development, Atlantic Richfield maintains deposits of over $1 million in minority-owned financial institutions across the country.

Atlantic Richfield reported purchases of $3.2 million from minority suppliers in 1974. This was double its 1973 purchases.

Contributions
Its $5.5 million of charitable contributions in 1974 supported a large number of educational, health and cultural organizations in the United States.

Atlantic Richfield matches, dollar for dollar, employee contributions to educational institutions.

One unusual grant in 1974 was $10,000 to the Council on Economic Priorities, an organization that monitors corporate social responsibility.

Community organizations backed by Atlantic Richfield Foundation grants include the Boy Scouts, YMCA, Junior Achievement, Urban Coalition, American Red Cross, Salvation Army and Urban League.

Shareholder Information
The firm's Form 10K financial report, which contains more detailed information than the annual report and which all corporations must file with the Securities and Exchange Commission, was offered free of charge to all shareholders in 1972 and 1973.

Environment and Conservation
Atlantic Richfield was the first company in the petroleum industry to announce that it would make a lead-free gasoline.

In the interests of what it called "America's natural beauty," the Company in 1972 cancelled its entire out-door advertising – 1,000 billboards in 36 states.

Its Cherry Point refinery in the state of Washington has been recognized as a model nonpolluter.

It has emphasized energy conservation in its own operations.

Consumerism
It was one of the first companies in the petroleum industry to post the octane levels of its gasolines at the pump.

Social Management
The Company's public affairs program in Alaska is outstanding, far surpassing any comparable effort by Atlantic Richfield in the lower 48 states both in the range and depth of activities. The Company has made its presence felt in Alaska as a concerned corporate citizen.

LIABILITIES

Most minorities and women who work for Atlantic Richfield hold low-level jobs. There is not a single black or female officer.

More than 70 major U.S. companies have elected blacks to their boards of directors. Many have also named women directors. The petroleum industry has resisted this trend – and so has Atlantic Richfield. Its board is all-white, all-male, all-Christian.

The Company has not been aggressive or innovative in its support of minority enterprise. Standard Oil of Indiana, for example, requires its purchasing agents to set goals and goes out of its way to help fledgling companies. Result: Indiana Standard spends four or five times what Atlantic Richfield spends in purchases from minority suppliers.

To encourage charitable contributions, the Internal revenue Service allows corporations a deduction of up to 5% on pretax profits. At least two companies – Dayton Hudson and Cummins Engine – takes this full deduction. Other companies – Aetna Life & Casualty, for example – have sharply increased their giving. Atlantic Richfield gives away 1.3% of pretax profits.

The pattern of Atlantic Richfield's giving is in the traditional mold, with most money going to old-line, established institutions. Of the $850,000 committed to education in 1973, for example, more than a quarter went to one school, the Massachusetts Institute of Technology.

Black colleges receive only minimal support.

The Company's annual report has been niggardly in providing meaningful details of pollution control programs or specific information about social responsibility activities. The tendency has been to substitute rhetoric for hard data. Shell Oil Company has consistently released far more information.

Atlantic Richfield was slow to comprehend the environmental problems connected with the Alaskan pipeline and for too long resisted protection measures later incorporated into the project.

The Company, while paying its respects to the conservation ethic in solving our energy problems, persists in the view that more development and more growth can solve our energy problems.

At many U.S. companies the concept of social responsibility has been institutionalized at least to the extent that new positions and/or committees have been created, some of them with high standing in the table of organization. Atlantic Richfield has floundered through a series of organizational reshuffles, with the social responsibility functions still scattered, relegated to lower levels of the Company and concerned largely with peripheral areas outside the mainstream activities.

CONCLUSION
As the youngest of the petroleum giants, the Company carries less baggage from the past. As a company still in transition, it is more conscious that its future lies ahead. And that is perhaps what is most hopeful; it is a company not yet fully formed. When oil from Alaska begins to flow and Atlantic Richfield becomes even bigger than it is today, it will have a splendid opportunity to demonstrate that social concerns can be built into the day-to-day operations of a petroleum company. More than most giant companies, it has its future in its hands. It need not relive or repeat the mistakes of the past.

Exhibit 5.3 Summary of the Atlantic Richfield Company's social report, 1977.
Source: *Participation II*, Atlantic Richfield Company, 1977. Used with permission.

unsurprisingly, from the USA. These are the reports from the Scovill Corporation Social Action Report (which has been extensively reported; see, for example, Estes, 1976; Jensen, 1976) and the Atlantic Richfield Company. The Atlantic Richfield Report is sixty plus pages. Exhibit 5.3 contains the summary of this report, entitled 'Social Responsibility at ARCO – a critique' by Milton Moskowitz. (See also McComb, 1978.)

The Atlantic Richfield and Scovill reports have some notable similarities. They both attempt to provide some indication of the benefits ('assets') *and* costs ('liabilities') arising from their activities, they are both wide-ranging and touch on matters of interest to at least part of each of the constituency or stakeholder groups. They are both, however, *ad hoc*, partial, and lacking a statement of objectives. The Scovill report is also highly likely to be selective and biased in that it is internally prepared and subject to no outside audit or yardstick. The 'summary' section of the Atlantic Richfield report, though, is particularly distinctive and noteworthy in having been 'audited'. Upon completion of the report the company asked a well-known journalist, Milton Moskowitz, famous for his critical attitude to companies, to comment on the report. This comment was published alongside the company's report (the 'liabilities'). While the audit successfully highlights the selective and biased nature of the report (and by implication should make one cautious in reading unaudited reports), its inclusion must make the Atlantic Richfield report probably the best of the narrative approaches.

A final element of CSR in the narrative disclosure format which deserves separate mention is the disclosure of charitable donations. A review of American examples of CSR shows a fairly high emphasis on a company's support of charities and other not-for-profit organizations. One of the peculiarities of UK company reporting is that disclosure of donations to charities is required by the Companies Acts. Apart from the reporting to and about employees this is the only area of CSR in the UK which has found its way onto the statute books. (For details see Cowton, 1983.)

STATISTICAL SUMMARIES

Moving up a stage in sophistication from the relatively straightforward narrative approach to CSR we meet attempts to communicate the social aspects of organizational activity via statistical summaries (although typically supported by some narrative). The major emphasis in this category tends to be on statistics about the labour force – pay, accidents, turnover, absenteeism, and so forth. However, not-for-profit organizations in the UK also commonly use this approach in their reporting of service delivery – i.e. customer orientation.

In so far as there is any guiding rationale for CSR based on statistical summaries, the idea seems to be to provide the reader with some systematic indication of the *input* to and/or *activities* (processes) of an organization. (As

RTZ's main interest in the Republic of South Africa is its 39 per cent shareholding in the Palabora Mining Company Limited. Palabora Mining operates an open-pit copper mine, smelter and refinery in the north eastern Transvaal where there were 3938 employees and 78 apprentices at 1 March 1985.

Remuneration structure

Although Palabora has had unified salary scales for all employees since 1980 it was decided to convert from the conventional points system of job evaluation to the well-known and internationally recognised Paterson system. This is based on the level of decision-making involved in each job and allows a quicker evaluation for grading purposes. Elected employee representatives sit on the job evaluation committee. Minor structural changes took place as a result of the change to the Paterson system but the vast majority of jobs remained at the same levels as before.

The current levels of remuneration together with the actual numbers employed in the various salary grades under the new system are as follows:

Notes
(1) Monthly paid employees qualify for an annual service increment equal to 1½% of the minimum rate for the salary group for each year of service, subject to a maximum after ten years of 15%.

(2) Monthly paid employees qualify for overtime payment when overtime is worked.

(3) All employees receive a holiday bonus equivalent to 8⅓% of their salary including service increments, a double cheque in effect.

(4) All employees are granted paid annual leave ranging from 21 calendar days to 40 calendar days, depending on their salary group and length of service.

(5) Apprentices' monthly earnings are paid on the following basis:
1st year R380   3rd year R525
2nd year R450   4th year R620

Should an employee be over 21 years of age at the start of his apprenticeship, the following incremental bonuses will apply:
21 years and over 10% increase
22 years and over 20% increase
23 years and over 30% increase
24 years and over 40% increase
25 years and over 50% increase

Adult artisan trainees continue to receive a salary according to their grade prior to commencing training; those who earn less than apprentices automatically receive the higher salary on starting.

Number of employees

Group	Salary range Rand/month	Salaried Staff White	Salaried Staff Black	Monthly Paid White	Monthly Paid Black	Total White	Total Black
A1	300– 450	—	—	—	302	—	302
A2	350– 525	—	—	—	1080	—	1080
A3	410– 615	—	2	—	421	—	423
B1	485– 725	6	14	—	335	6	349
B2	570– 855	11	17	—	249	11	266
B3	670–1005	41	29	6	413	47	442
B4	785–1180	15	22	4	6	19	28
B5	920–1380	21	27	38	—	59	27
C1	1085–1630	35	12	61	—	96	12
C2	1265–1900	88	2	304	—	392	2
C3	1485–2225	112	1	74	—	186	1
C4*	1750–2625	118	—	—	—	118	—
C5	2060–3090	20	—	—	—	20	—
Conf.	–	52	—	—	—	52	—
		519	126	487	2806	1006	2932

* C4 includes 21 Group
Tech employees

Total	3938
Plus Apprentices	45
Adult artisan trainees	33
	4016

Household subsistence level

Professor Potgieter of the Institute for Planning Research, University of Port Elizabeth, has carried out annual *Household Subsistence Level* (HSL) studies for Palabora since October, 1974.

The Household Subsistence Level for employees, resident in Namakgale the local black township, which is calculated for a family consisting of an adult man, an adult woman and four children of varying ages, amounted to R273.03 per month in the October, 1984 survey. HSL is an estimate of minimum requirements to meet primary needs. It should not be seen as an absolute norm, but as a guideline to establish minimum monetary income requirements. As HSL does not allow for any expenditure on items such as recreation, education, savings, holidays and other secondary needs, the higher level of income required to meet primary plus secondary needs, has been termed by Professor Potgieter as the *Household Effective Level* (HEL). This approximates HSL plus 50% or R408.05 in the October, 1984 survey. The minimum wage paid at Palabora when uplifted in accordance with the formula used by Professor Potgieter yields an HEL income of R416.25 compared to his HEL of R408.05.

Housing

Palabora's black employees live at Namakgale. The Government has allocated 1,356 South Africa Development Trust (SADT) houses to Palabora to house its own employees. In addition, the company has provided 770 houses of which 210 were financed jointly by Palabora and the SADT. All houses provided by the company are 2, 3 and 4 bedroomed, fully electrified and equipped with electric stoves, immersion heaters, lighting, power points, etc.

Exhibit 5.4 Rio Tinti-Zinc Corporation plc (Rossing Uranium Ltd): statistical disclosure. Source: *RTZ in South Africa – Employment Practices 1985*. Used with permission.

opposed to the *output* or *impact* of its activities.) The advantages to the reporting organization are that the data are relatively cheap to collect (much of it should be known already), and the results can be reported simply, clearly, and (most importantly) selectively. The reader of such reports gains advantages and disadvantages compared with the narrative approach. The advantages are the clarity and (purported) precision of the specific information communicated. The disadvantages lie in the absence of any frame of reference from which to judge the statistics themselves, the omissions and the trends (if any). Exhibit 5.4 shows one approach to reporting labour force statistics by RTZ.[3] Examples of statistical information on UK employees are fairly common and this type of information is covered in detail in Chapters 8 and 9.

In contrast, the not-for-profit organizations have tended to focus their reporting on service delivery and the customer. Exhibit 5.5 gives a not untypical extract from the annual report of a district health authority.

There are clearly problems with this approach as numerical data of this kind in isolation mean virtually nothing to a lay reader and do not *necessarily* relate directly to the extent to which the organizations have discharged their responsibility, i.e. to the organization's required *output*. Attempts to set data of this sort in context *have* been made, and this is reviewed in the next section.

For the more developed and sophisticated forms of CSR employing statistical summaries, we must again turn to the USA. Probably the best examples are the attempts by the First Pennsylvania Bank (1973) and Eastern Gas and Fuel Associates (1972 *et seq.*).

The First Pennsylvania Bank used a combination of statistics, narrative and financial information to provide a general view of their social performance. Being piecemeal, biased and selective, the report represents a perhaps useful first-step experiment. Typically, the experiment was not, however, developed and thus is subject to all the criticisms we have made of previous examples. (For a detailed report see Epstein *et al.*, 1977.) A more systematic approach is taken by Eastern Gas and Fuel Associates. Four specific areas were taken for analysis and attempts made to give both qualitative and the comparative aspects of the information. Begun originally as an MBA project in 1971 the social report ran until 1974 although (again perhaps typically) there is little evidence of serious development. Exhibit 5.6 shows an extract from the 1972 report.

Eastern Gas and Fuel Associates are worth a special mention also because they conducted one of the very few serious attempts to judge shareholder reaction to CSR. This they did by means of a questionnaire enclosed with the 1972 report. (See also Chapter 7 for Social Audit's experience in this field.) Estes (1976) reports that the results from the questionnaire:

> suggested that the shareholders were impressed by the company's honesty and openness in voluntarily revealing disappointing results. Many shareholders apparently judged Eastern a progressive company because it was working toward social accounting.   p. 37

SECTION III
A PROFILE OF LEICESTERSHIRE HEALTH AUTHORITY

An indication of the 1983 workload can be seen in the following key statistics for Hospital and Community Services:-

Main Hospital Statistics by Care Group

Care Group	In-Patient Days	Cases	Out-Patient Attend's	Day Cases	Regular Day Patients	Accident & Emergency Attend's
Acute	413,545	59,170	401,276	17,186	13,638	155,205
Geriatric	310,907	4,925	5,115	47	19,629	—
Maternity	83,512	16,333	64,983	146	—	—
Mental Illness	382,009	2,842	25,978	—	43,041	—
Mental Handicap	237,798	448	212	—	5,573	—
Regional Specialities	55,152	6,318	49,717	2,041	—	—
TOTALS	1,482,923	90,036	547,281	19,420	81,881	155,205

Community Services

Total Home Nurse visits	764,143
Total Health Visitor visits	194,903
Total Vaccinations and Immunisations	69,553
Total Family Planning Clinic attendances	40,153
Total Chiropody Treatments	98,356

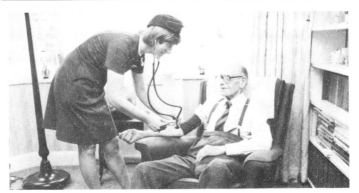

Community Nursing at work.

Exhibit 5.5 Leicestershire Health Authority. Source: *Leicestershire Health Authority Annual Financial Report and Accounts 1983/4.* Used with permission.

Toward Social Accounting

TO OUR SHAREHOLDERS:
There has been much talk in recent years of corporate social responsibility and of the need to develop some sort of social accounting to gauge how well a given firm is performing – not just as an economic unit but as a citizen. Indeed, some have suggested that these measures of corporate performance beyond net profit should be subjected to an independent social audit.

This insert for the 1972 Annual Report of Eastern Gas and Fuel Associates has been designed as an experimental exploration of two aspects of social accounting for "self-auditing" purposes:

(1) What are some internal topics on which management can presently assemble and organize reasonably accurate and coherent data?
(2) Which issues of social accountability are of external interest and to what extent are shareholders in particular interested, if at all?

To explore the first of these aspects we have gathered statistical information that covers four topics from among the many that are currently of concern to those studying corporate social responsibility:

● Industrial safety
● Minority employment
● Charitable giving
● Pensions

To explore the second aspect we have included, at the end of this insert, a short questionnaire which, if you will mail it back, will serve as a useful measure of shareholder concern with corporate social responsibility and the reporting of it. No generally accepted standards or methods of presentation have been developed for shareholder reporting on such topics nor is there clear evidence as to shareholder interest.

The topics for this first report were not chosen because they are necessarily the most important ones, or the ones that might make us look good, but because they are the most readily measurable, because our goals with respect to them are comparatively simple and clear, and because they lie in areas where management can rather directly influence results. In addition, managerial decisions on these topics can have a significant impact on earnings per share.

In the process of making this first consolidation of social data from our various operations, we found that our records were less complete and less certain than we had believed. We also found that even inadequate disclosure begins to exert a useful pressure on management to comply with new public expectations as to the conduct of large corporations. It may also be some of the best evidence that management is sincerely concerned and making an effort to meet proper expectations.

Four major recurring principles for the quantification of social responsibility have been suggested:

The first is that our priorities have been changing with some rapidity. Many of our political, economic and commercial measures of progress have become obsolescent. We need a new kind of social accounting that goes beyond GNP for the nation and goes beyond net profit for the firm.

Second, while we think of our current economic and accounting measures of GNP and net profit as very precise when you really get into the nitty gritty of how they are put together, their certainty is delusive.

Third, many proposed imprecise measures of social accounting can be sufficiently accurate to be instructive. They are not hopelessly less accurate than GNP or net profit, and so they can be quite useful, even though they lack precision, for many purposes for which we cannot use GNP and net profit.

And finally, while our efforts to calibrate our concerns by social accounting will reflect this new sense of priorities, without personal observation in the field and a weighing of the figures that we create with moral concerns, social accounting itself becomes only a new numbers game.

As we proceed with these early attempts to develop some form of internal social accounting, we should acquire additional useful insights into this new art.

Eli Goldston, *President*

1   INDUSTRIAL SAFETY
Recent legislation has demonstrated that a major current public concern, especially in the heavy industries in which Eastern is involved, is the health and safety of employees.

Our industrial accident record in recent years has not been very good. One standard measurement is the accident frequency rate (number of accidents versus hours worked), and our rate has almost doubled in the last three years, going up most dramatically in gas operations. It is clear that our safety performance has been slipping. In addition it seems that our record is poorer than that of a number of firms with whom we have compared specific records. Just where we stand in our various industries is difficult to gauge because meaningful comparative figures are not available.

ACCIDENT FREQUENCY RATE
(Lost time accidents per million employee hours)

	1970	1971	1972
Coal & Coke	43	61	78
Gas	14	26	30
Marine	34	41	43
EGFA Avg.	36	50	64

Another measure of safety performance is the severity rate, which takes into account time lost as a result of accidents. Here Eastern's record has been steadier, and apparently more in line with other firms for our industries. But much room for improvement remains.

ACCIDENT SEVERITY RATE
(Employee days lost per million employee hours)*

	1970	1971	1972
Coal & Coke	2,948	3,427	4,209
Gas	222	191	303
Marine	1,707	2,015	1,423
EGFA Avg.	2,225	2,516	3,033

*Excluding days charged for fatalities.

Exhibit 5.6 Eastern Gas and Fuel Associates. Source: insert for the 1972 *Annual Report of Eastern Gas and Fuel Associates*. Used with permission.

Frequency and severity rates, either for a single firm or for an industry, are rather elusive statistics. They may appear worse simply from improved reporting, or may appear better if excessive pressure to improve the record results in variable reporting practices. Comparisons are complicated by numerous variables. Our river towboat crews, for instance, live aboard the boats and so are at their workplace even when not actually working. A greater awareness by both employees and management of the importance of safety may increase the number of reported accidents. Improved benefits could encourage accident reporting. Comparisons are also difficult because of different bases of reporting. We are trying for 1973 to improve both our performance and our ability to supply managers with comparable industry statistics.

Job related fatalities, of course, are the most salient and tragic accidents. We require full reports to top management on all serious injuries and fatalities along with proposals to prevent recurrence. At Eastern we are constantly trying to develop more effective ways to impress on all our people the need to guard against the ever present hazards in their particular line of work. Here is our recent record of fatalities:

FATALITIES

	1970	1971	1972
Coal & Coke	8	3	4
Gas	0	0	0
Marine	1	1	2
EGFA Total	9	4	6

Critics of industry often assume that management has more ability to reduce accident frequency and severity and to eliminate accidents than may be the case. We do not accept at all the rationalization that "accidents just happen" and we would be the last to suggest that a victim alone is at fault. But it is obvious that we need to be better persuaders and to improve training, motivation and enforcement when it is considered that in at least five of the six 1972 fatalities, the victim was an experienced employee who was clearly violating a standard safety work rule of the company at the time of his death. The need for and difficulty of broad safety indoctrination is evidenced by the fact that 11 employees were fatally injured in 1972 in accidents off the job.

The economics of safety reinforces our social/humanitarian concerns. Compensation of employees injured on the job cost Eastern at least $3,600,000 last year, or about 20¢ in earnings per share.

We are continuing to increase our commitment of men and money to ongoing safety programs in all operations. One of our headquarters officers has been assigned to regular field checks of safety practices and the compilation and analysis of accident statistics. Eastern Associated Coal Corp. has further strengthened its existing safety program by engaging the highly respected safety department of a firm in another industry to help us improve our safety performance in coal operations. In Boston Gas Company, a safety campaign has commenced that focuses not only on safe work habits but also on continuing "defensive" use of equipment and procedures to avoid dangerous situations.

2 MINORITY EMPLOYMENT

An important thrust of Eastern's social concerns effort is to respond positively to the apparently clear national desire to bring an end to discrimination in employment and promotion because of race, religion or other difference from that elusive notion of "the majority."

It is difficult to generalize fairly and judiciously about Eastern's minority employment statistics. Numerically, minority employment in the company has increased in recent years, but has not quite maintained its percentage proportion. This has been particularly noticeable in coal operations, but in this instance, the increased employment has come in areas where there has been a smaller minority proportion in the local population. And it may be that the improving employment prospects for minority members either with our competitors or in fields previously closed to them have reduced the relative attractiveness of jobs with us. Boston Gas has had an excellent record of integrating its work force, but the addition of new territory with a different population mix has appeared to slow the trend.

MINORITY EMPLOYMENT

	1970	1971	1972
Coal & Coke			
Total	5,703	6,050	6,448
Minority	526	544	517
% Minority	9.2%	9.0%	8.0%
Gas			
Total	1,466	1,500	1,611
Minority	66	96	115
% Minority	4.5%	6.4%	7.1%
Marine			
Total Employees	1,077	1,332	1,358
Minority	64	84	79
% Minority	5.9%	6.3%	5.8%
EGFA*			
Total Employees	8,349	8,995	9,526
Minority	659	727	716
% Minority	7.9%	8.3%	7.5%

* Includes Boston Office

Measuring progress in integration is further complicated by the fact that companies were forbidden to record the race of employees until quite recently. Many of our operations are so geographically scattered that it is difficult to determine in many cases if our percentages of minority employment are in line with the minority population in reasonably relevant areas, although this does seem to be true.

MINORITY EMPLOYMENT LEVELS

	1971	1972	1972 Total in Category	1972 % of Total
Officers & Managers	15	12	1,229	1%
Professional & Technical	19	34	648	4.9%
Clerical	58	56	895	6.1%
Skilled	364	398	5,091	7.8%
Unskilled	271	216	1,663	1.3%

Passing over complicated matters of definition, the figures seem to indicate that Eastern has done a reasonable job but still has some distance to go in reaching a fair proportion of minorities in the work force and in levels of employment. Our effort in recruitment and advancement is to give due recognition to merit and performance while still showing concern for the need to achieve appropriate representation of minorities. There are local instances in our operations which will require continuing attention and prodding if this is to be accomplished.

The Eastern Gas report also deserves particular note because of the choice of areas which the report addresses. These were chosen because 'they are the most readily measurable'. Notable by its absence is any mention of pollution. This is the area that is likely to have the most immediate impact, in an organization in this industry, on employees, the community, and the environment. Apart from general statements of good intention, pollution failed to materialize as an element in any of their reports.

SOCIAL INDICATORS

Of all the methods of preparing and communicating information that are touched on by CSR, social indicators are the most developed (although the development was not carried out with CSR in mind). As Horn (1980) points out, definitions of social indicators vary, but the following gives the basic idea:

> Social indicators are constructs, based on observations and usually quantitative, which tell us something about an aspect of life in which we are interested or about changes that are taking place in it. Such information may be objective in the sense that it purports to show what the position is or how it is changing; or it may be subjective in the sense that it purports to show how the objective position, or changes in it are regarded by the community in general or by different constituent groups.   UN, 1975

Social indicators (SIs) are typically concerned with describing particular aspects of society's well-being (or otherwise) at the macro (national or regional) level.[4] As Russell (1981) points out, SIs in their crudest form go back to the earliest censuses although as a more sophisticated device to 'take society's pulse' their inception is more recent – usually identified as the United Nations' 1954 study, *Report on International Definition and Measurement of Standards and Levels of Living* and Bauer's Classic text *Social Indicators* (1966). A more recent OECD report (1980; quoted in Horn, 1980) gives a list of the areas for which SIs might be calculated:

● Health, including health care
● Education and learning
● Employment and quality of working life
● Time and leisure, including free time use
● Income, wealth and command over goods and services
● Physical environment, including housing and pollution
● Social attachments, including family situation
● Personal safety and administration of justice
● Social opportunity and participation, including socio-economic mobility.

The study and use of SIs has spawned a vast literature and yet despite this, there are significant problems associated with their use. The first stems from one of the basic ideas underlying SIs. Gross (1966) contributed one essay to

Bauer's text in which he argued that just as a system of national income accounts and associated economic indicators made it possible to measure and monitor economic performance a similar system of social indicators could be used to measure and monitor social performance. However, social 'performance' is not that straightforward. As Russell (1981) argues, we *cannot* measure welfare and happiness. As Parke and Peterson (1981) similarly point out, while it is possible to identify measures of illness and death, measures of vigour and life are not so easy.

There is also an important difference between statistics and SIs. SIs are goal or need orientated refinements of statistics (e.g. number of perinatal deaths per thousand live births) and they ideally require that some theory as to what is important precedes the measurement. That is, why, for example, measure X, Y and Z rather than say A, B and C? Which set best captures the important characteristics of social welfare? Other problems include:

● emphasis on what is measurable rather than what is important (Russell, 1981)
● how to cope with data overload (Glatzer, 1981)
● how to deal with interrelationships between SIs (Parke and Peterson, 1981)
● the feeling that discrete quantitative measures *cannot* capture social welfare, that such measures may mislead and distract and may be misused and abused (Beesley and Evans, 1978)

Applying macro SIs directly to CSR at the organizational level is not straightforward. To illustrate this point consider a number of haphazardly selected SIs which could be taken as indicative of a nation's social well-being:

Proportion of households with one car
Proportion of households with more than one car
Proportion of households below the poverty line
Number per thousand of the population who are homeless
Still births per thousand live births
Number per thousand of the population educated beyond age 16
Measures of level of crime
Proportion of waterways unable to support fish life through pollution

The question is: how can these be applied to an organization? And are they, in fact, relevant? Many of the above SIs are socio-economic indicators; that is, they are some reflection of economic prosperity and are therefore indirectly related to the economic activities of organizations. In most cases, each SI will relate *directly* to only a small number of organizations – motor manufacturers, house builders, medical instrument manufacturers, housing departments of local authorities. etc., but in so far as the SIs *are* a function of economic activity they relate in some general way to *all* organizations. That is, the level of employment, rates of pay, taxes to Central Government, etc. are all functions of economic prosperity and contributed to by organizations.

Corporate Social Reporting

It is this relationship that has lead to a number of influential theorists suggesting SIs as a basis for CSR (Preston and Post, 1975; AICPA, 1977; Ramanathan and Schreuder (reported in Mathews, 1984), and Belkaoui, 1984). The difficulty lies in devising some means of reflecting these relationships in a systematic (but finite) set of information which can be understood by readers. Brief thought will show that the list of SIs above could be applied to organizations (for example, proportion of employees/community with a car, etc.), but would the information be collectable, be useful, or simply beg more questions than it answers? As yet no practical attempts in this field have been made and so whether the promise exceeds the problems of the approach remains an undecided question. It stands, however, as a potentially fascinating approach to CSR.

Key Service Indicators

Item No.		Gwynedd 1981–82	Average Welsh 1980–81 Counties	Other Authorities 1980–81			
				Dyfed	Powys	Cumbria	Northumberland
	All services						
1	Net rate and grant borne expenditure per 1,000 population	£391,120	£357,666 £340,821	£325,934	£433,327	£311,300	£343,326
	Manpower – employees per 1,000 population –						
2	Full-time	26.5	27.0 24.6	24.8	29.8	22.2	24.1
3	Part-time	14.7	15.9 16.1	15.3	16.4	16.8	14.8
	Education						
4	Primary – pupil/teacher ratio	19.2	19.9 21.7	18.8	18.7	22.3	23.5
5	Primary – gross cost per pupil	£678	£563 £592	£644	£722	£545	£558
6	Secondary –pupil/teacher ratio	16.2	16.1 16.6	16.6	15.9	16.4	18.0
7	Secondary – gross cost per pupil	£917	£817 £827	£828	£924	£806	£748
8	Further Education – net cost per 1,000 population*	£47,859	£42,806 £42,439	£44,156	£49,545	£41,801	£38,215
9	School meals – revenue/cost ratio	41.0	39.6 38.4	47.8	42.5	44.3	36.4
10	School meals – pupils receiving free meals as % of school roll	13.9	12.3 11.9	8.4	7.1	8.5	6.8
	Personal social services						
11	Children in care as % of population under 18	0.52	0.53 0.70	0.42	0.33	0.57	0.51
12	Gross cost per child in care	£2,373	£2,455 £3,789	£3,170	£3,153	£3,365	£6,263
13	Supported residents aged 75+ in residential homes as % of population aged 75+	4.2	4.2 3.7	4.0	4.9	4.1	4.7
14	Gross cost per resident week in local authority homes for the elderly	£81.46	£70.85 £73.92	£70.13	£79.01	£77.72	£76.32
15	Social Work staff per 1,000 population	0.46	0.45 0.45	0.39	0.39	0.37	0.42
16	Home Helps – contact hours per 1,000 population over 65	11,639	11,785 13,700	11,938	10,373	10,229	15,968
17	Rate and grant borne expenditure per 1,000 population	£41,365	£37,240 £33,830	£29,590	£34,020	£29,350	£32,430
	* Including contributions to the National Education Pool.						

Exhibit 5.7 Cyngor Sir Gwynedd. Source: the County Council's 1981/2 *Annual Report and Abstract of Accounts.*

Even if macro SIs cannot be (or have not been) used directly, extensive use *has* been made of the principles behind them. Many organizations, especially in the UK public sector, have calculated indicators of general (social and/or economic) performance, sometimes relating them to macro SIs, sometimes not. These indicators, which are more usually called performance indicators (PIs) are actually a required element of reporting by local authorities and national industries. Exhibit 5.7 is an extract from a local authority annual report. The use of the regional (or national, depending on your point of view) average SIs provides a useful yardstick for comparison.

The use of macro SIs and other organizations' PIs as comparators does raise problems, not least about the actual comparability, difficulties and differences in measurement and possible information inductance effects (see Chapter 4). For example, it is not uncommon to find the more specific elements of local authority reports explaining why those PIs on which the organization performs badly are really inappropriate to that particular county.

Nationalized industries are required by Government to produce performance indicators. Whilst many interesting examples can be found (see, for example, the *British Railways Board Annual Report and Accounts 1984/5*, or the *Post Office Report and Accounts 1983/4*), they continue to emphasize service delivery at the expense of reporting on the environment and community. Furthermore, as Likierman (1979) and Perks and Glendenning (1981) demonstrate disclosure of these indicators is far from universal.

For the record, therefore, the figures for the intervening three months, January–March 1982 are given below:

		%
Taste and Decency	214	49.9
Language	58	13.5
Accuracy	5	1.2
Impartiality	28	6.5
Violence	12	2.8
Scheduling	25	5.8
General and others	87	20.3
	429	100%

The high figures for 'taste and decency' during these months represent public reaction to Central's experimental series *OTT*, which was reported on last year. The series was amongst those considered by the Authority itself (see below) and by its General Advisory Council. No further series of *OTT* was undertaken though *Saturday Stayback* was thought by some to be a development of it.

The figures for the twelve month period April 1982–March 1983 are as follows:

		%
Taste and Decency	521	21.1
Language	270	10.9
Accuracy	80	3.2
Impartiality	721	29.2
Violence	87	3.5
Scheduling	238	9.6
General and others	554	22.4
	2,471	100%

Exhibit 5.8 The Independent Broadcasting Authority complaints about television programmes. Source: *Independent Broadcasting Authority Annual Report and Accounts 1982/3*. Used with permission.

A different approach is shown in Exhibit 5.8. The analysis of complaints is, in a sense, an analysis of negative performance, of failures. It corresponds with the reporting of accidents and the (rather rarer) reporting of failures to control pollution, for example. As such, this type of reporting provides an illustration of Parke and Peterson's (1981) point that negative measures are easier to find than positive ones.

Throughout these and other examples there is an apparent tendency towards selective and signle constituency emphasis. In PI (and other) CSR, this is by no means confined to the UK. The Eastern Gas and Fuel Associates report (Exhibit 5.6) and similar experiments reported by Preston (1981) and Heard and Bolce (1981) show the same tendency amongst US companies.

As stated at the start of the chapter, the division or typology of approaches to CSR is somewhat arbitrary. In particular the distinction between statistical summaries and SIs (or PIs) may frequently blur. A useful development from SI CSR (although not a universal practice) is the employment of some form of yardstick by which to judge performance. Earlier examples have shown previous years' figures, national/regional averages, the organization's own targets, or other organizations' performance figures. Despite the problems associated with comparators, carefully chosen and explained yardsticks should provide additional information to the reader. We saw another approach to this in The Atlantic Richfield 'audit' and the following section (and Chapter 7) shows how legal and other standards can be used to set information in context. Probably the most widely quoted (though not necessarily the most convincing) experiment with CSR using SIs in one form or another is that of First National Bank of Minneapolis. Allowing performance to be judged against previous performance and stated targets, the approach is one of the more developed (and continuous) examples of CSR. The bank's reports began in 1974 and have run since. They are so widely quoted that it is not necessary to give them precious space here (see Belkaoui, 1984; Estes, 1976; Epstein *et al.*, 1977; Blake *et al.*, 1976) although a few points are worthy of mention. The bank's report was derived initially from an attitude survey of what the community saw as important. Attitude surveys are a further way of setting information in context by testing opinion on one's performance. They are, however, expensive and cumbersome and, as is the case with the First National Bank, they are very rarely integrated in the CSR.

The bank's report captures many of the advantages and disadvantages of SI (or PI) reporting. The advantages lie in it being systematic, synthesized and 'objective'.

The disadvantages are many. Butcher (1973) lists his objections:

> The first is the reliability of the social indicators themselves: Does an increase in the number of high school graduates going to college really indicate higher quality education? Does an increase in home ownership really indicate better housing? This type of basic question has been troubling social scientists for years. The second limitation is that it will be next to impossible for these banks to determine what impact their individual programs have had on changes observed in the community. There are so many variables at work in any community that the input of one company will more than likely be obscured.   p. 12

Belkaoui (1984) in his critique of the bank's approach adds:

> The macro–micro social indicator audit rests on the main assumption that social indicators can be developed to reflect the impact of various areas on the overall 'quality of life' and that the activities of business firms may be traced to discover their impacts on these indicators. This presents problems related to both the availability and reliability of the social indicators. Use of the macro–micro social indicator units has, however, certain benefits, namely, in allowing all firms to compare their activity to a rational set of goals and indicators ensuring consistency and comparability of the reports of various business organisations.   p. 264

The First National Bank's reports are not audited and are selective with no explicit statement of objectives. There are no *external* yardsticks and, particularly, they are not easy reports to read.

The social indicator/performance indicator approach has certainly been a diverse and rich source of experimentation. With a more systematic approach it may be possible to derive a manageable CSR approach based on SIs/PIs that *does* discharge accountability but no such attempt has yet been made.

COMPLIANCE WITH STANDARDS

If we had to pin our colours to the mast of one single approach to CSR, the choice would be compliance with standards (CWS). The approach is not without difficulties, but it does overcome most of the problems associated with other methods and comes closest to satisfying the criteria we deduced in Chapter 4. The basic idea is that standards of performance derived from *outside* the reporting entity (partly from law and partly from other sources) are used as yardsticks to judge the results of the organization's activities.[5] Now the idea is not, in principle at least, a particularly original one. However, while the idea has been touched upon frequently in the CSR literature it has generally only emerged as practice in the case of the so-called social audits by both governmental and non-governmental bodies. (These are reviewed in Chapter 7.)

The law and the standards contained therein are thus the cornerstone of a CWS approach. The principle of the approach is the axiom that the law is a 'first approximation' of a society's preferences. It therefore constitutes the basic terms of the 'social contract' between the organization and the society.[6] As such it specifies the *responsibilities* expected of the entity. A CWS report, in reporting on the extent to which the responsibilities are met, thus becomes, by definition, the means of discharging the associated *accountability* (see Chapter 1).

There are, however, significant theoretical and practical problems with treating the law as a full and proper specification of the terms of the social contract. Lindblom (1984) provides one particularly useful discussion on this issue, but see also Stone (1975). At least part of the problem is expressed by Dowling and Pfeffer (1975):

Though in a democratic polity laws are likely to be correlated with societal norms and values, their correlations are less than perfect. There are at least three reasons why this is so. First, we have the dynamic nature of norms which change over time whereas legal change which is much more formal, is delayed and must await a specific statutory or common law enactment. Second, norms may be and are contradictory whereas there is a greater presumption of consistency in the legal code. Third, there is the question of the formal nature of law; societies may be prepared to tolerate certain behaviour informally but not to give them legal sanction.   p. 124

These are significant problems but the most significant stem from a more fundamental difficulty which relates to the distribution of power within a society and the resultant bias in the legal system. The legal systems of (for example) the UK and the USA favour property ownership and emphasize the rights of capital over those of labour or any other interest groups (Mac-Pherson, 1973). In addition, power is unevenly distributed within societies (thus allowing the views of some to dominate those of others) and the state is by no means an even-handed agent of the members of the society. Therefore law (and all apparently authoritative standards) are biased in favour of the dominant groups, the élite or the system (depending on your views). Thus it is argued, for instance, that the CWS report *can* only discharge a biased accountability – the 'true' responsibilities of the organization remain hidden.

Such a critique brings us right back to the comments we made in the Introduction to this book and in Chapter 1 – *accountability* as we have defined it is a function of a particular society at a particular time. As Rawls (1972) says:

> thus we are to imagine that those who engage in social co-operation choose together, in one joint act, the principles which are to assign basic rights and duties and determine the division of social benefits.   p. 11

That such principles are warped in favour of some over others is, we would submit, not particularly surprising or contentious. They are however, the 'rules of the game' by which, whether through choice or accident, we find ourselves governed. To seek a more radical expression of a society's views means identifying terms of some implied contract *outside* the status quo. (For example, based upon a Marxist view to sweep aside contemporary capitalist society.) While such terms *may* more accurately reflect the 'true' views of society (but be concealed by 'false conciousness') resolution of the matter is highly problematic and, to a great extent, throws one back onto the particular views of individuals and groups. This, we saw in Chapter 1, produces the sort of confusion that has typified CSR to date. We seek to avoid this by suggesting that a CWS approach which uses the law as a starting point is the *only* generally acceptable basis for CSR.

The practical problems of a CWS approach to CSR can be most conveniently divided into problems with standards themselves and problems with communicating and monitoring performance against those standards. In the first place, law does not (especially in the UK) necessarily contain specific levels of required performance. This is either because the legislators have deliberately avoided specificity, or because specific levels of performance seem inappropriate. Thus, for example, levels of permissible air pollution are not enshrined in statute but are periodically established by the Government body empowered to set and monitor standards – the Industrial Air Pollution Inspectorate (formerly the Alkali Inspectorate).

On the other hand, for example, it would appear inappropriate to specify an 'acceptable' level of fatal accidents at work (zero accidents would be the most appropriate target). As a result, the factory inspectorate lays down only general guidelines about the prevention of accidents. Therefore, in most cases standards must be derived from those set by quangos rather than direct from statute, and/or surrogate standards must be found. Where this is not possible some, preferably independent, authoritative source must be found. From these a full CWS report should contain: (a) a range of standards from different sources, and (b) performance in required areas for which no standards exist, e.g. accidents. In the latter case, social indicators may be used to set information in some sort of context.

From this two further problems arise. First, as Belkaoui (1984, p. 219) argues there is a danger that standards of (say) 'acceptable' air pollution fail to address the more serious and direct problem of controlling *emission* levels. That is, rather than monitoring the quality of air around a factory or the water in a lake or river, the emissions from factories should be monitored. By being more direct, such measures are easier to enforce. Second, standards do not apply equally to all organizations and industries. For example, the lending policy of a bank, the purchasing policy of a health authority, or the advertising of a particular agency may have just as far-reaching social consequences as the pollution practices of an industrial company but will be governed by less social legislation as the social consequences are less obvious and immediate. This latter point is a particular problem with all CSR and is the major area in which the charges from the more radical commentators to the effect that CSR does not address the *real* issues (such as ownership, control, and power), have the greatest validity.

Monitoring and communicating CWS raises obvious difficulties, but these are no different from any other reporting. On the whole, most of the difficulties we have raised are not insuperable, and can and have been solved to some degree (see Chapter 7). What is needed is practical experience in this field – but of that there is so far little outside the social audits.

Despite the frequent, if usually oblique, references to CWS CSR the cases of organizations producing such reports are rare indeed. Suggestions by (*inter alia*) Marlin (1973), Dilley and Weygandt (1973), the Council for Economic Priorities (1973), Blake *et al.* (1976), SSRC (1976), AICPA (1977), and Gray and Perks (1982) have not resulted in organizations reporting in this way. Therefore, in order to illustrate that the method *is* possible, we have chosen one of the examples that strictly speaking should fall in Chapter 7 (social audits). Exhibit 5.9 shows the pollution audit conducted on the Phillips Screw Company in 1973. A clear and straightforward, if

Pollution Audit

The information herein has been extracted from a comprehensive pollution audit conducted by the undersigned on the Phillips Screw Company subsidiary Phillips Metallurgical, Inc. (PMI) and its subsidiary, Shell Cast Corp. (SCC). The audit included consideration of air, water, noise and solid waste effluents and consisted of engineering and economic segments. Preliminary technical equipment needs and costs were projected to provide management with parameters for determining the economic impact on the Company and its operations. Experience suggests that these preliminary cost estimates will prove to be within normally accepted deviation ranges.

Where required, effluent testing was conducted in accordance with standardized techniques applicable to the circumstances encountered at each site. For the business/economic analysis, not presented in the summary. Company financial data on PMI and SCC were provided and integrated with proposed abatement equipment capital and operating costs as estimated by the undersigned. Based upon our technical and economic analysis, the following significant conclusions have been drawn:

PMI has two effluent liabilities.

1. The plant exceeds Vermont air pollution standards – particulate emissions calculated at 7.0 lbs/hr compared to a maximum allowable level of 2.8 lbs/hr.

2. The plant exceeds Federal OSHA air contaminant standards – particulate concentration of at 25.2 mg/m3 compared to a maximum allowable level of 10.0 mg/m3.

SCC has two effluent liabilities.

1. The plant exceeds Connecticut air pollution standards – particulate emissions calculated at 3.0 lbs/hr compared to a maximum allowable level of 1.53 lbs/hr.

2. The plant emits at the Federal OSHA air contaminant standard – particulate concentration of at 10.0 mg/m3 compared to a maximum allowable level of 10 mg/m3.

No effluent liabilities in the areas of water, solid waste or noise pollution were observed.

Financial liabilities are as follows:

1. PMI to meet State and Federal air pollution standards requires a capital investment of $32,500 and annual operating expenses of $3,700.

2. SCC to meet State and Federal air pollution standards requires a capital investment of $25,500 and annual operating expenses of $3,200. (These estimated costs are before tax and do not include amortization of capital equipment.)

In our opinion, expenditures of the levels cited for a remedial program of air pollution control will bring the current foundry operations into compliance with the respective State and Federal standards as they now exist. Furthermore, these expenditures are expected to provide sufficient margin to permit continued compliance in the event of any change in air pollution standards which we consider reasonably forseeable. Additionally, the nature and volume of solid waste effluents from current operations provide a sufficient margin for continued compliance in the event of reasonable changes to those standards.

Resource Planning Associates, Inc.

Cambridge, Mass.
June 1, 1973

Exhibit 5.9 Example of compliance with standard. Source: *Phillips Screw Company Annual Report 1973.*

limited, example of CSR, it demonstrates the possibility of CWS, albeit in its simplest form. The report is, we should note, about the only example of CSR published by the reporting entity which comes close to satisfying our criteria from Chapter 4.

OTHER APPROACHES TO CSR

As we have seen, CSR can employ virtually any medium of communication – pictures, words, numbers or a combination of these. More recently companies have used audio and video cassettes to communicate their financial accounts and/or their chairman's statement and review of operations. Such media could be equally employed for CSR. Thus our separation of CSR into narrative, statistical, social indicators, and compliance with standards approaches is really rather artificial but, with the exception of social income statements and balance sheets (covered in Chapter 6), they do cover all the major approaches to CSR. A word needs to be said, however, about advertising. When is CSR really no more than advertising? And does the distinction matter? We saw in Chapter 1 an example of advertising with a 'social slant'. Television and other media advertising frequently adopts this approach – especially in advertising the 'corporate image' – and in principle it is little different from the one-sided self-congratulatory reports we have seen in this chapter. Neither have much to do with *accountability* and neither approach places much emphasis on information. Exhibit 5.10 is an example of where advertising and CSR seem to meet. This extract from British Telecom's 1985 *Report to Customers*, circulated to all customers following 'privatization', is as much CSR as many of our earlier examples but is clearly intended as advertising.

We should be grateful, one supposes, for the existence of such reports and the fact that they do indicate that business recognizes a relevance for CSR. However, if CSR is to ever be anything other than effectively clever advertising, a more systematic, balanced and independent approach to accountability will have to be adopted.

SUMMARY AND CONCLUSIONS

In this chapter we have examined a heterogeneous array of approaches to CSR. The principal observation we should make from this review is that CSR comes in a very wide variety of forms, that few of these have much to do with accountability and virtually none come close to the criteria we deduced in Chapter 4.

The variety of approaches to CSR makes categorization difficult but the separation into narrative disclosure (including pictorial 'reporting'), statistical summaries, social indicators, CWS and (perhaps) advertising provided a

British Telecom in the community

Our deep involvement with the community is shown by the 999 service and the vital, 24-hours, coastal radio services for shipping. But also:

The chairman of British Telecom, Sir George Jefferson, is on the governing council of Business in the Community, which tries to stimulate job creation through local, small-scale business enterprise.

Our unit for overseeing the needs of disabled people, BTAID, is looking at aids to help the hard-of-hearing, and those with speech difficulties, to use the phone; text systems for the deaf, cheaper information technology for the blind, and emergency alarms for the elderly. We provide pagers for hospitals.

To help pupils gain a better understanding of new technologies, our education service provides teaching material and other help to schools and colleges. And Prestel, our viewdata system, has launched an education service.

Top: Monita is a new aid being developed for the elderly: it will set off an alarm.

Right: customers with speech difficulties will be able to use 'Claudius Converse' with a choice of 64 recorded phrases.

Left: doing homework with the help of Prestel, British Telecom's viewdata system which has just launched an education service.

5

Exhibit 5.10 British Telecom. Source: *British Telecom 1985.* Used with permission.

. . . and value for money

How our bills compare with other countries

The charts compare typical British Telecom bills with other countries' charges —
conversions into sterling take into account domestic purchasing powers. The variations
are given in percentages — eg for the residential bill, F R Germany is 35% dearer than
the UK. Among those countries the UK is the 3rd cheapest for the business bill and 4th
for the residential one.

How our charges compare with UK retail prices

The chart shows the way retail prices have risen over 14 years in comparison with
telecommunications charges. The Retail Prices Index — a "basket" of prices — is up 4
times; while stamps are 5½ times dearer, bread, 3 times, and telecoms charges, 2½
times dearer than 14 years ago.

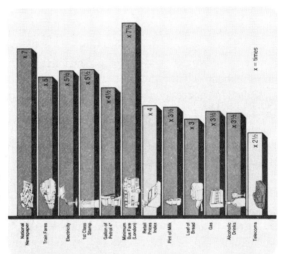

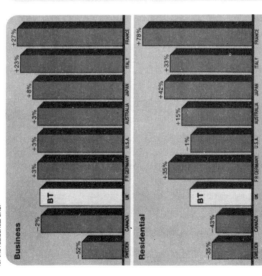

Exhibit 5.10 continued

useful framework for discussion. It is unfortunate, moreover, that a distinction between the approaches to CSR by commercial and not-for-proft organizations seems to be justified. That is, not-for-profit organizations appear to concentrate on their service delivery – the principal objective of such organizations – to the detriment of consideration of the wider implications of their activity. In contrasting commercial organizations and non-commercial organizations we should remember that, despite sermons to the contrary, commercial organizations have commercial goals and CSR will often be considered by them as secondary at best, irrelevant at worst. We might reasonably expect not-for-proft organizations to be more sensitive to their social impact. We are generally disappointed in this to judge by their reporting.

We should also remember that we have concentrated on visible reporting. Given the quality of such reporting and the low incidence of audit of CSR we must be careful in drawing conclusions about any changes in the social impact of organizational activity from this. Given an example of CSR we are unable to judge whether this is the tip of a social responsibility iceberg, behind which lies an extensive and genuine commitment to social performance (Hargreaves and Dauman, 1975; Humble, 1973), or whether it is a PR exercise – a false tip of a false iceberg – which bears little relationship with reality (Wiseman, 1982; Rockness, 1985). Promising experiments with CSR do not necessarily mean one is looking at an organization pursuing a goal of social betterment; a lack of CSR does not mean that one is faced with a socially irresponsible company. Only full and systematic CSR would allow such questions to be judged. A CWS with audit should (in principle at least) allow such judgements to be made.

NOTES

1. Bownman and Haire (1976), Estes (1976) and AICPA (1977) provide a large number of US examples. Further UK examples can be found in Maunders (1981), and recent reporting by RTZ, ICI and BP is worthy of note. Most annual reports from local authorities and health authorities include interesting examples.
2. One of the most quoted examples is that of Quaker Oats (1973), of which details can be found in Glautier and Underdown (1976, p. 703). A variation on the theme is the 'socially responsible' investment fund. The Dreyfus Third Century Fund in the US is widely quoted (see, for example, Seidler and Seidler (1975)) and the mid-1980s saw a similar development in the UK – The Friends Provident's Stewardship Fund.
3. RTZ's own reporting gives the impression that they are a fine employer and an asset to the host country. This may well be true, but the reader has no opportunity to verify it. A hair-raising contrary view is given by Counter Information Services' *Anti-Report on RTZ* (see Chapter 7).
4. The UK collects statistics from censuses, public sector and business surveys etc. which are collated and published in a variety of forms. The Central Statistical Office's annual *Social Trends* is probably the best source of UK national SIs.

5. Standards are to be distinguished from SIs in that they set a level of required performance (normative) as opposed to a current average level of performance (positive) as is the case with SIs.

6. The social contrast is defined by the *Oxford English Dictionary* as 'an agreement of mankind to submit to restrictions on individual liberty assumed as a basis of social life'.

7. We would wish to acknowledge the comments of Sten Jonsson of the University of Gothenburg for drawing attention to this point. For more detail see Tinker (1984a, 1985).

Chapter 6

Social reporting II – financial information

Whereas in the previous chapter we noted the considerable number of companies in both Europe and the United States that have experimented with some form of non-financial social reporting, it will also be recalled, from our earlier survey of international developments, that certain companies have gone further in producing social reports containing at least some financially quantified information. Our purpose in this chapter is to investigate the extent to which financially quantified reports are able to give a comprehensive picture of a company's overall social performance. Our focus will be particularly placed on a number of proposed 'models' for financially quantified social reports, illustrated where applicable by reference to any practical implementations of such proposals.

There are potential advantages accruing to companies able to produce financially quantified reports capable of presenting an objective measure of social performance. As Estes (1976) points out, such reports produced for external stakeholders would make socially responsible companies look better on the 'bottom line' than their irresponsible competitors – a result exactly the opposite of that produced by traditional financial statements. Furthermore, an objective measure of results obtained from expenditure for social purposes would be useful in enabling management to make rational decisions concerning the amount and direction of expenditure on matters such as pollution control and community relations (Solomons, 1974). However, it is of course essential that information produced is indeed useful for the decision-making purposes of both management and external stakeholders. A particular word of warning for accountants is voiced by Perks and Gray (1979) here, who quite rightly point out that their reputation is likely to suffer severely if they are associated with the production of half-baked and inconsistent social reports using spurious measures to support dubious assertions about social impact! Whether it is possible to produce comprehensive financially quantified social reports which avoid this pitfall is a question we shall address in this chapter.

AN IDEAL MEASURE

Solomons (1974) considers the most important component of social performance to be the production of goods and services that the company is in business to supply. He further suggests that value added presents the most suitable point of departure for developing a measure of corporate social performance. In this way the company is given full credit for the value of goods and services it provides for society's enjoyment, whilst at the same time incomes generated within the company are not deducted as employment provided cannot of course represent a diminution of corporate social performance.[1] To get from such a basic value added measure to a complete financially quantified measure of social performance it is necessary: (a) to add any unappropriable benefits generated by the company, i.e. corporate expenditure which benefits society but from which the company itself derives no direct benefit; and (b) to deduct any external costs which the company inflicts on society but does not bear, or only partially bears, itself. In the former category one would include corporate spending on charitable concerns and conservation projects for example, and in the latter category would be included externalities such as pollution of air and water arising from the production process together with any adverse effects on the health of employees.

Solomons' analysis can be summarized as follows:

Statement of social income	£
Value added generated by the productive process	x
Add Unappropriable benefits	x
Less External costs imposed on the community	x
Net social profit/loss	x

Such a format is similar to that put forward by Seidler (1973).

The works of Solomons and Seidler effectively provide us with an 'ideal' financially quantified measure of corporate social performance. However, there are major practical problems encountered when one attempts to place monetary values on both unappropriable benefits (for example, how does one place a value on the aesthetic pleasure provided by an office block which is an outstanding piece of architecture?) and more particularly externalities, notably the cost of pollution. These problems have been encountered in the public sector where the technique of cost–benefit analysis (CBA) has been employed as a means of appraising investment projects in terms of the net social benefits accruing from the investment. In attempting to allow for all gains and losses from a project as viewed from the standpoint of society CBA both describes and *quantifies* social advantages and disadvantages in terms of a common monetary unit. The decision model utilized can be described as follows:

$$V = \sum_{t=1}^{\alpha} \frac{B_t - C_t}{(1 + r)^t}$$

where V = net social surplus/deficit
       B_t = benefit in year t
       C_t = cost in year t
       r = social discount rate
       t = life of project.

Thus, the present value of a project is arrived at by discounting the net surplus/deficit of benefits over costs for each year of the project using a social discount rate.

In addition to these valuation problems (which we shall shortly consider in more detail) choice of a suitable social discount rate provides another major hurdle to be overcome. Different approaches adopted have included the use of a social time preference rate (STPR) which reflects society's preference for present as against future benefits, or alternatively the use of a social opportunity cost rate (SOCR), being the rate of return foregone in the private sector by using limited resources in the public sector. Both these methods have serious shortcomings. For example, use of STPR may lead to undue weight being given to present benefits due to factors such as pure myopia, i.e. a simple preference for the present for no apparent reason; risk of death; and the belief that future generations will be wealthier than present generations and hence in less need of benefits that could be provided today. On the other hand, use of SOCR raises the problem of determining rates of return in the private sector and making suitable adjustments for taxation and differences in risk characteristics between private and public sector investment. Also, of course, to compare like with like, the rate of return on investment foregone in the private sector should be measured in terms of social, rather than merely private, values which again poses severe practical problems. One possible solution to the problems involved in choosing a discount rate is to use 'test' discount rates which reflect national objectives regarding long-term growth rates and national policies regarding time and risk preference.[2]

Despite severe practical difficulties there have been a number of well documented attempts to use cost–benefit techniques in appraising public investment projects in the United Kingdom. Major examples are provided by the studies carried out prior to the construction of the M1 Motorway and Victoria underground line as well as the Roskill Commission Report on the siting of a third London airport. Whether such techniques, however, are practicably feasible as a basis for developing a comprehensive corporate social reporting system is very much open to question. Interestingly, Estes (1976) has made a notable attempt to utilize CBA methodology in constructing the following corporate social benefit/cost model which, rather than reflecting the view of the entity looking out toward society, takes the view of society looking at the entity, with social benefits equal to the values or utilities received by society and social costs reflecting the full detriments to society, paid and unpaid.

Estes' comprehensive social accounting model

$$SS = \sum_{i=1}^{n} \sum_{t=1}^{\infty} \frac{B_i}{(1 + r)^t} - \sum_{j=1}^{m} \sum_{t=1}^{\infty} \frac{C_j}{(1 + r)^t}$$

where SS = social surplus or deficit
B_i = the ith social benefit
C_j = the jth social cost
r = an appropriate discount rate
t = time period in which benefit or cost is expected to occur.

He further develops a format for a comprehensive annual social report, termed a social impact statement, based on the above model (Figure 6.1).

Whereas one must certainly agree with Belkaoui's (1984) assessment that Estes' social impact statement does represent a comprehensive format for companies experimenting with social accounting, the measurement problems it presents are so severe that very few companies indeed would be likely to follow such a path. Some of the more major measurement problems are:[3]

1. *Products and services provided.* Whereas exchange price provides a starting point for valuing the benefit to society of products and services supplied by the company, such a figure only reflects value to the marginal customer, i.e. the one who would not buy at a higher price. For a product having a downward sloping demand curve there are other customers who would be willing to pay more than the market price, and who therefore benefit from a market price lower than their expected value for the good. This excess of value, or utility, received over the amount paid is termed 'consumer surplus', a measure of which must be obtained to arrive at a figure for social value of production. Direct measurement of consumer surplus, it has been argued, entails construction of a demand schedule intersecting the price axis, which in practice would be virtually infeasible. However, studies have been performed on changes in consumer surplus – for example, a study of benefits accruing from constructing a Channel Tunnel concluded that an increase in consumer surplus of £294 million

The Progressive Company
Social impact statement for the year ended December 31, 19x1

Social Benefits

Products and services provided		$xxx	
Payments to other elements of society			
Employment provided (salaries and wages)	$xxx		
Payments for goods and other services	xxx		
Taxes paid	xxx		
Contributions	xxx		
Dividends and interest paid	xxx		
Loans and other payments	xxx		
	———	xxx	
Additional direct employee benefits		xxx	
Staff, equipment, and facility services donated		xxx	
Environmental improvements		xxx	
Other benefits		xxx	
Total social benefits		———	$xxx

Social Costs

Goods and materials acquired		$xxx	
Buildings and equipment purchased		xxx	
Labour and services used		xxx	
Discrimination			
In hiring (external)	$xxx		
In placement and promotion (internal)	xxx		
	———	xxx	
Work-related injuries and illness		xxx	
Public services and facilities used		xxx	
Other resources used		xxx	
Environmental damage			
Terrain damage	$xxx		
Air pollution	xxx		
Water pollution	xxx		
Noise pollution	xxx		
Solid waste	xxx		
Visual and aesthetic pollution	xxx		
Other environmental damage	xxx		
	———	xxx	
Payments from other elements of society			
Payments for goods and services provided	$xxx		
Additional capital investment	xxx		
Loans	xxx		
Other payments received	xxx		
	———	xxx	
Other costs		xxx	
Total social costs		———	xxx
Social surplus (deficit) for the year			$xxx
Accumulated surplus (deficit) December 31, 19x0			xxx
			———
Accumulated surplus (deficit) December 31, 19x1			$xxx

Figure 6.1 The Progressive Company social impact statement. Source: Estes, R.W., *Corporate Social Accounting*, John Wiley & Sons, 1976, p. 96. Reproduced by permission.

would be produced (see Mishan, 1975, pp. 20–23). An alternative approach is that of surrogate valuation which attempts to identify the alternative goods and services customers would be forced to use if those being valued were not available. For example, the cost savings achievable from installing a computer to replace manual processing of data would provide a measure of consumer surplus, and the total cost of manual processing would serve as a surrogate valuation for the computer installation.

2. *Goods and services acquired.* Just as exchange price generally understates value to the consumer, so it may also overstate value to the seller in terms of scarificed utility in cases where the supplier would have accepted lower prices for his output. This excess income is termed 'producer surplus'. Measuring producer surplus entails attempting to construct a supply schedule or, as an alternative, to approximate producer surplus by obtaining some estimate of the sacrifice incurred by seller in terms of his cost function, including a reasonable return on investment.

3. *Environmental damage.* The major problem involved here is quite simply trying to establish a market price where no market exists. Among techniques that can be employed to estimate the costs of environmental damage imposed through the company's productive process are:

● Surveys – to determine the amounts people would pay to avoid pollution, or alternatively the amounts they would have to be paid to endure pollution.

● Analysis – an encompassing technique that pulls together information from a variety of sources. For example: the cost of air pollution to houseowners may be estimated by an analysis of the decline in property values; the cost of water pollution may be estimated by reference to numbers of fish killed and their associated market value; the cost of noise pollution may be estimated by analyzing compensation payments, accidents, inefficiency and absenteeism.

● Use of avoidance costs – i.e. the costs that would have been incurred in preventing the damage. For example, the cost of purchasing safety equipment to prevent industrial injury could be used as a surrogate for the social cost of the accident. Also costs of air pollution control equipment and water treatment facilities could be used to represent the costs of air and water pollution.

● Restoration cost – the cost of repairing damage done. Thus the cost of air pollution may be estimated by totalling costs of consequent medical expenses and the painting, cleaning and refinishing of surfaces, etc.

● Surrogate valuation and shadow pricing – for example, the social costs of environmental damage may be estimated by using shadow prices for recreational activities foregone, such as the cost of a day's boating, which may then be subsequently used to justify costs incurred in cleaning up a polluted river.

Corporate Social Reporting

The above, necessarily brief, analysis gives some indication of the very real practical difficulties encountered in attempting to follow Estes' essentially welfare theoretical approach to social reporting. Other measurement problems not considered above include those of valuing direct employee benefits, such as recreational facilities and training programmes, as well as measuring the social costs of labour used, discrimination, accidents at work, and public services and facilities used. The difficulty of adopting such an approach is indeed well exemplified by the experiences of Abt Associates Inc., an American public relations company, which throughout the 1970s published integrated social and financial accounts (Abt, 1977). A later example is that of the Cement Corporation of India Ltd, whose social accounts for 1981 are reproduced in Chapter 1.

Erwerbswirtschaftliche Erfolgsrechnung		
Costs	Revenues
Profit	

Gesellschaftsbezogene Erfolgsrechnung		
Social costs	Social benefits
Net social benefits	

Geseuschaftsbezogene
Erfolgsrechnung

Social costs
I Producer's surplus for:
   1. labour performances
   2. fixed assets
   3. materials
   4. capital
   5. entrepreneurial performances
   6. bought-in performances

II Value of negative external effects on:
   1. employees
   2. population
   3. companies
   4. public entities

III Net social benefits

Social benefits
I Consumers' surplus for:
   1. product A
   2. product B
   3. product C
   4. product D

II Value of positive external effects on:
   1. employees
   2. population
   3. companies
   4. public entities

III Net social costs

Figure 6.2 Eichhorn's societal profit and loss account. Source: Schreuder, H., Corporate social reporting in the Federal Republic of Germany: an overview, *Accounting, Organizations and Society*, Vol. 4, no. 1/2, 1979, p. 110. Copyright Pergamon Press; reproduced by permission.

A similar theoretical structure to that of Estes is suggested by Eichorn (Figure 6.2) which again entails measures of consumer and producer surplus being made, as well as valuing externalities. Schreuder's (1979) comments on this comprehensive, financially quantified approach to social reporting seem to us particularly apposite:

The measurement and valuation problems caused mainly by the impossibility of interpersonal and intemporal comparisons of utility have as yet not been sufficiently met by economic theory to render (such an approach) practical. Nevertheless, the welfare theoretical approach has a very important function. It produces ideal/typical models, which can serve as a frame of reference for the evaluation of less ambitious proposals   p. 111

It is to a consideration of two widely canvassed 'less ambitious', but nevertheless comprehensive in terms of social issues considered, proposals that we now turn our attention.

LINOWES' SOCIO-ECONOMIC OPERATING STATEMENT

Like the proposals of Estes and Eichorn considered above. Linowes has developed a reporting model (Figure 6.3) which relies exclusively on financial quantification and produces a single 'bottom line' measure of corporate social performance. Under Linowes' scheme, social performance is considered under three headings: relations with people; relations with the environment; relations with the product. Under each heading expenditure voluntarily undertaken to improve welfare is netted off against 'detriments' which reflect the cost avoided, or not incurred, for necessary action brought to management's attention by a responsible authority, including socially beneficial action required by law. Necessary action is regarded as that which a reasonably prudent and socially aware management would undertake (Linowes, 1972a). It should also be noted that under the 'improvements' heading are included a pro-rated portion of salaries and expenses of company personnel who spend time on socially beneficial actions, as well as cash or other contributions made by the company to social institutions, such as educational establishments.

Whereas Linowes' proposal has the merit of ensuring that the performance of a socially responsible company appears in a favourable light, rather than the company being penalized for undertaking voluntary expenditure in areas of social concern, as is the case in a traditional income statement, it also has two major drawbacks. Firstly, as writers such as Estes (1976) and Jensen (1976) point out, there is a large element of subjectivity involved in deciding upon what should be included under the heading 'detriments'. Secondly, and probably more fundamentally, by focusing exclusively on costs incurred or avoided by the company, Linowes' model does not disclose the benefits or costs imposed on society by the company. For example, as our analysis of Estes' work showed, cost savings from not undertaking necessary expenditure on pollution control do not adequately reflect the cost of pollution thereby caused which are imposed on the community. Furthermore, merely disclosing expenditure incurred gives no indication of the efficiency of the company in areas of social performance. Indeed, the company which manages to

X Corporation
Socio-economic operating statement for the year ending December 31 19x1

I Relations with people

A. Improvements

1. Training program for handicapped workers	$10,000
2. Contribution to educational institution	4,000
3. Extra turnover costs because of minority hiring program	5,000
4. Cost of nursery school for children of employees voluntarily set up	11,000
Total improvements	$30,000

B. *Less* Detriments

1. Postponed installing new safety devices on cutting machines (cost of the devices)	$14,000

C. Net improvements in people actions for the year $16,000

II Relations with environment

A. Improvements

1. Cost of reclaiming and landscaping old dump on company property	$70,000
2. Cost of installing pollution control devices on Plant A smokestacks	4,000
3. Cost of detoxifying waste from finishing process this year	9,000
A. Total improvements	$83,000

B. *Less* Detriments

1. Cost that would have been incurred to relandscape strip-mining site used this year	$80,000
2. Estimated costs to have installed purification process to neutralize poisonous liquid being dumped into stream	100,000
	$180,000

C. Net deficit in environment actions for the year $97,000

III Relations with product

A. Improvements

1. Salary of vice-president while serving on government Product Safety Commission	$25,000
2. Cost of Substituting leadfree paint for previously used poisonous lead paint	9,000
Total improvements	$34,000

B. *Less* Detriments

1. Safety device recommended by Safety Council but not added to product	$22,000

C. Net improvements in product actions for the year $12,000

Total socio-economic deficit for the year $69,000

Add Net cumulative socio-economic improvements as of January 1, 19x1 $249,000

Grand total net socio-economic actions to December 31, 19x1 $180,000

Figure 6.3 Socio-economic operating statement. Source: Linowes, D.F., An approach to socio-economic accounting, *Conference Board Record*, November 1972, p.60. Reproduced by permission.

Utility Company
Statement of funds flow for socially relevant activities 19x1
Environmental

Installation of electrostatic precipitators (Note 1)	$26,000
Construction of power plants (Note 2)	2,089,000
Construction of transmission lines (Note 3)	35,000
Electrical substation beautification (Note 4)	142,000
Incremental cost of low-sulfur coal (Note 5)	33,670
Conversion of service vehicles to use of propane gas (Note 6)	3,700
Incremental cost of underground electrical installations (Note 7)	737,000
Incremental cost of silent jackhammers (Note 8)	100

Environmental research

Thermal	$17,000	
Nuclear	1,955	
Other	38,575	
Subtotal		57,530

Total environmental funds flow	$3,124,000

Other benefits

Charitable contributions	$26,940
Employee educational and recreational expenditure (Note 9)	6,000
Total other benefits	32,940
Total 1971 funds flow for socially relevant activities	$3,156,940
As a percentage of 1971 operating revenues	7.9%
As a percentage of 1971 advertising expenses	8,500%

Notes to funds statement
1. The company will complete installation of two electostatic precipitators in 1973. Costs in 1971 totaled $26,000.
2. The company is building power plants which will begin operation in the middle to late 1970's. Incremental cash costs of environmental controls installed in these plants during 1971 totaled $2,089,000.
3. The company is constructing a high-voltage transmission line from another community to the company's service area. Environmental cash costs resulting from wider spacing of line towers totaled $35,000 in 1971.
4. The company constructed a new substation in 1971 with an enclosed structure rather than open exposure of the electric transformers. The cost of this enclosure along with landscaping of existing substations totaled $142,000 in 1971.
5. The company used approximately 150,000 tons of coal during 1971 for electric power generation. Low-sulfur content coal comprised 8.6 percent of this coal consumption with the remaining 91.4 percent being coal of a higher sulfur content. The low-sulfur coal cost approximately $2.61/ton more than the high-sulfur coal.
6. Motor vehicles fueled with propane gas contribute substantially less air pollutants to the atmosphere than gasoline-fueled vehicles. During 1971 the company converted 9 more of its fleet of 115 vehicles to use of propane gas. The cost of this conversion was $3,700. Seventeen company vehicles are now operated on propane gas.
7. Underground installation of electric transmission lines has increased since environmental attention has focused on the aesthetic pollution of poles and wires. During 1971 the company installed underground electric transmission lines, which cost $737,000 more than putting the same lines above ground.
8. Jackhammers used by the company are, with one exception, of the normal, noise-polluting type. One jackhammer purchased during 1971 with noise controls cost $100 more than the regular jackhammer.
9. The company reimburses employees for educational expenditures and provides recreational opportunities such as the annual company picnic. Such expenditures amounted to approximately $6,000 in 1971.

Figure 6.4 Statement of funds flow. Source: Dilley, S.C., and Weygandt, 1973. Reproduced by permission. Opinions expressed in the *Journal of Accountancy* are those of the editors and contributors. Publication in the journal does not constitute endorsement by the AICPA or its committees.

achieve a level of social improvement equivalent to its competitors but at a lower cost would be effectively penalized under the Linowes' proposals.

DILLEY AND WEYGANDT'S SOCIAL RESPONSIBILITY ANNUAL REPORT

Dilley and Weygandt adopt a somewhat similar approach to that of Linowes in utilizing a cost outlay methodology towards social reporting. They do in fact recommend publication of a comprehensive set of statements giving background information on the company and the community in which it operates, air pollution and water consumption figures (physical units), occupational health and safety, and minority recruitment and promotion, together with a funds flow statement for socially relevant activities. The latter is the only statement that is both financially quantified and attempts to integrate social information concerning environmental, employee and other areas of concern. It is upon the funds flow statement that we shall therefore focus our attention[4] (Figure 6.4).

At the outset it should be noted that the Dilley and Weygandt report was prepared specifically for a gas and electric utility company, hence the categorization of socially relevant expenditure into 'environmental' and 'other'. Dilley and Weygandt point out that different statements would be necessary for firms in different industries. Nevertheless one must presume that the basic format, based on expenditure incurred, could be adhered to for any company. Such an approach, although less subjective, has the same major drawbacks associated with it as that of Linowes. Namely costs incurred by the company give little indication of benefits accruing to the community or efficiency of the company's social performance. Presumably the expression funds flow for socially relevant activities as a percentage of operating revenues and advertising expenses respectively is designed to show the degree of corporate commitment to areas of social concern. However, it does little to remedy the basic defects of a cost outlay approach to social reporting. It is perhaps relevant to add as a footnote here the fact that the original version of the report, prepared by Dilley as part of a doctoral dissertation, did indeed attempt to financially quantify the cost of the adverse effects of air pollution upon the community. Controversy over the particular methodology adopted however led to this aspect of the report being deleted on subsequent publication (Dilley and Weygandt, 1973).[5]

FINANCIAL MEASUREMENT: A CRITIQUE

A major difficulty facing proponents of a comprehensive, financially quantified approach to social reporting is clearly highlighted by our discussion of the above four models. Whereas the welfare theoretical approach of Estes and

Eichorn is conceptually valid, in that a societal, rather than corporate, view of company performance is taken, it is at the present time operationally infeasible. On the other hand the models of Linowes and Dilley and Weygandt, whilst being certainly capable of practical implementation, fail to adopt a societal perspective due largely to their adoption of a corporate cost outlay approach. Inevitably the question must be posed as to whether effort expended on developing conceptually valid monetary measures of direct externalities is futile because of the inevitable ultimate failure of such attempts, as Benston (1982) argues, or alternatively whether the search should go on. In arguing the latter viewpoint Schreuder and Ramanathan (1984a) suggest that perfect measures of externalities are not necessary and the use of subjective and imprecise indicators is quite acceptable as long as the current situation is thereby improved. They also point out that accountants have found temporarily acceptable solutions to other conceptually difficult measurement problems although the search for better measures of course continues (Schreuder and Ramanathan, 1984b).

However, as Bauer (1973) argues, the long history of welfare economics in struggling unsuccessfully with the monetarization of social benefits provides little encouragement for accountants attempting to develop conceptually valid financially-based measuring techniques for externalities. There are dangers inherent in the premature adoption of any such techniques, in that bias is likely to enter the measurement process through the introduction of value judgements on the part of the measurer, and the conscious or unconscious suppression of more relevant but non-commensurable measures (Spicer, 1978a). Furthermore, as indicated by Dierkes and Preston (1977), the integration of precise data into artificial indices of social welfare, or arbitrary monetary valuations, effectively hides rather than provides information, and ultimately serves as a barrier to understanding and decision making.

There is, however, a more fundamental objection to comprehensive monetarization, raised by Bauer, which concerns its inevitable emphasis on market price, or surrogates for market price, whereas social reporting largely purports to be a response to widespread societal questioning of the propriety of measuring things solely in terms of their market value! Gray (1973) echoes this view arguing that

> The notion of recording all relevant human and social phenomena into dollar amounts ... seems to us basically unsound. ... The reason why it seems basically unsound to us to try to apply traditional business accounting to these 'externalities' is that prevailing accounting is married to and therefore bounded by the same limits as the prevailing theory of a market economy. Like that theory it focuses on the world of transactions. But the very problems we want this accounting to cover have become problems precisely because they lie outside the world of transactions. Profit and loss accounts derive directly from a theory that could only achieve closure by expressly excluding what it calls 'external diseconomies' and we call 'unrequited social demands'. It will not take an act of stretching but an act of invention to produce a calculus that will encompass such demands.   p. 316

We ourselves see little prospect of such an act of invention ever being performed. This does not mean that financial quantification has no role to play in the development of social reporting practice, but rather suggests that financial data should be combined with other information, both quantitative and qualitative, in order to give a reasonably comprehensive perspective on a company's social performance. Thus a cost outlay approach towards reporting environmental performance, although certainly not geared towards producing a single 'bottom line' measure, together with information on pollution emittants, quantified in terms of physical units for example, may well prove useful to a variety of stakeholder groups. Such an approach has underpinned the work of a number of researchers, notably Nikolai *et al.* (1976) and Dierkes and Preston (1977). Corcoran and Leininger's (1970) proposed Environmental Exchange Report focusing on the exchange of human and physical resources between the firm and its environment, together with selected financial data of relevance to areas of social concern, provides another example of progress in this area.

Alternative approaches to partial financial quantification include making adjustments to the financial accounts in order to reflect particular aspects of corporate social performance, such as Beams' (1970) proposal for recognition in the accounts of industrial site deterioration caused by pollution, or the production of separate, financially quantified reports dealing with specific areas of social performance. An example of the latter development is provided by the relatively recent phenomenon of local authority produced social cost analyses which attempt to measure in financial terms the contribution made to the public cost of unemployment by individual companies implementing plant closure decisions.[6] Indeed, the employment aspect of corporate social performance appears particularly to lend itself to financial quantification.[7] As we saw in Chapter 2 in the case of Volvo, such information seems potentially very useful for management decision-making purposes, for through financial quantification the major impact of particular social factors on the company's cost structure may be brought to management's attention, and hence economical ways of combatting problem areas sought out. It should also be pointed out that internal management reports provide a particularly useful area in which to experiment with financial quantification of individual aspects of corporate social performance as objectivity takes second place to decision usefulness, which appears not to be the case with external reporting!

SURPLUS ACCOUNTING: A PRACTICAL ADVANCE?

The above analysis tends to suggest that the impossibility of financially quantifying all aspects of a company's social performance must lead to a degree of segregation of financial and social reporting, and consequent abandonment of the quest to find some common base by which to express overall corporate performance. There is, however, a completely new concept of

1 Profit statement

	Profit statement year 1			Profit statement year 2		
	Quantities	Unit Price (Fr)	Total (Fr)	Quantities	Unit Price (Fr)	Total (Fr)
Sales	200,000	50	10,000,000	220,000	50	11,000,000
Purchases	1,000	5,000	5,000,000	1,050	5,714	5,999,700
Salaries	200,000	15	3,000,000	205,000	17.56	3,599,800
Profit			2,000,000			1,400,500

2 Changes in distribution between stakeholders

	Unit price year 1 (Fr)	Unit price year 2 (Fr)	Variance (Fr)	Quantities year 2	Distribution (Fr)	Stakeholders
Sales	50	50	0	220,000	0	Customers
Purchases	5,000	5,714	714	1,050	749,700	Suppliers
Salaries	15	17.56	2.56	205,000	524,800	Employees
Total					1,274,500	

3 Productivity surplus

	Quantities year 1	Quantities year 2	Variance Quantities	%	Price year 1 (Fr)	Total (Fr)
Sales	200,000	220,000	20,000	10	50	1,000,000
Purchases	1,000	1,050	50	5	5,000	250,000
Salaries	200,000	205,000	5,000	2.5	15	75,000
Productivity surplus						675,000

Figure 6.5   An illustration of surplus accounting. Source: Glautier, M.W.E., and Roy, J.L., Social responsibility reporting, in Lee, T.A., ed., *Developments in Financial Reporting*, Philip Allan, 1981, pp.246–7. Reproduced by permission.

social reporting pioneered in France in the 1970s which does seek to interpret the firm's social role in financial terms, and hence relate social to financial
performance.[8] This method, called surplus accounting, seeks to measure
performance in terms of productivity improvement and the distribution of
new wealth created amongst social partners participating in the production
process. Thus it places great emphasis on production (which Solomons
(1974) considered the most important component of social performance)
whilst ignoring the vexed question of external economies and diseconomies.
Surplus accounting therefore, as Maitre (1978) points out, shares the limitations inherent in every accounting model, as it represents only a new way of
organizing available quantitative data whilst not attempting to quantify
additional factors such as environmental dimensions of performance. Nevertheless, Maitre considers the surplus accounting model to offer,

> an original and realistic response to the growing requirement for an effective
> social accounting.   p. 236

Figure 6.5 presents a simplified example of the main principles involved in
surplus accounting. Part 1 shows how profit has been affected by price and
quantity changes in inputs and outputs. Part 2 focuses on the price change
element and indicates the impact on different stakeholders, in particular the
benefit accruing to suppliers and employees. Part 3 then focuses on the
productivity surplus by holding prices constant at their level at the beginning
of the accounting period. Taken together the tables show that whilst a
productivity surplus, or wealth creation, of Fr 675,000 has been achieved,
there has been an increase in income distributed to suppliers and employees
of Fr 1,274,500. This has been financed by the shareholder group through a
consequent reduction in profits of Fr 599,500. Thus a comprehensive picture
of the wealth created by the firm and its distribution amongst stakeholder
groups is clearly presented.[9]

Despite the somewhat limited interpretation of the term 'social performance' adopted in the surplus accounting model it does offer a number of
advantages. As Glautier and Roy (1981) point out, it reflects the reality of
the firm's environment, in that it has to make profits to be viable and meet the
social constraints with which it is faced. Furthermore it explains clearly the
social role of the firm with regard to income distribution by relating changes
in the latter to changes in productivity. Finally, it recognizes the utility of an
analysis in terms of value and volume, hence integrating the main inflation
accounting methods whilst emphasizing the importance of volume changes
in the economic accounts (Maitre, 1978). However, despite its practical
advantages the surplus accounting method has achieved little recognition
outside France. Intriguingly Maitre provides us with a possible explanation
for this, which suggests that the concept of volume performance may be
considered of limited relevance in liberal economies based on concepts of
market value and monetary performance. These very concepts, of course,
represent the major obstacles to the recognition of social performance itself as
a vital element of overall corporate performance!

SUMMARY AND CONCLUSIONS

Our survey of a number of comprehensive models of financially quantified social reporting has indicated that whereas conceptually valid welfare theoretical models (notably those of Estes and Eichorn) have been developed, such proposals raise major problems of practical implementation so that one must probably regard them as being of little use in the real world. On the other hand, less ambitious models, although still comprehensive in terms of the range of issues covered and development of a 'bottom line' measure of performance (such as those of Linowes, and Dilley and Weygandt) fail to provide a societal perspective on corporate social performance.

In view of the above it is perhaps not surprising that in recent years researchers have tended to abandon the quest for a comprehensive financial reporting model. Instead there have been proposals for combining monetary and physical data with more qualitative reporting and, more recently, an increased interest in quantifying, from a societal viewpoint, certain individual aspects of corporate social performance, notably in the area of employment ramifications of company decision making. We foresee further developments in this sphere, for example in the increasing use of social cost analysis by stakeholders such as local authorities, which we consider in the next chapter. An alternative approach which seeks to integrate social and economic performance so as to produce a common base by which to express overall corporate performance is that of surplus accounting. Whereas much theoretical and empirical work has been conducted in this area in France very little has been done elsewhere. Nevertheless we feel that surplus accounting provides a rich source of ideas for both researchers and practitioners.

In conclusion it seems safe to say that the over-ambitious attempts of early researchers to develop financial statements, in the form of income statements and balance sheets, purporting to show the costs and benefit impact of an organization's social behaviour have largely led us up a blind alley. However, more cautious initiatives such as social cost analysis and surplus accounting seem ripe for further development.

NOTES

1. Whilst being immeasurably superior to profit as a measure of social performance, value added still has its imperfections. For example, as Solomons points out, a successful monopolistic company may exploit its market dominance by pushing up prices and thereby appear to be generating more value added whilst in effect diminishing social welfare.
2. Further discussion of this problem can be found in Pearce (1971) Chapter 6 which provides an excellent concise introduction to the field of cost–benefit analysis. More detailed coverage of the major issues involved in cost–benefit analysis can be found in Layard (1972) and Mishan (1975).
3. The treatment presented here is of necessity somewhat brief and sketchy. For a fuller analysis of the issues involved see Estes (1976) pp. 95–149.

4. The other statements suggested by Dilley and Weygandt are reproduced in Estes (1976) and Belkaoui (1984).
5. For a fuller discussion of this matter see Jensen (1976) p. 48.
6. Local authority initiatives in this area are discussed further in Chapter 7.
7. The 1975 American Accounting Association *Report of the Committee on Social Costs* appeared to reach a similar conclusion in considering the areas of affirmative action programmes (designed to secure equal employment opportunities for minority groups) and the community impact of plant closures as areas of social performance which appeared particularly conducive to financial quantification.
8. The method was first tested in the state-owned railway, electricity, gas and coal industries. A number of private companies have since studied the possibility of using the method as an important element in their management information system (Maitre, 1978).
9. See Maitre (1978) pp. 230–235 for a more rigorous analysis of the principles involved in surplus accounting.

Chapter 7

Externally-prepared social reports – the social audits

In Chapter 1 we noted that the term 'social audit' was used to mean a number of different things:

● as a synonymous term for CSR
● as an internal-to-the organization monitoring of social performance (as suggested by Humble, 1973, and Hargreaves and Dauman, 1975 – mentioned in Chapter 5)
● as an independent attestation of a CSR statement (a rare event, but see Atlantic Richfield in Chapter 5)
● as an external-to-the organization preparation of CSR reports (for example the Philips Screw report in Chapter 5).

The first of these we have simply referred to as CSR, the second we have touched upon as seemed appropriate. In neither case was the term 'social audit' used as we consider it to be misleading in these contexts. It is with the last two meanings that this chapter is concerned. In particular, the emphasis will be on the externally-prepared CSR – an area in which the UK has considerable experience.

An individual or group seeking to collect and prepare social data on an organization is faced with very real difficulties and this represents something of a theme to this chapter. The Council for Economic Priorities who conducted a number of social audits in the United States pointed to this problem. Stephenson, a member of the Council says:

> it appears that government cannot effectively evaluate and regulate big business. And it seems unwise to place the burden of the corporate conscience on executives who are responsible for maximising profit, or on the stockholders who are normally motivated even more singularly by profits. The best place to

start correcting this situation is in making more information available to the public. But federal and state governments do not have all the necessary information to begin with, and much of what they do have is confidential. Thus, any citizen or public interest group that tries to evaluate these questions will find the task frustrating.   Stephenson, 1973, p. 69

This echoes closely the experience of organizations in the UK, as we shall see. This chapter is divided into five sections:

● the work of Social Audit Ltd
● the work of Counter Information Services
● local authority social audits
● the role of Government bodies in monitoring social performance
● other types of 'social audit'.

The examples in this chapter are nearly all from the UK but there are also the USA examples of Atlantic Richfield and Philips Screw already touched upon in Chapter 5 (and for a contrasting national perspective see Teoh and Thong, 1984).

SOCIAL AUDIT LTD

Of the British attempts in the field of CSR, the work of Social Audit is probably the best known. The organization was formed in 1971 by Michael Young,[1] the founder of the Consumer's Association (CA). Charles Medawar, another of the leading figures in Social Audit, had previously worked with the CA and with Ralph Nader (the consumer campaigner) in the USA. Social Audit describe themselves as:

an independent non-profit making body concerned with improving government and corporate responsiveness to the public generally.

and initially defined their objectives thus:

it will be one of our objectives to illustrate the feasibility of progress towards the day when reasonable safeguards for economic democracy will be embodied in law and social audits universal.   *Social Audit*, No. 1, p. 3

Their work conveniently splits into two: the *Social Audit* quarterlies (containing, amongst other things, 'social audits' of specific organizations), and the later (post-1976) books and pamphlets. The *Social Audit* quarterlies contain general articles reviewing such things as armaments and industry, the social cost of advertising and company law reform as well as their best-known work – the social audits of Tube Investments Ltd, the Alkali Inspectorate (as was), Cable & Wireless Ltd, Coalite & Chemical Products Ltd, and the famous (or infamous) *Avon Rubber Company Ltd Report*. Since 1976, Social Audit Ltd has performed no social audit as such. Later work can again be conveniently split into that intended to help others perform social audits (for example, the handbooks on pollution and consumer audits and the guide to chemical hazards – Medawar, 1978b; Frankel, 1978, 1982) and detailed investigation of various social issues (for example, chemical suppliers' health and safety information (Frankel, 1981), the marketing and advertising of food and drugs in the Third World (Medawar, 1979), various aspects of pharmaceuticals (Medawar and Freese, 1982; Blum *et al.*, 1983; Medawar, 1984) and the problems facing nurses in mental health institutions (Beardshaw, 1981)).

We noted in Chapter 5 that there is frequently a hazy dividing line between company-produced CSR and advertising. There is a similar difficulty in distinguishing between social audits on the one hand and investigative journalism and specialized and/or commissioned reports on the other. Accounting as a discipline maintains a focus on the *entity* concept as a central principle. Generally speaking, CSR has also tended to adopt this principle (rightly or wrongly). The emphasis in this chapter is therefore on the entity-based social audits although a number of the local authority 'social audits' eschew this principle. We would wish to encourage the reader not to ignore the possibilities raised by a wider definition of 'social audit'.[2]

The social audit of organizations produced by Social Audit Ltd are a far cry from the one or two page reports that have been the norm in the examples we reviewed in Chapters 5 and 6. The report on Tube Investments is about sixty pages long (about thirty thousand words) and that on Avon Rubber is about ninety pages long (about one hundred thousand words). The reports are mainly narrative although photographs, cartoons, statistical summaries, compliance with standard and financial data are also employed. We can give only the briefest of reviews of the work of Social Audit here but the following description of salient points of the Avon Rubber report (and a brief synopsis of the Tube Investments and Alkali Inspectorate report) gives the general idea.

Avon Rubber Company Ltd

The Avon Rubber report is unique in that, in the initial stages at least, it was carried out with the full co-operation of the management of the company (this co-operation was later withdrawn with a number of consequences which are discussed below). The report reflects both this co-operation and the experience gained by Social Audit from their previous investigations. Exhibit 7.1 indicates the areas covered by the report.

The introduction to the report contains the objectives Social Audit Ltd set for themselves.

> The aim of the report goes beyond a description of what a single company has done, at a certain point in time. The report has been prepared also: (i) to show to what extent it may be possible to assess what, in social terms, a company gives to and takes from the community in which it operates; (ii) to advance understanding about the practical problems and possibilities that may be involved in making assessments of this kind; and (iii) to establish precedents for the disclosure of more, hard information about what companies do, why they do it, and to what general effect.   p. 2

Social Audit on Avon

Most sections of this report have been organised into three parts: an introduction, which includes details of yardsticks of performance used; a report, which includes statements (or representations) of fact; and a discussion, which summarises and comments on the main findings.

Contents

Social Audit Spring 1976   1

Exhibit 7.1   Contents of the Social Audit Ltd's Avon Rubber Company report. Source: *Social Audit*, spring 1976. Social Audit Ltd, P.O. Box 111, London NW1 8XG. Used with permission.

and then reviews their experiences of the company's co-operation and, again, the problems of extracting information from Government bodies. The report makes fascinating reading in its attempts both to catalogue Social Audit's attempts to gain access to information held by public bodies and, in a genuine attempt at frankness, to communicate the biases that Social Audit perceived as informing their work.

The review and analysis of Avon Rubber's business which follows is a useful background to the social audit of the company. In a general sense this section amounts to a simplified interpretation of the annual report and accounts for the previous few years. One notable inclusion is the analysis of value added.

As with previous reports there is extensive and thorough analysis of employees and employment conditions. The report examines problems of motivation and productivity, the effectiveness of the union representations and the extent and effectiveness of employee participation. There is a useful analysis of safety. The description and analysis of Avon Rubber's products and services which follow seem to show the company as one of the 'better' organizations in their industry, although industry-wide practices with regard to advertising and keeping consumers informed about the products they buy are heavily criticised.

The section of the report on the environment uses statistical summaries and compliance with standard approaches as a major theme and to good effect. Exhibit 7.2a shows the results of water authority analysis of effluent from one plant. Social Audit point out, however, that the use of independent figures is essential – the company's figures cannot necessarily be trusted (Exhibit 7.2b)

The report also examined noise pollution, reporting Avon Rubber's performance against Government standards, then setting the standards in context for the layman by reference to the noise levels typically generated by everyday things.

The Avon Rubber report concludes with a summary of the problems that resulted from the company's withdrawal of co-operation. The company's response to the draft report was:

> Having read the draft copy of the Social Audit of Avon Rubber Company Limited, the reaction of the Management and most of the Trade Union Representatives in the Avon Companies involved in the Audit, is one of acute disappointment and concern at the enormous number of inaccuracies and misinterpretations that it contains. This, in spite of the very considerable assistance given to the Social Audit researchers and the many hundreds of hours of interview time and volumes of correspondence.
>
> A detailed correction of the report would in our opinion result in a document as voluminous as the draft report itself.
>
> In these circumstances, and whilst appropriate action has and will be taken on any criticisms which we believe are justified, both Management and most Union Representatives in the Avon Companies concerned feel they must disassociate themselves from the general contents of the report and do not wish to have any further discussions or correspondence on it.

**Results of sampling of trade effluent discharged into sewers
from the Bradford-on-Avon factory.**
(Results of 9 analyses between November 1974 and August 1975;
together with conditions of consent issued in March 1975.)

Parameter	Limit imposed	Range of samples
	(parts per million, unless indicated)	
pH	6–10pH	3.2–9.5pH
Temperature	43.3°C	—
Volume	100cu.m/day	—
BOD	—	4–70
COD	—	28–432
Phenols	—	3–8
NH₃	200	1.5–224
Suspended solids	400	49–220
SO₃	500	21–970
Cl	—	8.4–294
Total Heavy metals	20	<1.5–12.1
Zinc	10	0.4–10.5

Effluent discharges from Avon Medicals

Date of sampling	Source	pH (limit 6–12)	Suspended solids (limit 400ppm)	Chemical oxygen demand (limit 600ppm)
15.7.74	Avon	8.5	6	0
8.8.74	*Water Authority*	*7.9*	*72*	*5,735*
25.10.74	Avon	8.3	5	5
19.12.74	Avon	7.7	2	0

Exhibit 7.2 Effluent discharge reporting and the sample problem. Source: *Social Audit*, spring 1976, pp.3 and 77. Social Audit Ltd, P.O. Box 111, London, NW1 8XG. Used with permission.

Having received and considered these reactions from our Subsidiary Companies, the Board of Avon Rubber Company Ltd, endorses their viewpoint.

Social Audit amended the draft report in the light of such comments as they did receive and conclude:

> this report on Avon represents what we believe to be an accurate and fair record of some of the Group's principal activities, as they were observed over the Winter of 1974 and 1975.   p. 89[3]

This aspect of the Avon report does raise the important practical problems of how to avoid bias (through providing partial information) and inaccuracy (through difficulties of measurement and monitoring). It seems highly unlikely that an outside body without the full co-operation of the organization concerned and the appropriate Government bodies can realistically hope to produce a wholly 'accurate and unbiased' report. In addition, of course, every 'social auditor' is likely to bring his or her own personal values and bias to all matters of selection and description. It is likely, therefore, that the objective of 'freedom from bias' is little more than a pious hope.

> For all this, there have been encouraging responses to the report, not as much from home but from abroad. In the UK, the publication of the Avon report has certainly not gone unnoticed, even if it has failed to provoke the discussion in public we might have hoped for. Possibly, this lack of an open response is indicative of the kind of cover up with which the British business (and other) establishments characteristically seek to hide their embarrassment, confusion and dismay. Alternatively, the report may simply have been published in the wrong place and at the wrong time. In Sweden, by contrast, the report has led to extensive and continuing discussion about social accountability which has been evident to us, not least, through the arrival of several delegations from 'big business' (Volvo and two state-owned manufacturing concerns among them) from across the North Sea.   Medawar, 1976, p. 391

Tube Investments and the Alkali Inspectorate

Whilst the Avon report was the most substantial (and famous) of Social Audit's investigations, the reports on Tube Investments (TI) and the Alkali Inspectorate deserve comment.

TI was the first organization to be subject to the 'full glare' of Social Audit's investigation (*Social Audit*, No. 3, Winter 1973/74). The report consists of:

- a review of the TI group, its profitability and its structure
- a discussion of the problems of gaining the company's co-operation (in which Social Audit Ltd failed) and touches on the difficulties of acquiring information about a company without that company's co-operation
- a review of employee relations, redundancies, pensions, and race relations
- an analysis of health and safety at work statistics
- some analysis of TI's overseas activities, particularly in South Africa.
- a description and assessment of TI's consumer goods
- a section on military contracting
- a section on the environment.

The emphasis given to each section appears to be largely a function of data availability thus allowing, for example, accidents to be given extensive analysis.

The TI report attempts to be fair-handed. The accident statistics, for example, are far from unilaterally damning and the section on products is, on the whole, complimentary.

Social Audit had more difficulty with environmental information on TI and thus concentrated on only one or two issues. Exhibit 7.3 illustrates the style of the report as well as the frequently *ad hoc* structure of the information and presentation.

Exhibit 7.3 Using any information available. Source: *Social Audit*, winter 1973/4, p.57. Social Audit Ltd, P.O. Box 111, London NW1 8XG. Used with permission.

The TI report, apart from being Social Audit's first full investigation, was noteworthy for its survey of shareholder attitudes to 'social issues' (*Social Audit*, No. 4, Spring 1974). Their aim in this was put thus:

Shareholders put to the test
This report takes up where the 'social audit' of the Tube Investments left off. It describes how shareholders in TI reacted to the various recommendations we made, and it looks at the wider issue of shareholder participation.

We approached 1,000 shareholders in TI asking for support for two almost symbolic resolutions: one requesting the Company to publish more information about the social impact of its business, the other asking for substantial wage increases for African employees in South Africa.

The 1,000 shareholders were carefully chosen. The total sample comprised 15 sub-samples – including, for example, 25 clergymen, 50 charities, 100 women – and we report here on the response we got from each.

The approach to shareholders was made not to ask for support for the motions but rather to ask for support in getting the motions tabled at the AGM. The responses were illuminating in that no charity, university, trade union or local authority supported the motion and support was scant even from clergymen. Less than 5% of the shareholders supported the motions and they thus failed.

The detailed reasons given by the major institutional shareholders make discouraging reading. The Church Commissioners' response, for example, is one of the more encouraging:

> Although the Commissioners are in broad sympathy with the general aims of your organisation, they consider that they should adhere to their well established practice of dealing direct with the managements of companies on ethical as on other matters. . . . Your report does, of course, comment on a number of issues which the Commissioners have already raised with the company . . . but in following up any of the points which your report raises, the Commissioners would prefer to do this in their own particular way.

We would believe this lends support to our contention in Chapter 4 that shareholder response has not much relevance to CSR and, furthermore, is a most unlikely agent for change in this field.

Whilst the media coverage of response to the TI report was extensive, the company itself appears to have been little affected (*The Accountant*, 23 May 1974, p. 671), although Medawar (1976) says that the TI report 'led directly to a setting up by the SSRC of a committee of enquiry into the social responsibility of business', and 'contributed also to the decision of several other companies to pre-empt any possible outside interference by carrying out enquiries of their own'.

The Alkali Inspectorate, now known as the Industrial Air Pollution Inspectorate, is a Government body appointed under statute to monitor air pollution emissions in co-operation with local authorities. The Social Audit report of 1974 was an attempt to answer the perennial question – *quis custodiat custodians?* The report, almost entirely narrative, is an analysis of the history of the Inspectorate, their *modus operandi* and their effectiveness and fairness in controlling air pollution.

The Inspectorate does not fare well in the investigation. Social Audit finds it ineffective and, most importantly, secretive and unaccountable. The continual difficulty of gathering data prompted Social Audit to survey local authorities for their views on this:

> We asked local authorities whether they were satisfied with the control of registered works. About half of the 200 authorities replied that they were totally satisfied; the others, to a greater or lesser degree, were not. As might be expected the dissatisfied authorities tended to be those whose registered works were the source of more regular public complaints: their answers form the basis of the following report.

The largest single complaint, from 37 local authorities, was that the Alkali Inspector did not pay enough attention to local problems. 'Although it may not be true' wrote one Chief Public Health Inspector, 'one is always left with the impression that premises are not being visited often enough.'

The great majority of local authorities reported that they were well satisfied with their relationship with the Alkali Inspectorate, and many stressed the value of the help they had received with problems concerning non-registered works.

However ten local authorities told us that past requests to the Inspectorate for information had either been refused or evaded.

'This reluctance on the part of the Inspectorate to impart information – presumably on the grounds of confidentiality – could have had the most serious consequences for the general public.'   pp. 39–40

The report emphasizes the difficulty of acquiring information and thus largely relies upon *ad hoc* incidents and examples. Again there was extensive media coverage of the report which at least achieved one of Social Audit's aims in this case – namely publicizing the activities of this little-known body. The difficulties of extracting information from Government bodies, such as the Alkali Inspectorate (who purportedly monitor social activities on behalf of the public), is central to much of Social Audit Ltd's work and also features extensively in the Avon Rubber report.

Critique of Social Audit

The reports of Social Audit come closer to meeting the criteria we deduced in Chapter 4 than does most CSR we have examined. The reports all include a statement of objectives, whilst the overriding objective is the pursuit of the discharge of accountability. Assessing how well the reports relate to these objectives is less easy. A comprehensive range of major constituencies and issues are addressed but difficulty in acquiring information has often led to uneven treatment of the different categories. In addition, whether deliberately or not, Social Audit did *not* specify the exact range and type of information they intended their reports to include and therefore assessment of 'completeness' by the reader is difficult. The information is in the form of raw, unmanipulated data on the whole, although the *ad hoc* use of anecdotal evidence and the frequent expression of writers' opinions could be viewed as defects in the communication process. This, together with the difficulties of gathering information and the inevitable lack of any general independent attestation of the report mean that the reports' 'correspondence with reality' cannot be wholly relied upon.

The reports are eminently readable and no expert knowledge is required. A variety of presentations were used – photographs, narrative etc. The length of the report raises problems however. First, as a basis for the development of CSR the production of reports like that of Avon Rubber is clearly impracticable – the Avon Rubber report took something in the region of five man-years to prepare not including the time given by Avon personnel. Second, the length of the reports has been referred to by many commentators as a negative element – being too long to read and digest. Given the complexity of the issues underlying CSR, however, whether length is a critical advantage or disadvantage is clearly a debatable point.

Over a decade later, the Avon Rubber report remains the most thorough and important example of CSR in the UK. This report plus Social Audit's later work provide a 'toolbox' of information and ideas which mean that CSR in a form not incompatible with Chapter 4's criteria *is* a practicable possibility – although further experimentation would be necessary to develop the idea. The problems, as Medawar (1976) says, are not really practical but political – organizations, including Government, are highly reluctant to embark on CSR and as they control the information they effectively have the power over its development. Despite their efforts, Social Audit do not, as an organization, have much power, thus allowing subjects to dismiss them as irrelevant.

COUNTER INFORMATION SERVICES

Counter Information Services (CIS) are a rather different organization from Social Audit. They describe themselves as:

> a collective of journalists dedicated to publishing information not covered or collated by the established media. It is [our] aim to investigate the major social and economic institutions that govern our daily lives, in order that the basic facts and assumptions behind them can be as widely known as possible.
>
> *Anti-Report No. 12*

Ridgers (1979) – a member of CIS – gives the goals of the organization as:

> providing information resources for workers engaged in specific struggles, and exposing the nature of the social and economic system which is the cause and content of these struggles.   p. 326

CIS are therefore concerned directly with one constituency – labour – and are an example of the 'anti-capital' or 'radical' group from Chapter 1. They share with Social Audit a belief that corporate social accounting, through the straightjacket of 'objective verifiable measurement techniques' can be no vehicle for change, but unlike Social Audit Ltd, are looking for revolutionary change in western capitalist society in line with a Marxian view. Therefore, assessment and analysis of their work within the framework of Chapter 4 would be impossible and inappropriate.

Whilst the CIS reports cover a wide variety of topics – including for example, South Africa, nuclear technology, the Queen's Jubilee and the position of women in society – their best known reports broadly in the CSR field are the 'Anti-Reports' which have focused on (*inter alia*) Lucas, Ford, British Leyland, Unilever, RTZ, Consolidated Gold Fields, Courtaulds, GEC and the NHS.

The reports are deliberately undated and Gray (1980), from an interview with CIS members, identified the priorities of the reports as being, 'a good story', readable, and encouraging to employees. As a result they are quite deliberately selective and biassed.

The reports are largely of a narrative format with tables of financial and statistical data as available. The effects of redundancies, strikes and working conditions are given high priority.

But the power of the report lies in the photographs and frequent quotations. These give a better indication of the tenor of the reports:

> The history of Consolidated Gold Fields is one of brutal and inhuman exploitation which still continues. It is a case history of our current economic system operating in its purest form.   *Anti-Report No. 3*, p. 35, circa 1973

> Occasionally men did die. One, a man about forty, lay by the side of the lines as his mates worked. 'We were in the locker room before the shift had started and he collapsed with a pain in his chest. He went an awful colour but then he reckoned he was alright. We went down the stairs onto the shopfloor, walked across the line and he collapsed again. Y'know – flat on the floor. His face was an awful grey colour. We all rushed around him and the buzzer went. The line started. The foreman came across shouting "get to work ... get on the line". And there we were sticking things on the cars and he was lying there ... dead ... in front of us.'   *Anti-Report No. 5: British Leyland*, p. 23, circa 1974

Photographs will frequently be used in direct appeal to the emotions; a portrait of Franco 'fascist dictator of Spain' appears in the Ford Anti-Report (p. 9, circa 1978); Hitler appears in the Lucas and Unilever Anti-Reports (p. 11, circa 1976 and p. 81, circa 1976); a caption reading 'the effects of bombing in Vietnam' appears over the picture of a burnt out hospital in the GEC Anti-Report (p. 31, circa 1973); and graphic photographs of indigenous populations, particularly blacks in South Africa, suffering various 'indignities' from extreme physical violence to starvation are not uncommon.

The Anti-Reports clearly have little, if anything, to do with the production of nicely turned social income statements and social balance sheets, and they have little relevance to CSR as a form of 'objective', 'balanced' and 'unbiassed' communication. They are, however, important to CSR as a particular example of the 'radical approach' and provide a critical contrast to what could be seen as the more conventional CSR we have touched upon in earlier chapters. Exhibit 7.4 is an extract from the RTZ Anti-Report (circa 1973) and provides a striking contrast to the extracts from that company's own CSR. (Recall that Chapter 5 included several references to RTZ's social reporting and suggested that the company are probably the UK leader in company-generated CSR.)

It comes as no surprise to learn that companies have not responded positively to the CIS Anti-Reports – 'inaccurate', 'wrong', 'distorted', 'without integrity', 'glib' and 'aggravating' were frequent descriptions employed by the 'victims' of the reports (Gray, 1980). Whilst sales of the reports remain buoyant (thus indicating demand for the CIS approach), the companies were of the expressed view that even the employees and unions were largely unaffected by the material.

Nevertheless, however much the CIS approach fails to fit 'conventional' CSR, has more in common with journalism than accounting and is biassed and sensationalist, it cannot (and should not) be ignored and most clearly will not go away.

North Wales: The Angelsey Aluminium Smelter

"We intend to be good neighbours and to bring a benefit to this community", Duncan Dewdney, Chairman of Angelsey Aluminium Company, and executive director of RTZ. (Angelsey Mail, 2/7/72)

1. The Angelsey Aluminium Company comprises holdings by BICC, Kaiser Aluminium, and RTZ (27%, 30% and 43% respectively). Its main industrial function is to smelt alumina shipped from the giant refinery at Gladstone (Queensland), operated by the RTZ groups Comalco in which Kaiser is also a partner, and fed by the bauxite from Comalco's Weipa deposits again in Queensland. These are the largest known deposits of bauxite in the world, at present rates of consumption (which are certain to be increased, with improvements in mining technology) they will be exhausted inside 35 years. (Ecologist, June 1971).

2. "By 1964 detailed plans for the building of a smelter had been prepared whilst the people of Angelsey still had no idea of their existence. The plans proposed the immediate construction at Penrhos, Holyhead, of a smelter with an initial capacity of 120,000 tons per annum, as well as extensive modifications to Holyhead harbour. A later phase was planned, to increase capacity to 300,000 tons with the further development of a bauxite refinery. No mention of these plans was made in the 1966 annual report." (Ecologist, June 1971)

3. One of the main problems initially, however, was finding a supply of cheap electricity, as every pound of aluminium "takes about 8kWh to produce – the equivalent of running a two bar fire for four hours." (Guardian, 17/2/72). The original plan was for RTZ to build its own nuclear power station jointly with the Atomic Energy Authority (Times, 26/5/67). Instead, the Wilson government arranged to provide a loan for the purchase of one third of an atomic power station, the nearby Wylfa, with an option on a further third should the company wish to increase production in the future. Since Wylfa was not yet built, it was decided to peg the price and terms of the agreement to the production of electricity at the Dungeness 'B' station then just coming on tap.

4. Thus the government was pegging the price of the AA Co.'s electricity (a way of giving them cut-price power without officially doing so), then handing over the money to pay for it (£33 million at 7%); they were thus technically not subsidising an industry in competition with Norway, which would have been in contravention of EFTA agreements.

5. "The aluminium smelting process consists of the electrolytic reduction of alumina . . . dissolved in a bath of molten fluorides at 950°C. It is technically possible to scrub both the low level emission of gases from the pot-rooms and the high level emission from the main stack to an efficiency of 95%; however, because of the type of cell or pot chosen for use in the Angelsey smelter (using 'prebaked' anodes), efficient extraction is made more difficult." (Ecologist, June 1971)

6. "Fluorine contamination from atmospheric fall out can cause severe damage to most forms of life; it is cumulative and therefore the degree of damage is dependent upon the length of exposure to the contaminant, as well as its concentration. For these reasons the Medical Research Council Memorandum No. 22 on Industrial Fluorosis concludes that '. . . it is only prudent to site new developments in such a way that, so far as is possible, residents are kept out of the zone known to be liable to contamination' . . . Presumably RTZ ignored these facts when they made their plans, for the smelter stands contiguous with Holyhead town; primary schools are only a few hundred yards away and 16,000 people live within the fallout area." (Ecologist, June 1971)

7. A public inquiry was held in 1968; however, the inquiry never seems to have been intended to have much significance attached to it, either by RTZ, or by the government. When the smelter went into production, total emissions of pollution were up 54.7%, while fluoride emissions from the main stack were up more than 3 times on the figures submitted by the company at the inquiry.

8. "The official reason for the increase seems to have been that, since the inquiry, smelting capacity had been reduced from a maximum of 120,000 tons per annum to 100,000 tons and the height of the stack increased from 300 feet to 400 feet . . . (The original) recommendations were based on a data provided by RTZ and on a stack height of 525 feet". (Ecologist, June 1971). The chief Alkali Inspector wrote to a resident of Angelsey who expressed alarm at the increase: "We do not accept that the estimates submitted by the company at the public inquiry were binding in any way". (Nov. 1970) Duncan Dewdney, in a personal interview in 1969 told the same resident (who had purchased some shares in RTZ), that the level of pollution control originally promised by them (95%) could have been achieved with the expenditure of only another £250,000.

10. A major hazard from aluminium smelting is the possibility of fluoride pollution. Heavy doses of fluoride are injurious both to animals and human beings. "In the vicinity of industrial plants (high doses) can give rise to thickening of the bones and ossification of the ligaments (osteoscelarosis)." (Chemical and Process Engineering, June 1971).

There are a number of pieces of admittedly circumstantial evidence that this could possibly be affecting the area. Residents have reported that cars parked near the smelter have suffered windscreen "etching" characteristic of fluoride corrosion. Trees used to landscape the plant site are also reported to have been renewed more than once. Under inversion conditions residents of Rhoscolyn, four miles from the smelter, found the air so contaminated as to produce gasping for breath and a burning sensation in the throat. The curling leaves of a dogwood shrub corresponded exactly to a photograph of the effects of fluoride poisoning.

As has been emphasised this evidence is totally circumstantial, but the fears of the residents are greatly compounded by RTZ's insistence on monitoring its own pollution figures and refusing either to publish them or to show them to interested local bodies, like the Farmers Union of Wales and the Angelsey Resident's Association.

On the evidence of Avonmouth and Swansea the residents have little reason to feel that their interests are properly protected by a Combination of RTZ and the Alkali Inspectorate.

Exhibit 7.4 CIS Anti-Report – RTZ Ltd. Source: *Anti-Report No. 1: RTZ,* pp.18–19, circa 1973.

LOCAL AUTHORITY SOCIAL AUDITS

Local authorities (LAs) fulfil a number of social roles as we mentioned in Chapter 3. Two of their most important in the present context are:

● their monitoring of compliance with law and other standards;
● their social cost–benefit analyses of local commercial activity.

The former falls more easily into the broad 'role of government' section which follows. This section will therefore concentrate on the relatively recent phenomena of LAs taking initiatives to investigate the effects of local and regional 'deindustrialization'. The stimulus for LAs to enter this field is the serious and rapid decline in the contribution of (particularly) manufacturing industry to the national and local economy. By the mid-1980s in the UK, plant closures and rising unemployment were important features of many local economies and the LAs were faced not only with a declining (rate) income and deteriorating industrial infrastructure but also with an increased pressure from their local populations. Some LAs deduced that they needed to try and bring pressure on the big companies and the Government in an attempt to halt the decline.

The problem they recognized is this. A company generally owes its primary accountability to its shareholders. As we have pointed out, the broader social responsibility is rarely treated as a primary objective of organizations in the private sector. A decline in a company's short-run returns will prompt decisions to close 'marginal' or 'inefficient' plants, cutting back its industrial base or moving operations elsewhere. 'Good economic sense' you say. However, the local effects (unfelt by most shareholders) can be catastrophic. Plant closure decisions are often based on short-term information and take no account of the 'externalities' – the knock-on effect to other businesses and the LA rate income, the unemployment, the reduction of the Government's tax income and the myriad social problems that result from this. It is to the problem of increased unemployment in the local community and the consequent costs incurred by the public purse, in having to maintain a higher pool of unemployed people, that LA social audits seek to draw attention.

The problem may be seen in many different ways. Tinker (1985) and CIS would, for example, see this as a result of decisions taken in the immediate interests of capital and, more pertinently to our present concerns, decisions which were based on accounting information which emphasizes short-run gains for capital and ignores the wider implications of the accounting myopia. However, to try and persuade companies and (particularly right-wing) Governments with arguments of such a Marxist slant is clearly doomed to failure. What the LAs (and the trade unions) sought to do was represent information about these problems in terms potentially acceptable to the 'status quo'. Owen and Harte (1984) and Harte and Owen (1986) have discussed these issues and documented the LAs attempts to turn the tide.

Harte and Owen (1986) review ten local authority 'social audits' which attempt to assess the impact of plant closures. These reports cover elements such as:

- accountability to the work-force
- accountability to the community
- the role of pension funds (as shareholders and as agents of employees – see Chapter 4)
- the economic effects on other businesses
- the costs to the Government in reduced taxation and national insurance and increased unemployment benefit
- the social costs to the individuals and their families
- the 'spin-offs' in terms of increased need for health, personal social services, and public order provision etc.

Such analyses are notoriously difficult, and despite effective support from the House of Lords (1982) appear to have had little direct effect in persuading either companies or Government to change their behaviour. Their effect, if any, will possibly be educative – drawing attention to the limits of traditional accounting and attempting to force, by pressure of opinion, an accountability to work-force and LA upon Governments and companies. (See Chapter 8 for a fuller discussion of some of these issues.)

The central issue raised by the LA (and trade union) attempts at 'social audits' is again one of power – both over information and over resources. An LA has not the access to the detailed costs upon which a company may make a plant closure decision and, in any event, *any* attempt to quantify costs and benefits from a plant's continuance or closure is bound to be highly subjective (House of Lords, 1982, Ch. 6). Furthermore, no matter how persuasive the social audit might be, or how strong the arguments for developing accountability might appear, without involvement from Government, LAs are unable to enforce their views. One reason is an example of the question we touched upon at the end of Chapter 4 – capital is not geographically tied – it can move easily; labour and communities cannot.

The whole range of issues here were most graphically illustrated in 1985 by the National Coal Board's decision to close pits, the Miner's Strike and attendant debate (if such a word is not too mild for the vitriolic exchanges that resulted). Party political issues aside, the question was: What is the cost of closing a pit?, and running alongside this: Which pits are 'uneconomic'? The answer is 'it depends'. The debate showed so very clearly that:

- 'social' and 'private' costs are inextricably linked
- assessing the costs and benefits from economic decisions depends as much on value judgements as accounting
- information, no matter how persuasive, is not enough to cause powerful groups (in this case the NCB and the Government) to change their behaviour (see, for example, Berry *et al.*, 1985; Glyn, 1985; and in a different context, Rowthorn and Ward, 1979).

It would appear that despite the apparent lack of effects from such 'social audits' LAs and trade unions will continue with their efforts, whether intended to educate, change decisions, put pressure on Government or, in a more radical vein, seek to change accountabilities and even the relative powers of capital and labour.[4] Of particular interest is the importance of the political climate of a country upon the issues. Political change may tend to make these debates more balanced and progressive (see, for example, the more recent Scandinavian experience with respect to changing legislation, for example the 1983 Wage Earner Funds and access to information).

Placing LA and trade union audits within the main corpus of CSR is not easy. The reports tend to be one-off and prompted by a particular action by a company – plant closure. They are not, therefore, intended as a regular feature of the mechanism of accountability. They are, however, capable of bringing pressure to bear in order to allow a formal mechanism of accountability to develop. To that extent, they may be seen as a precursor to CSR. On the other hand, to the extent that such reports are aimed directly at changing the 'status quo', they must be seen as CSR in the 'radical' vein and treated as similar to the CIS work.

Specifically, though, LA and trade union reports raise a number of challenging questions. First, they are concerned with change in the economy and society rather than with the static model upon which most CSR is predicated. Second, their emphasis is largely on the public externalities of private economic decisions, that is, on the effects rather than on information itself (see Chapter 4). Their approach, therefore, is close to the material reviewed in Chapter 6 and reflects the advantages and disadvantages discussed there. Third, the LA and trade union reports are concerned first and foremost with the economic health of a country or region and focus on the problems that result from the *absence* of industrial and commercial activity. Most CSR is concerned with problems arising from the *existence* of such activity. (Thus, for example, pollution is rarely a feature of these reports.) In the light of the 'radical' elements of these reports it is perhaps surprising that they all appear to hold the need for a healthy and growing economy, in the sense of traditional manufacturing and commercial activity, as an underlying and self-evident assumption. Such an assumption is not uncontestable (see, for example, Dickson, 1974; Schumacher, 1973; Robertson, 1978).

But we should not leave this section giving the impression that LA activity in the 'social realm' is entirely limited to plant closure analyses. Apart from their role of monitoring compliance with social legislation (see below) LAs have taken other initiatives. One such is reported by Ward (1985). She reports on the LAs enterprise boards' attempts to vet new business proposals for their 'social usefulness' and to encourage those which pass the test. In particular the 'socialist' authorities of Greater London and the West Midlands were, Ward suggests, extremely successful in emphasizing and generating a 'social contract' attitude from business. This relates back to our earlier discussion. Many of the problems faced by the LAs and their 'social audits' arose due to a lack of any recognized social accountability from the businesses. Under these schemes, not only are businesses which are socially orientated encouraged, but a contract of accountability can be established in order that LAs have some say over any future decisions the businesses take which may affect the community.

GOVERNMENT MONITORING OF SOCIAL PERFORMANCE

The role of the state in the development of social accountability is a complex and ambivalent one. At the risk of considerable oversimplification we can describe the state's role in terms of the principal–agent model of account-ability from Chapter 1. Parliament (the agent) ostensibly acts on behalf of the society (the principal) in determining the rules of social action and social relationships. These rules, frequently established in law (or what we called quasi-law) are enacted by Government departments, Local authorities, and/ or by quasi-autonomous Government bodies (quangos) – as 'agents' of Parliament. The rules are imposed on the various organizations and moni-tored by the 'Parliamentary agents'. The organizations – companies, health authorities etc. – as 'agents', ostensibly discharge their accountability on the specific issues to their immediate 'principals' – the Parliamentary agents. The need for CSR and, in particular, the work of organizations like Social Audit would evaporate if:

● the 'rules' were universally accepted as a complete specification of a society's terms of social interaction
● the rules were satisfactorily monitored
● society received the information about the monitoring (i.e. the indirect accountability was discharged to the primary principals – society).

Of course, none of these conditions hold. As we have seen, a substantial minority not only disagree with the 'rules' but, in a far more radical sense, disagree with the very basis from which the rules are deduced. In addition, the work of Social Audit shows quite clearly that monitoring is inadequate in many instances and members of society will frequently not be allowed access to the information purported to discharge accountability. It is argument along these lines that may lead to the conclusion that the least accountable of all organizations is the Government itself and if the Government do not discharge their accountability then the democratic ideal, of which Medawar (1976) says accountability is an essential and necessary (if not sufficient) prerequisite, remains unfulfilled.

The state has established and monitors rules across a very wide range of 'social issues'. In the UK these include:

race relations
sexual discrimination
air pollution
water pollution
health and safety at work
protection of consumers
rights of employees
implementation of mental health legislation
public protection (i.e. police)

The information thus (purportedly) collected by the 'parliamentary agency' would, in principle at least, go a long way towards satisfying the needs of most CSR or social audit requirements. As far as it is possible to assess, however, the data are not properly collected, are not collated, appear to be rarely examined and, most importantly, are rarely made public – *quis custodiat custodians?* The example of the UK water authority exemplifies the issue.

The *Control of Pollution Act 1974* lays down that water authorities (who monitor river effluents under the *Rivers (Prevention of Pollution) Act, 1961*) should keep public registers of who is polluting what. As Geoffrey Lean reports in *The Observer* in 1985 (11 August, p. 5) – eleven years later – the authorities were taking 'the first faltering steps towards allowing the public to find out who is polluting the environment'. Until 1985, polluters could be fined up to a derisory £100 and anyone making the information public was liable to imprisonment!

Such secrecy, as Social Audit discovered, is likely to apply to all forms of pollution and health and safety information (for example) and applies equally to public sector bodies (such as the water authorities who are themselves polluters from sewage works) as it applies to companies. If the Government is secretive in matters in which it is purportedly acting on behalf of society, it should come as no surprise that companies are highly reluctant to take serious initiatives with CSR (see, for example, Beesley and Evans, 1978; Medawar, 1978a; Frankel, 1978). It is concern with issues of this sort that has lead to calls for a 'Freedom of Information' Act – calls which have succeeded in the USA, but which still sound hollow in the UK and Australasia.

Therefore, although Government social audits are potentially an extremely important element of CSR and may in fact be important in constraining organizational behaviour, in terms of broad social accountability, the lack of publicly available information means state monitoring of social performance is, generally speaking, a negligible element in CSR practice.[5]

OTHER SOCIAL AUDITS

Defined broadly enough, social audits can encompass anything from investigative journalism to systematic analyses of specific and general issues of social accountability. Viewed in this way, the possible number of social audits at any one time is vast indeed. In this last section of this chapter we can very briefly review a few further, more general examples.

Some of the best known examples of the less systematic social audits are conducted by special interest groups. The Royal Society for the Protection of Birds has investigated the effects of oil spillage and 'flaming' from North Sea oil platforms on, particularly, migrating birds. The Friends of the Earth have mounted many investigative campaigns including, for example, the 'externalities' of the use of nuclear power. The UK Green Party came to brief prominence with their investigations into the manufacture and use of 2–4–5T (the defoliation 'Agent Orange' used in Vietnam). Similarly, trade unions have carried out their own investigations into issues and organizations and, indeed, the TUC has more than once proposed the more widespread use of social audits.

A more systematic approach has been taken by the End Loans to Southern Africa organization (reported by Wells, 1985). Since 1981, this group has produced a 'Shadow Report' of Barclays Bank. This is in effect an 'Anti-Report' bearing some similarities to the CIS reports but rather less vitriolic in tone. The Shadow Reports are modelled loosely on the Bank's own 'Report and accounts' and purport to 'provide a substantial dossier exposing the bank's support for apartheid' in an attempt to embarrass Barclays into withdrawing from South Africa and Namibia. The contents of the report are *ad hoc* and vary from the simply provocative to the apparently factual.

A very different role is played in the UK by the Consumers Association. Best known for their magazine *Which?*, this private sector body concentrates principally on collecting and publishing information about products and services (public and private sector) and through keeping the public informed and campaigning in its own right, provides a form of social audit for consumers.

These few examples can give but a flavour of the whole range of social audits, whether they be investigative journalism, commissioned research, special interest group campaigns or produced by self-appointed 'watchdog' organizations. All are part of the broad, if usually partisan and *ad hoc*, process of opening up, exposing, explaining, developing and attempting to control the myriad aspects of complex social interactions in a society. And, it is worth repeating, the visible elements of social audits are, quite possibly, only the tip of the iceberg. It is impossible to evaluate just how much Government and other activity does take place in this field. Certainly we know that organizations themselves undertake some form of social monitoring, rather like an internal audit process and this, no matter how partial and partisan is still part (however negligible) of the development of CSR.

SUMMARY AND CONCLUSIONS

In this chapter we have concentrated on the work of Social Audit Ltd and, to a lesser extent, on the Anti-Reports of CIS. In addition, we have covered a number of other examples of externally-prepared social audits and the role of the Government in this context. If a focus of accountability is one's interest, then Social Audit Ltd's experiences represent an important step in the development of CSR – not least for the problems they encountered; gaining company and shareholder co-operation, obtaining information and in particular with prising information from the one purportedly public body who has it – the Government. It seems unlikely that CSR will make any real advances as long as the 'accountable' organizations, the Government, and quangos (as both agent of society and 'accountable' body in their own right) refuse to co-operate. Seeking to improve accountability and, in particular, make public the extent to which the rules of the 'social contract' (the law and quasi-law) are being satisfied, hardly seems an especially radical idea – at least in principle. Those with the power over information appear largely unpersuaded by such arguments and this should bother us if we mistakenly believe we live in a democratic society – we clearly do not.

In such a context the work of CIS begins to take on more meaning. The essentially 'reasonable' approach of Social Audit has not been overtly successful, then maybe CIS are right – the 'system' is not in the interests of society and should be attacked.

Only the hindsight of history will begin to answer this dilemma, because it may be that the 'dripping tap' of pressure groups, and special interest investigations etc., *are* slowly turning the tide of 'socially responsible' behaviour. In the meantime, various bodies and groups continue their attempts to develop CSR and social audits, pursuing their own particular cause, in the (hopefully not mistaken) optimistic belief that information and education *can* change behaviour and that accountability and democracy are worthy ideals.

NOTES

1. The name 'Social Audit' whilst being the title by which the organization is best known, strictly speaking refers to the publishing arm of the Public Interest Research Centre (PIRC) – a registered charity, and is the title given to their early periodic publications. We will use 'Social Audit' as a general reference to both Social Audit Ltd and PIRC.
2. Limiting CSR to an entity-based approach does have its problems (Tinker, 1985) but space prevents an analysis of this question. Similarly an analysis of 'social journalism' and specialist 'social reviews and investigations' would necessitate an expansion of this book out of all recognition. The interested reader is recommended to read the referenced publications from Social Audit Ltd and the non-entity reports produced by Counter Information Services.
3. The similarity to a standard audit report is probably not coincidental.
4. The frequent assumption that such questions of power are *only* a function of two groups (capital and labour) struggling for ascendancy (see, for example, Cooper and Sherer, 1984; Tinker, 1985) is not it must be emphasized, uncontroversial (see, for example, Gray, 1985).

5. The apparent excitement generated in the early to mid-1980s (in the UK and elsewhere) by the so-called value-for-money audits (VFM) of public sector organizations is unlikely to provide a significant improvement in public accountability. Its focus on spending – generally unrelated to performance measures – might improve the efficiency of services from local authorities etc., but appears to have little to do with the quality of service and virtually nothing to do with the broader social issues of the community, the labour force, and general accountability (Glynn, 1985).

Chapter 8

Accountability to the work-force I – reporting information

There is much debate at present concerning the real level of accountability towards their work-forces currently acknowledged by many companies. The survey of business objectives undertaken by the Technical Directorate of the Institute of Chartered Accountants in England and Wales,[1] referred to in Chapter 3, as part of the work involved in producing *The Corporate Report*, indicated that slightly more companies recognized a responsibility towards employees (71% of those responding) than towards shareholders (69%). However, events occurring since this survey was carried out, particularly the rapid de-industrialization experienced in the United Kingdom since the late-1970s and consequent massive increase in unemployment levels, have led some writers to question the validity of such findings. Thus Bryer *et al.* (1984b) present an analysis suggesting that UK manufacturing industry has been run down in the interests of investors, whilst Glyn and Harrison (1980) cite the use of private profit as the criterion for employment, rather than the social value of production, as a major factor promoting de-industrialization.

Certainly there seems a large measure of agreement on the part of influential bodies representing both labour (e.g. TUC–Labour Party Liaison Committee 1982) and capital (e.g. CBI 1981, 1982) as to the undesirable social and economic costs of rapid large scale de-industrialization and consequent high levels of unemployment. The CBI Steering Group on Unemployment indeed unequivocally stated that,

> it is clear that current levels of unemployment represent an immense human and economic cost to the country ... unemployment should be regarded as our number one social problem   CBI, 1982, p. 45

Indications of the cost of unemployment at the macro-economic level in terms of Exchequer Costs are given in a report from the House of Lords

Select Committee on Unemployment (1982) which estimated a total Ex-chequer Cost for the UK in 1981/82 of some £13,000 million, equivalent to a cost per person unemployed per year in the range of £4,500–£5,000. A later study by the Centre for Alternative Industrial and Technological Systems (CAITS, 1984) arrived at a figure of £4,943 for an adult male taking a period of thirty-three weeks as the median period of unemployment.

The above studies were essentially concerned with measuring two major costs of unemployment to the state: transfer payments (i.e. benefits paid to the unemployed) together with their attendant administration costs, and the loss of government revenue in direct and indirect taxes together with national insurance contributions. An alternative presentation of the public cost of unemployment is given by Glyn and Harrison (1980) who point out that full employment would permit production of £43.5 billion extra goods and services (in 1980 prices) enabling a 50% increase in pensions and social security benefits to be made, a 75% increase in house building, a 25% increase in expenditure on health and education and a 50% increase in manufacturing and construction investment.

In addition to such economic costs to the nation there are a number of social costs arising from what the House of Lords Select Committee term 'a more than plausible' connection between unemployment and higher rates of ill health, mortality, crime and civil disorder. Whilst accepting that the precise magnitude of these effects is difficult to quantify, a study by Rowthorn and Ward (1979), which draws on earlier work in the United States by Bremmer (1976), estimates that a substantial rise in unemployment of one million could, over a five year period in the United Kingdom, lead to something like fifty thousand more deaths, over sixty thousand additional cases of mental illness, and fourteen thousand more people receiving prison sentences. In addition to the personal burdens laid upon families directly affected, such figures also have severe implications for future government spending on prisons, the police, the law courts and the National Health Service.

Despite heightened public awareness of the immense economic and social costs associated with ever-increasing rates of unemployment, current cor-porate reporting practice gives no indication whatsoever of the contribution to such costs made by individual companies implementing plant closure and redundancy decisions. The only figures that are given relate to costs incurred by the company, mainly redundancy costs, which generally appear as extra-ordinary or, more usually, exceptional items in the profit and loss account. Indeed the narrow concentration on shareholders interests in the develop-ment of current reporting practices has led to a situation in which very little attention is paid generally in company reports to factors such as job security, income opportunity and employee purchasing power.

Whereas Benston (1982) believes that both shareholders and employees are nevertheless likely to be well served by current accounting procedures adopted by corporate management, Kern (1975) in a paper on labour orien-tated business management (AOEWL)[2] (a concept developed by the German

Federation of Trade Unions (*Deutscher Gewerkschaftsbund*)) provides us with an alternative viewpoint. The proponents of AOEWL vigorously question whether corporate management in planning future, and evaluating past, courses of action consider goals which represent the interests of employees and society. They argue that the achievement of such goals is hampered by the capital orientated profit goals of private enterprises in capitalistic systems. Furthermore, it is pointed out that the typical corporate accounting system plays a vital role in perpetuating such a situation in that it fails to indicate the degree of achievement of these new goals due to its presumed biased conceptual basis which neglects labour interests as well as the general public welfare.

The important role that accounting systems can play in influencing management's actions was also referred to by the authors of *The Corporate Report* who expressed the view that because managements naturally respond to those indicators by which they consider their performance is to be judged, their attitudes and objectives can be profoundly affected by changes in reporting practices. Thus it would appear that accountants must at least consider the possibility that the systems they presently operate and the procedures they apply, which pay little attention to labour interests and wider social ramifications of decision making, have made some contribution to the major problem of de-industrialization, and its attendant social strains, that the United Kingdom is now experiencing. However, it would equally appear to be the case that the accountant does have a potential role to play in developing the concept of accountability to the work-force, particularly in view of Shanks (1978) remark that,

> Objectives of a social nature can be set, and some … can be quantified, particularly those that deal with relationships with employees.   p. 9

Our purpose in the remainder of this chapter is to consider the extent to which accountants have begun to promote the concept of accountability to the work-force via the voluntary provision of information which could be used for forming judgements on matters of corporate performance affecting their interests, and the prospects for further developments in this area. To this end it is necessary to consider and assess the significance of developments in recent years in two major areas:

● The reporting of employment information
● The provision of corporate information to employees.

THE REPORTING OF EMPLOYMENT INFORMATION

The employment report
The authors of *The Corporate Report* felt that the inclusion of an employment report within the published annual report of companies would:

assist users in assessing the performance of the entity, evaluating its ecomonic function and performance in relation to society, assessing its capacity to make reallocations of resources and evaluating managerial performance, efficiency and objectives.   para. 6.5

Furthermore, it was envisaged that:

The report will make available information of use not only in judging efficiency and productivity but will also provide significant information concerning the workforce of the reporting entity, its personnel policies and industrial relations record.   para. 6.21

We have already outlined the suggested contents of an employment report, and discussed the reactions of various interested parties to the Boothman Committee's proposals in Chapter 3. With the exception of the then Labour Government's Green Paper (Cmnd. 6888), there seemed to be a general measure of agreement amongst the principal parties concerned with financial reporting over the inappropriateness of employment reports being included in company annual reports, the Stock Exchange and CBI in particular expressing very negative attitudes. Furthermore, an initial research study undertaken for the Accounting Standards Committee by Thompson and Knell (1979), whilst also questioning whether a company's annual report is a practical and relevant means through which to provide the information required by the Green Paper, went on to suggest that it was unlikely that the concept of an employment report so envisaged would be valuable or practicable for the majority of companies, their shareholders, or employees. Given such reactions it is hardly surprising that there has been a muted response on the part of most companies towards providing comprehensive employment reports.[3] (There have been some notable exceptions to this general rule, one example of which can be found in Appendix I.)

However, there have been some signs of renewed interest in the publication of employment information on the part of the accounting profession, as exemplified by the appearance of a recent study prepared for the research board of the ICAEW (Maunders, 1984) which draws very different conclusions from those of Thompson and Knell. Maunders presents a rigorous analysis which clearly demonstrates a role for employment reports in satisfying the information needs of a number of potential users, including both employees and shareholders. For example, he argues that labour force data of the type covered by the employment report would aid the employee in forecasting expected changes in the whole structure of terms and conditions of employment arising as a result of collective bargaining. Furthermore, information on matters such as training and education arrangements and health and safety conditions would also enable employees to make predictions concerning future income from employment together with associated risks.[4] Turning to the shareholder group, Maunders argues that employment information appears relevant for predicting the systematic risk of the undertaking's securities together with the earnings of the undertaking, and the variability or total risk attached to these, as well as being useful in evaluating and predicting social performance. The latter performance dimension can be expected to become a matter of growing interest to an increasingly important category of equity investor, namely pension funds. In this context Hughes (1981) has called for trade unions to bargain for joint control of pension funds, so that the flow of pension fund money can be treated as long-run Workers' Capital Funds, and a number of local authorities and trade unions have forcibly expressed the view that their pension fund resources should be channelled into enterprises that preserve and create jobs rather than destroy them.[5]

Maunders concludes his study by recommending that the Accounting Standards Committee should, in the short term, issue 'guidelines' or 'advice' on the appropriate definition, measurement and reporting of employment information items which currently have to be, or are being, included in annual reports. In the longer term he suggests that the ASC should move towards a position of attempting to anticipate emerging concerns about user needs for employment information. This could result in further 'guidelines' and 'advice' being issued, or even accounting standards where intervention by Government could otherwise be expected.

A further study worthy of note is that of Fanning (1979) who, having highlighted the general tendency of industrial and commercial companies to give just the minimum employment information required by legislation, recommends that the reporting of such information should be done in a clear and specific quantitative way facilitating comparison between organizations and with *targets* and *objectives*. Schoenfeld (1978) similarly stresses the importance of goal definition and publication, also pointing out that if goals were known for the actions reported, then at least the degree of goal attainment could be assessed in particular cases. Arguments such as these suggest that the employment report should not be considered in isolation. More useful information would be presented if quantified, medium-term, strategic targets and future prospects for the year following balance sheet date relating to matters such as future employment levels and the purchasing power of wages paid to employees, were to be published for subsequent comparison with performance in the employment report itself. The authors of *The Corporate Report* envisaged the publication of information concerning employment issues within the statement of future prospects and statement of corporate objectives. However, they tended to cloud the issue somewhat by suggesting a wealth of other information to be included in such statements, with the inevitable result that their recommendations, as we have seen, have been widely ignored.

The above, necessarily brief, analysis of the work of writers such as Maunders and Fanning has suggested that publication of an employment report, along the lines suggested by the Boothman Committee, would provide relevant and useful information for annual report users. Indeed, a number of steps could be taken to improve the presentation of employment information beyond *The Corporate Report* recommendations. Such steps would involve providing information on changes in the purchasing power of wages paid to employees, as a number of French companies now do in the Bilan Social, providing more external comparison data and linking more closely the publication of an employment report with statements of future prospects and corporate objectives. Nevertheless, much of the human re-source information so presented would remain non-financially quantified. It may be that still more meaningful information could be produced if financially quantified measures of the human resources in an enterprise could be arrived at. Human asset accounting provides us with an illustration of this process, which its proponents believe provides information relevant to de-cisions involving employees.

Human asset accounting

Human asset accounting, or as it is sometimes termed 'human resource accounting', has been defined as:

> the process of identifying and measuring data about human resources and communicating this information to interested parties.
> American Accounting Association, 1973b, p. 169

The concept was originally popularized by an American social pysychologist, Rensis Likert, who adopted a behavioural science approach to human re-source measurement in investigating the relationship between the system of management used and productivity of the organization. Likert (1967) went on to advocate incorporating human resource accounting in the formal organizational accounting system. The challenge set for accountants, to develop suitable measurement methods for evaluating the human resource, was rapidly taken up. However, Likert's broad definition of the term 'human resources', which included the value of assets such as a firm's human organ-ization, customer loyalty, and reputation in the local community, was also narrowed down to a concentration on the valuation of the firm's human capital, i.e. its work-force.

The aim of developing measures was to provide the data necessary to convert 'qualitative' decision making, inherent in the management of human resources, into a more quantitative framework (American Accounting Association, 1973b). One can see in this development the influence of scientific management principles which seek to make the most efficient use of all resources, including human resources, employing quantitative method-ology. However, Gambling (1976) considers that a fundamental aspect of human asset accounting, as revealed by the practical demand for it, encompasses a form of stewardship accounting, or accountability, which can be used to justify an organization's personnel policies to outsiders. Jurkus (1979) echoes this viewpoint, arguing that the more assets can be quantified in the input–output productivity model the better the accountability to be achieved:

> Thus human resources accounting promises more information with which to make better decisions and more data to better evaluate those decisions, all for the sake of improved accountability.   p. 73

The pioneering work of Likert[6]

Likert's work arose from a concern that traditional accounting systems, with their emphasis on short-term profit maximization, tended to encourage managers to misuse human resources by ignoring factors such as the need for employee participation in decision making and for more training of subordinates. He argued that short-term profit increases generated in this way were largely illusory as the resultant increases in employee turnover and consequent additional spending on hiring and training more than offset the immediate savings. Likert developed a behavioural model of management which identified four basic management systems:

System 1 – exploitive authoritative
System 2 – benevolent authoritative
System 3 – consultative
System 4 – participative group

The first three systems represent varying degrees of authoritarian management, whilst the fourth involves the type of supportive and participative management recommended by modern organization theorists. Likert suggested that an organization's management style can be classified into one of the above systems through the observation of certain variables consisting of three broad classes:

(i) Causal variables, which include organizational structure, managerial leadership styles and organizational policies, are independent variables which can be directly or purposely altered by the organization and its management and in turn determine the quality and capabilities of the human organization.

(ii) Intervening variables which reflect the internal state, health and performance capabilities of the organization, for example the attitudes, motivations, perceptions, and performance goals of the members of the organization.

(iii) End result variables which are dependent variables and reflect the results achieved by management such as productivity, costs, scrap loss, growth, market share, and earnings.

Briefly, Likert argued that changes in causal variables would produce, after a time lag, changes in the intervening variables, which again after a time lag produce changes in the end result variables. His basic thesis is that a firm in which the causal variables display system 4 characteristics will generate more effective intervening variables and therefore more desirable end result variables in the long run. However, management accounting systems which overemphasize short-run profits and cost reductions may penalize the manager who is making the greatest long-term contribution to the organization and reward the manager who achieves impressive short-term results at the cost of using up human assets. To correctly evaluate the performance of a system 4 manager the causal and intervening variables must be measured and periodically reported so that their impact may be considered at least subjectively. One suggested way of measuring intervening variables is by means of employee attitude surveys, covering items such as job satisfaction levels. Experiments have been conducted in this area in the United States (Preston, 1981), Canada (Brooks, 1980) and Sweden (Grojer and Stark, 1977). Ultimately Likert believed that human resources could be measured by predicting a firm's future earnings, based on the current status of causal and intervening variables, and then discounting to net present value, a portion of which is allocated to human assets.

The complexity of behavioural relationships tends to limit the practical value of Likert's model, as Groves (1981) points out. Nevertheless, as indicated earlier, Likert's work did lead to the development of a number of accounting-based methods for measuring human asset values. Much of this development work, which took place in the decade from the mid-1960s to the mid-1970s, has, however, made little continuing practical impact. Indeed, interest in human asset accounting appears to have declined markedly in recent years and there seems little point in devoting precious space to an exhaustive treatment of suggested models. However, we shall give the reader a flavour of the debate by outlining very briefly some of the more widely canvassed models, which may be conveniently classified as cost-based or value-based.[7]

Cost-based methods

The simplest method to operate in practice is that of *historical or acquisition cost*. Under this method costs incurred in recruiting, selecting, hiring, training, placing, and developing employees of the firm, instead of being written off in the year incurred, are capitalized and amortized over the expected useful life of the asset, i.e. the employee. In the income statement this addition to 'investment in human resources' is added back to income before taxation.

Such a method of course suffers the same drawbacks as historic cost accounting generally. An alternative is to use *replacement cost* which focuses on the costs incurred in replacing existing employees with others of equivalent ability and experience. These include the acquisition cost of replacement, learning costs involved in bringing the new employee to the required level of productivity, and separation costs resulting from factors such as short-term losses in production arising from the staff change (Flamholtz, 1973).

A third cost-based method, that of *opportunity cost*, is suggested by Hekimian and Jones (1967). Here, the value of human resources is approximated by a process of competitive bidding, involving departmental managers bidding for scarce employees with the successful manager including the bid price in his investment base. Whereas such a method provides a measurement of the human asset value of each employee whose services represent a scarce resource, it excludes all other employees together with individuals secured from outside the organization.

Value-based methods

Lev and Schwartz (1971) put forward a valuation method based on *discounting future salaries*. Their model may be represented as follows:

$$V_r = \sum_{t=r}^{T} \frac{I_t}{(1+r)^{t-r}}$$

where V_r = the human capital of a person r years old
       I_t = annual earnings up to retirement, represented by the
              earnings profile
       r = a discount rate specific to the person
       T = retirement age

The value of the total human resources of the firm is obtained by aggregating and averaging the earnings profile of homogeneous groups of employees. A more complex method of valuing human resources, which also involves capitalizing salaries, is suggested by Hermanson (1964). In Hermanson's model, discounted salaries for a given time period are adjusted by an 'efficiency factor', being a measure of the firm's rate of return in relation to the average rate of return for the industry.[8]

Brummett *et al.* (1968) suggest a *discounted earnings flow* method based on discounting future forecast earnings of the firm rather than wage payments. One procedure suggested involves forecasting future earnings for the firm in excess of industry averages. These forecasted deviations are then discounted to their present value and a portion allocated to human resources based on their relative contribution compared to non-human resources.

Hermanson (1964) favours a *market value* approach to human asset valuation in which the excess of the market value of a firm's securities over tangible asset value is used to approximate the value of human resources. The model may be summarized as follows:

$$MV_s - MV_a = I = HR$$

where MV_s = market value of firm's securities
       MV_a = market value of firm's tangible assets
       I = value of tangible assets
       HR = value of human resources

In a rare UK-based study in the field Giles and Robinson (1972) advocate the use of a *human asset multiplier*. The procedure envisaged is to multiply the company's annual earnings figure by the industry average P/E ratio to arrive at a valuation figure for the company. From this figure is deducted the amount of the net assets to give a balance which is assumed to represent the value of human resources. This 'value' is apportioned amongst the work-force by attaching a multiplier to each job grade, the size of the multiplier reflecting the relative importance of the job, and multiplying this figure by the total remuneration of each job grade. Totalling the resultant figures over all grades gives a value for human resources which can be checked against the earlier goodwill figure based on the P/E ratio.

The final, and most sophisticated, value-based method of human asset valuation worthy of note is Flamholtz's (1971) approach based on *service states*. A stochastic (probabilistic) model for the monetary valuation of individuals is presented based on the notion that a person is not valuable to an organization in the abstract, but in relation to roles, or service states, he is expected to occupy. An individual should move through various service states, with attached appropriate salary levels, during his employment with an organization, and is accordingly assessed for the probability of being in each service state at a given time. The model defines an individual's expected realizable value as being:

$$\sum_{t=1}^{n} \left[\sum_{i=1}^{m} \frac{R_i P(R_i)}{(1+r)^t} \right]$$

where R_i =   the rewards obtainable to the organization from the *i*th service state

$P(R_i)$ =   the probability that the person will occupy the *i*th service state

m =   the exit state

n =   number of years expected employment from the individual

r =   discount rate

Due to major practical difficulties in measuring the present value of expected services to the entity, surrogate measures, such as replacement cost, compensation and sales revenue, may be employed (Flamholtz, 1972).

Human asset accounting: a brief critique
It is not our purpose here to present a methodological critique of the above-suggested approaches to human resource valuation.[9] Instead, we shall concern ourselves with assessing the potential of the concept, as it has been developed in the literature, as a mechanism for promoting accountability. In this context, it is quite clear that the high degree of subjectivity involved in many of the suggested valuation procedures calls into question the utility of employing human asset accounting for external reporting purposes. Admittedly, there have been attempts to incorporate human asset valuations into published accounts, a notable example being that of the American R.G. Barry Corporation, which employed an acquisition cost approach,[10] and the American Accounting Association Committee on Human Resource Accounting (AAA, 1973) stressed that development of the concept should fully take into account its usefulness to external parties. However, it should be pointed out at this stage that such empirical studies as there are concerning the usefulness of human asset measures to external parties have focused

exclusively on the investor (e.g. Elias, 1972; Acland, 1976; Schwan, 1976) and ignored the issue of accountability to the work-force.

Despite studies such as the above, the majority of models developed for measuring human asset values, particularly the second group of models we looked at, have been concerned essentially with assisting management decision making.[11] This development accords with the view of Brummett *et al.* (1968) who see human asset accounting as a managerial tool not constrained by accounting conventions and legal regulations. Therefore the remainder of this discussion is concerned with questioning the role of human asset accounting as an input into management social reports and in promoting the welfare of employees.

Bauer and Fenn (1972) feel that human valuation is naturally included within the scope of a corporate social audit and Wright (1970) argues that accounting for people as capital assets leads the way to a more humanistic treatment of employees. In particular;

> Greater attention may be given to individual selection, development, placement, advancement, incentive and redevelopment. Greater care may be taken to avoid overtaxing man, under-utilising his talents and allowing managerial obsolescence.   p. 298

Certainly Likert's pioneering work was greatly motivated and influenced by similar thoughts. Giles and Robinson (1972) also believe that the dignity of the employee is enhanced by being recognized as a vital asset of the organization, and that the personnel manager is equipped with powerful new arguments, based on financial quantification, to justify the expense of training and development programmes and to indicate the contribution of personnel expenditure to corporate success. Similarly, Mirvis and Macey (1976) see a role for human asset accounting in providing relevant cost–benefit data justifying human resource development programmes.

Overall then, many proponents of human asset accounting point to its role in influencing management to think of people as an organizational resource, and that management therefore becomes sensitized to the influence of human variables in determining the success of the organization (Dobbins and Trussell, 1975). However, an alternative viewpoint is possible, in that managers may be tempted to act on the basis of the figures alone rather than going to the trouble of considering the human effects of their decisions. In other words, as Jurkus (1979) points out, they may treat human quantitative data no differently from quantitative data relating to the physical plant and equipment of the firm. Furthermore, Maunders (1984) argues that 'valuing' factors such as training and health and safety of employees may merely serve to obscure relevant information rather than highlight it.

A particularly damning critique of human asset accounting, as it has developed in practice, is provided by Glautier (1976). Analyzing many of the models we have previously considered, he points out that they have been concerned essentially with the problem of economic (as opposed to social) efficiency and further highlights the influence of powerful user groups in this development. Glautier argues that consideration should be given to the wider socio-economic goals that may be served by human asset accounting and, like Maunders, suggests that non-monetary measures may well provide a better indication of social effectiveness. He further feels that the potential of human asset accounting in promoting social effectiveness, for example in eroding the classical view that gives all advantages associated with capital to shareholders and in ensuring that individuals are placed in organizational tasks to which they are best suited, is not being realized.

Other writers such as Marques (1976) and Cherns (1978) have also pointed to the fact that most on-going human resource accounting research implicitly presumes classical capitalistic objectives, which means essentially maximization of shareholders' profit. For example, Cherns points out that when Flamholtz studies the individuals expected realizable value to a formal organization, he implicitly introduces the notion of contribution to a strictly capitalist objective. Cherns in particular attacks the 'practical' orientation of much accounting research in this area:

> Paradoxically, this very urge to be practical contributes to drawing the teeth of human resource accounting. Its use in legitimising to the outside critic the present framework of accounting theory and practice undermines its revolutionary potential. At its most ineffectual it becomes cosmetic; at its worst dangerously manipulative.   p. 111

Marques has posed the question, 'Are people a resource for the enterprise or is the enterprise a resource for people?' Practical applications of human asset accounting so far attempted, particularly in the United States, appear to favour the former view, and therefore it has tended to develop as a manipulative management tool rather than a vehicle for extending accountability to the work-force.[12]

THE PROVISION OF CORPORATE INFORMATION TO EMPLOYEES

An alternative to the reporting of employment information in demonstrating accountability to the work-force, may be to report corporate financial information to employees. *The Corporate Report* envisaged that special purpose reports would provide the most suitable medium for transmitting information to employees, rather than merely supplying them with copies of the annual report prepared for shareholder use.

The method of communicating financial information to employees by means of an 'employee report', which Hussey (1979) defines as 'a Statement produced at least annually, in written form, specifically for all employees, which provides information relating to a financial period of the undertaking', has become increasingly popular in recent years, particularly amongst larger companies. For example, a survey undertaken by Maunders (1982a) of the reporting practices of three hundred of the largest UK industrial and commercial companies found that 77% of companies responding had produced an employee report, or simplified financial statements for the use of both shareholders and employees, during 1981/82.

Whereas Hussey (1981) points to a few examples of companies giving information on financial performance to employees in the first half of this century, and to a quickening of interest in employee reporting in the 1940s, such practice did not become widespread until the 1970s. At the same time a growing literature in the subject area began to appear in the UK, whereas much of the earlier work had originated in the United States (Lewis *et al.*, 1984a). Undoubtedly the ill-fated *Industrial Relations Act* of 1971 played a large part in this process, section 57 of the Act providing that employers of more than 350 persons should make an annual written financial statement available to all employees. Whilst this statutory obligation never actually became operative it did spur many companies on towards reviewing their reporting policies. Further encouragement was provided by the CBI who in 1975 took the step of publishing guidelines for members on the provision of information to employees.

There are indeed a number of potential benefits accruing to companies from the publication of employee reports. For example, Parker (1977) points to their role in developing favourable employee impressions of the company and reducing resistance to change, as well as their educative function in broadening employee perspectives away from matters merely affecting their own particular part of the shopfloor, demonstrating the relevance of company finance and explaining the role of the shareholder to employees.

Looking at the exercise from an employee standpoint, Hussey (1979) considers that employee reports may both meet a desire on the part of employees for information and, perhaps more fundamentally, represent a demonstration of accountability by companies to their employees. It is to these latter issues that we will devote our attention in the remainder of this chapter.

Satisfying employee information needs

A study by Lyall (1982) based on sixty employee reports received from a random sample of companies chosen from the *Times 1,000* largest UK companies, indicated that generally only a very small amount of information is disclosed in the annual employee report, which is generally insufficient to meet employees basic information needs. Utilizing earlier work by Taylor (1976) and Jones (1977) an information checklist was drawn up under three main headings reflecting the major areas of employee interest (Figure 8.1), and the reports examined to determine whether information about each of the items on the list was disclosed.

It was found that on average the reports contained only four of the items on the checklist, with the fullest report giving only information on seven of the listed items. The most frequent disclosures were profitability (57

A. Job security

1. Profitability	8. Divisional information
2. Product development	9. Manpower information
3. Sales development	10. Cash flow (present)
4. Financial resources	11. Cash flow (future)
5. Budgets/long range plans	12. Research and development
6. Order levels	expenditure
7. Exports	13. Capital investment levels

B. Company performance

14. Production Costs (profitability)
15. Selling and distribution costs (divisional information)
16. Administration/management costs

C. Wealth sharing

17. Value added (capital investment)

Figure 8.1 Lyall's information checklist. Source: Disclosure practices in employee reports, *The Accountant's Magazine*, July 1982, p.246. Reproduced by permission.

companies), value added (43 companies), divisional information (29 companies), financial resources (21 companies) and capital investment (21 companies). It was also discovered that none of the reports contained information on budgets, future cash flows, or production, selling and administration costs. On weighting the information to take account of the fact that the level of provision under the various headings varied considerably, ranging in the case of profit, for example, from a comprehensive profit statement to a single profit figure, value added replaced profitability as the item receiving most attention in the reports, whilst financial resources replaced divisional information in third place. These findings are summarized in Table 8.1.

In assessing the significance of Table 8.1's findings it must be borne in mind that there is considerable evidence of employees experiencing great difficulty in understanding financial information (e.g. Hussey, 1979; Mitchell *et al.*, 1980). Therefore companies have to find a suitable balance between attempting to fully satisfy employee information needs and avoiding presenting an over-long and complex document causing 'information overload.' Hussey has suggested that three separate statements generally comprising:

1. a statement of financial highlights over a period of years;
2. either a simplified profit and loss account *or* a value added statement;
3. a balance sheet

provide a good balance, and should avoid information overload. An analysis of 302 employee reports undertaken by Marsh and Hussey (1979) did in fact indicate that the most frequent statement appearing was a financial highlights statement (77.2%) followed by a value added statement (40.7%) and a balance sheet (38.7%).

Table 8.1 Items most commonly disclosed in employee reports

Item	No. of companies disclosing item (out of 60)	Ranking	Weighted value of information given*	Ranking
Profitability	57	1	68	2
Value added	43	2	99	1
Divisional information	29	3	29	4
Financial resources	21	4=	47	3
Capital investment	21	4=	23	5

* Arbitrary weightings of 3, 2 or 1 are used, depending on whether the information took the form of a substantially full statement, an abridged statement or merely selected figures.
(Adapted from Lyall, D. (1982), *op. cit.* Reproduced by permission.

As well as producing simplified and abridged versions of a limited selection of the financial statements appearing in the full annual report and accounts, most companies take other steps to try to increase the readability of their employee reports. Fairly routine procedures here are the presentation of financial data in the form of bar charts, pie charts and line graphs as well as a fairly extensive use of photographs, line drawings and, in some cases, cartoons. A recent example of the ingenuity employed by some companies in producing eye-catching graphics is provided by Rowntree Mackintosh's 1984 employee report, part of which is reproduced in Exhibit 8.1.

Whereas readability is obviously important, there is a real danger, as Lyall's (1982) study highlights, that companies may tend to err on the side of over-simplification and a consequent underprovision of relevant information. The findings of Hussey's (1979) study, concerned with employees' reactions to employee reports, are illuminating in this context in that they indicate that the report most appreciated, and hence most likely to be read by employees is a report termed the 'heavy shareholder' type (i.e. a document very similar to the shareholders' report and accounts in appearance, presenting a wide range of information produced in a conservatively written style with an avoidance of gimmickry). Conversely the most highly criticized reports were those of

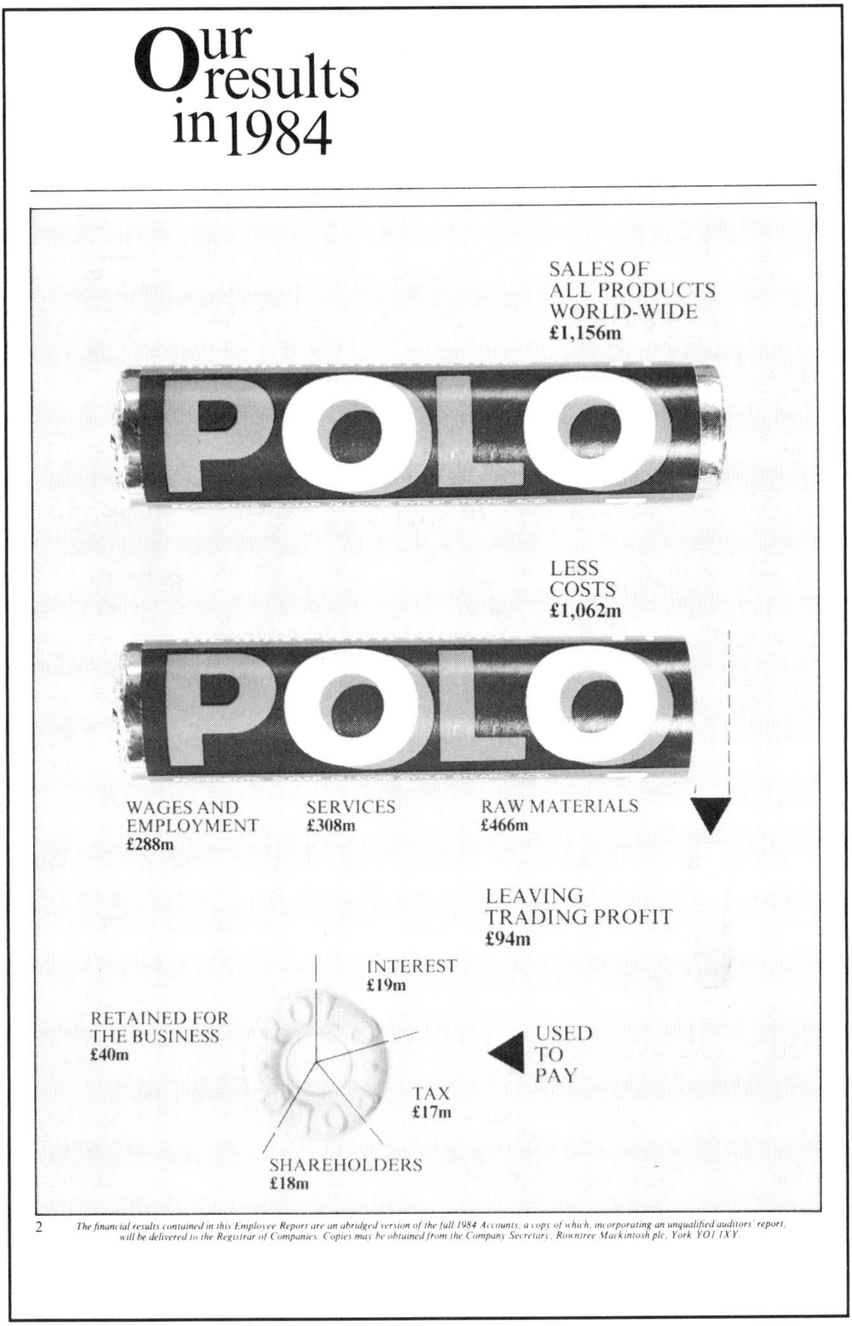

Exhibit 8.1 *Rowntree Mackintosh Report to Employees 1984.* Reproduced by permission.

the 'throw-away' type, often economy issues produced on a single sheet of paper and presenting the bare essentials of financial information.

Of course, employees are not a homogeneous group and some may well be ill-equipped to appreciate or understand a detailed report. One possible solution to this problem is for companies to produce a simplified report for both shareholders and employees, a development we touched on earlier, thus avoiding giving the impression that employees are regarded as a less sophisticated audience. At the same time it should be ensured, as many companies indeed do, that a copy of the full annual report is available to employees on request as theoretically they require access to the same range of financially predictive information as shareholders (Maunders, 1984).

A possible drawback to the above approach is that employees have certain needs which may not be common to many shareholders. For example, Hussey (1979) found that above all else an employee seems to want information about his own workplace, whether it be subsidiary company, division, department or factory. Maunders' (1982a) survey appears to indicate that many companies are attempting to satisfy this particular need in their employee reports, 77% of companies in his sample providing divisional or product line information. However, Lyall (1981) has pointed out that such data is generally restricted to disclosure of sales, profit and investment figures and is therefore inadequate for reaching any meaningful conclusions concerning job security and prospects. Security of employment depends on future product demand, and whilst sales and profit figures indicate the past success of the organization they provide no assurance of its future health. In this context Hussey (1979) concluded that the desire on the part of employees for information about future development and plans is the need least well satisfied in the reports he studied. One could indeed draw the same conclusion from our earlier discussion of the results of Lyall's (1982) study! Further evidence of employee information needs not currently being met is provided by the general lack of detailed employment data, referred to earlier in this chapter, and quantified comparative data, relating, for example, to the industry in which the firm operates, appearing in employee reports.

Further issues of accountability

As well as underprovision of relevant information, further criticisms of current practice in employee reports, which reflect on their role as a means of accountability to the work-force, have centred on a perceived degree of bias in the way information is presented.

A particular case in point is provided by value added statements, in which, the information shown, Lyall (1981) has argued, is frequently unhelpful and occasionally misleading. He points to the common practice of showing both company retentions and distributions to shareholders net of tax whilst the amount paid to employees is shown inclusive of tax, thus effectively overstating, by a considerable amount, the employees share of value added measured in terms of take home pay. Furthermore, the practice of including pension

A message from the Chairman

1984 was a year in which the Group continued to grow in sales and profits, with the biggest part of the increase coming from newly acquired companies in North America. But many other businesses did well and you will find their progress described in the report.

1984 was also a year in which we continued to invest heavily around the world. Capital expenditure on new plant and equipment was again a record, as was expenditure on advertising. Both are essential to the long term health of the Group businesses.

The need to reduce costs is as great as ever, for we can only continue to satisfy our consumers if we can offer our products at competitive prices and weights. In the end this is the only sustainable source of prosperity and job security, even though it may now mean reductions in the numbers of jobs in some factories and offices. I very much regret the anxiety and unhappiness these reductions can cause. But they are necessary if we are to achieve a secure future for the majority of employees.

Thank you all very much for your great efforts in 1984. The Group depends, as ever, on the energy and wide ranging technical and personal skills of you, its employees.

KENNETH DIXON
12th March 1985

Exhibit 8.2 *Rowntree Mackintosh Report to Employees 1984*. Reproduced by permission.

contributions, national insurance contributions, sickness benefits and other welfare expenditure in the employee share of value added also tends to overstate their position. An apparent increase in the employees share may be due to an increase in national insurance contributions, which of course really represents an increase in the Government's share of value added.

Further charges of biased information provision have been laid against the contents of chairman's statements included in many reports. Parker (1977) has identified a tendency to resort to clichés, exhortations, political dogma and managerial conventional wisdom, and suggests that such statements may well cause employees to reject the report in its entirety. The chairman's statement from the 1984 Rowntree Mackintosh employee report, whilst by no means as extreme as some, possibly illustrates Parker's point (Exhibit 8.2).

Whereas there can clearly be no such thing as complete neutrality in the presentation of information there are differing degrees of bias and management could, by avoiding presenting an overly political document, increase the credibility of information presented in the employee report. Suggestions for increasing credibility include forming a working committee composed of employees from all levels to contribute to the preparation of the report (Hussey, 1979), possibly enabling some degree of critical comment to be contained in the finished product, or giving trade union representatives the opportunity to contribute a statement (Parker, 1977; Hilton, 1978). The importance of taking union reactions to the report into account is stressed by Hilton who points out that unions may feel threatened by management attempts to communicate with the work-force over their heads. There are however very few examples of statements from union officials being included in employee reports (although the British Oxygen Company experimented with the idea of including a statement by a national union official some years ago) and indeed very few instances of really hard-hitting critical comment of management performance being included either.

The above analysis has raised a number of questions as to how far current employee reports succeed in satisfying employee information needs or can be regarded as exercises in accountability to the work-force. Drawing on his research in the area Lyall (1981) has in fact concluded that:

> There is little evidence of any widespread attempt to improve the quality of information contained in employee reports or to increase its relevance to the needs of employees. Whether this is due to an unwillingness on the part of management to disclose certain information or is merely an indication of a continuing lack of awareness of what information employees need is unclear. What is clear, however, is that until the contents of employee reports more closely reflect employees' interests and needs, they are unlikely to be warmly welcomed and used by employees, and indeed may represent wasted effort and money spent producing them.   p. 38

Accounting researchers must of course shoulder a large extent of the blame for any continuing unawareness of employee information needs. For, as Lewis *et al.* (1984b) have pointed out, employee preferences for information have been largely a neglected issue in accounting research and in particular, the rights of employees to information, their information demand and information needs, have not been integrated in any framework capable of empirical verification.   p. 232

Employee reports as part of the communication process

Lyall (1982) has suggested that the most likely explanation for the generally low level of information disclosure in employee reports is that such documents represent only the tip of the information iceberg and that the information employees seek is often provided in other forms. A study by Purdy (1981) indeed suggested that companies with a tradition of operating 'open' management styles view annual employee reports not as the centre-piece of information provision, but rather as an adjunct to the more frequent supply of information to employees utilizing means such as works councils, communication or briefing groups and site meetings. On the other hand, it was suggested that companies not adopting an open management philosophy tend to use employee reports in an effort to influence employees to accept management's views and hence reduce industrial conflict. Such companies seem particularly concerned to produce employee reports which foster in the employee the notion that they are operating an open management system and that employees are fairly treated. However, they tend to be somewhat disadvantaged in this respect in that they do not generally have suitable structures for feedback to enable them to assess employee reactions!

For production of employee reports to represent a meaningful exercise in accountability to the work-force there must obviously be an opportunity for employees to comment on the information presented to them and for management to respond to such comments. Parker (1977) points out that if the employee report is seen merely as an exercise in downward communication, employees may be unresponsive, since they will see the report as being something external to them and over which they have no influence, and in which therefore they have little interest. Hussey (1979) and Jones (1978) have also stressed the need for information in written form to be supported by oral communication involving group discussion.

A further problem arising from an over-reliance on the employee report as the major means of communication with the work-force is that information so provided will be somewhat out of date by the time employees receive it, particularly if production of the employee report is timed to coincide with that of the annual report for shareholders. This problem may be overcome to a certain extent if interim reports are issued during the year (Hilton, 1978; Parker, 1977) although Jones (1978) considers that information to be of any real use should be supplied more frequently still, probably monthly. Obviously the company is going to face cost constraints here, and also confidentiality constraints if the detailed cost information which Jones suggests employees need is to be provided, to say nothing of the problem of information overload. This raises the fundamental question of whether a meaningful extension in accountability can in fact be realized via the medium of communicating with the work-force in general.

Hussey (1979) has produced evidence suggesting that employee reports have a role to play in raising the morale of the work-force, by at least demonstrating to employees that management is aware of their existence, and that employees generally appreciate the information they receive, preferring more rather than less information provision. This would appear to suggest that efforts made to improve the quality of information provided in employee reports, and to eradicate some of the more obvious deficiencies referred to earlier, would be far from wasted. However, true accountability can really only be said to exist if employees have the capacity to actively influence managerial actions. Wilders and Heller (1981), whilst suggesting that companies with higher levels of information provision tend to have a more satisfied work-force, could find no evidence of employees in high information companies they studied having a significantly greater say in plant activities than employees in low information companies. It may well be that employees can only achieve a greater share in decision making via extensions in collective bargaining, and that information required in this context is better supplied to employee representatives rather than the work-force generally. It is to these issues we turn in the next chapter.

SUMMARY AND CONCLUSIONS

In this chapter we have been concerned with assessing the extent to which companies, via information provision, have begun to accept the concept of accountability to the work-force. For those who believe such a concept to be central to the operation of a truly democratic society the chapter makes depressing reading.

Very few companies have begun to supply the type of work-force data *The Corporate Report* envisaged could be supplied by means of employment reports, despite the potential usefulness of such information to groups such as employees and shareholders, whilst no suggested system of human asset accounting has achieved widespread acceptance. Indeed, human asset accounting has tended to develop narrowly as a managerial tool in the promotion of private economic efficiency despite its apparent potential for serving wider socio-economic objectives. Turning to the reporting of information to employees, whereas most large companies now produce employee reports, the limited research evidence available has cast considerble doubts on the effectiveness of these documents in satisfying employee information needs. One may thus be inevitably left with the impression that current reporting systems reflect the overall lack of accountability to the work-force many company managements appear to have exhibited in the recent years of de-industrialization!

NOTES

1. *The Corporate Report*, Appendix 4, pp. 92–96.
2. *Arbeitsorientierte Einzelwirtschaftslehre*, a concept developed by a study group operating in the Institute for Economic and Social Sciences of the German Federation of Trade Unions, and intended to be a counterpart to traditional business management.
3. Data on the number of companies producing employment reports along the lines suggested in *The Corporate Report* is given in Chapter 3.
4. See Maunders (1984) pp. 15–27, for a more detailed analysis of these issues.
5. A recent example of union ambitions in this area is provided by the widely reported case of Cowen v. Scargill (Chancery Division, 13 April 1984) in which trustees of the mineworkers pension scheme appointed by the National Union of Mineworkers opposed plans for an investment strategy which involved placement of funds overseas and investment in the competing oil and gas industries. Whereas the union was unsuccessful in this case, one may expect control of pension fund money to be a continuing trade union objective.
6. For a fuller discussion see Likert (1967).
7. For a fuller treatment see, for example, American Accounting Association (1975), Grove *et al.* (1977) and Groves (1981). A comprehensive biography of the literature in the field appears in *Accounting, Organizations and Society*, Vol. 1, no. 2/3, 1976, pp. 271–279.
8. For a worked example of such a calculation see Dobbins and Trussell (1975).
9. For such a critique see, for example, Groves (1981).
10. See Flamholtz (1974) for an extended discussion of the R.G. Barry Corporation approach and other practical initiatives.
11. It should be pointed out that the effectiveness of human asset accounting in this narrow context is far from conclusively proved. Thus, Flamholtz (1976) in a laboratory experiment, found that whilst non-monetary information on human resources influenced management decisions, it could not be established that monetary information had the same effect. A later study by Harrell and Flick (1980) focusing on a single decision making issue, namely the promotability of captains in the United States Air Force to the rank of major, did however find a greater emphasis placed on monetary measures.
12. Such applications have generally been attempted in service organizations where highly qualified and skilled personnel do indeed comprise the main productive assets, for example, firms of accountants! (e.g. Alexander, 1971). There has also been a noteworthy attempt to apply human asset valuation techniques to the personnel of Liverpool Football Club (see Dobbins and Trussell, 1975).
13. This latter practice is incidentally becoming more widespread, an impetus to such a move no doubt being provided by Lee and Tweedie's (1977) study which pointed to generally low levels of comprehension amongst shareholders of traditional annual reports and accounts.

APPENDIX I

Employment Report

CROWN HOUSE plc

for the year ended
31st March, 1985

Number employed	(a) Total employees	31st March, 1985		1st April, 1984	
		Male	*Female*	*Male*	*Female*
	Full time	4,946	1,003	4,492	1,048
	Part time	35	408	31	403
		4,981	1,411	4,523	1,451
	(b) *Functions of employees*				
	Engineering, production and service	4,377	388	3,935	388
	Distribution, selling and marketing	249	496	245	532
	Administration	355	527	343	531
		4,981	1,411	4,523	1,451

Location of employment at 31st March, 1985	(a) *United Kingdom*	*Engineering Production and Service*	*Distribution Selling and Marketing*	*Administration*
	England	2,805	597	657
	Scotland	418	93	61
	Wales	491	15	32
	Northern Ireland	153	1	7
		3,867	706	757
	(b) *Overseas*	898	39	125
		4,765	745	882

Remuneration	Gross pay	*U.K.*	*Overseas*	*Total*
		£43,573,502	£6,475,221	£50,048,723

Education and training	Total employee hours spent in training during the year within the company (excluding on-the-job-training)	*Hours*
		139,249
	External training courses	18,049
		157,298

	Cost of training	*£000*
	Training department	91
	Wages paid during training	204
	Training Board levy	119
	External courses	59
		473
	Less: Training Board grant	99
		374

Trade Unions

As at 31st March, 1985 the principal trade unions recognised by member companies of the group were:– Ceramic and Allied Trades Union; Electrical and Engineering Staff Association; Electrical, Electronics, Telecommunications and Plumbing Trades Union; National Union of Sheet Metal Workers, Coppersmiths, Heating and Domestic Engineers; General, Municipal, Boilermakers and Allied Trades Union; National Union of Flint Glassworkers; Transport and General Workers Union; Union of Construction Allied Trades and Technicians; Amalgamated Union of Engineering Workers; Association of Scientific, Technical and Managerial Staff; National Society of Metal Mechanics.

Accidents	(a) Number of reportable accidents during the year	54
	(b) Frequency of reportable industrial accidents (accidents/1000 hours worked)	0.0043

Disabled persons   At 31st March 1985, 45 registered disabled persons were employed by the group.

Source: Crown House plc Employment Report 1985. Reproduced by permission.

Chapter 9

Accountability to the work-force II – collective bargaining

In the previous chapter we were largely concerned with assessing the degree of reponsibility that companies had accepted towards their employees through the medium of voluntary provision of information, which could be used for forming judgements on matters of corporate performance affecting the interests of the work-force. However, as Stewart (1984) points out, true accountability requires not only the provision of information, but also the opportunity to take action on the basis of judgements formed. Employees are most able to take action when acting collectively, generally through the medium of a trade union. Therefore in this chapter we shall be looking at the role trade unions may play in broadening corporate accountability via the mechanism of collective bargaining.

Whereas the mere mention of the words trade union may be sufficient to raise the hackles of many accountants, and possibly readers of this text, it must nevertheless be acknowledged that unions are vitally concerned with many aspects of the social performance of business enterprises. For example, Pope and Peel (1981b), have suggested that the union may be regarded as an organization attempting, under conditions of uncertainty, to maximize an objective function having as key components the employment and real wages of its members. Support for the inclusion of the employment factor in this function is provided by Daniel (1981) who points to the high priority that union negotiators attach to the avoidance of any redundancies arising from pay settlements reached. Also, it is relevant to recall the attempts at social audits undertaken, or supported by, trade unions in cases of threatened plant closure described in Chapter 7. Indeed, other writers such as Cooper (1984) have argued that unions take a far broader social perspective still, as in striving to improve the welfare of their members union officials are concerned not only with wage levels and job security but also working conditions, industrial and community health, industrial democracy, national income and quality of life.

The above arguments suggest that it would be an act of omission to discuss the concept of social accountability whilst ignoring the role that trade unions could play in its development, particularly in view of the fact that much legislation which has sought to impose wider accountability on business enterprise in recent years has closely involved trade unions. It is one such piece of legislation enacted in the United Kingdom, the *Employment Protection Act 1975*, which provides us with a useful starting point for subsequent analysis.[1]

THE *EMPLOYMENT PROTECTION ACT 1975*

Essentially the Act encourages company management to engage in more 'open government' by placing upon them an obligation to disclose to trade unions:

● information without which trade union representatives would to a material extent be impeded in carrying out collective bargaining;
● information which it would be good industrial relations practice to disclose.

These disclosure provisions, which incidentally have been retained in subsequent Conservative legislation, were based on earlier, somewhat ill-fated, attempts to legislate in the industrial relations arena by both Labour and Conservative administrations.[2] Thus they seem to reflect an appreciable amount of political consensus that trade unions should be able to participate with management on equal terms in the extension of collective bargaining, and thus have a need for adequate information to enable them to form an independent judgement on management proposals, policies, and decisions. In particular it appears that there is a measure of agreement across the political spectrum that information disclosure has an important role to play in promoting more informed and rational bargaining.

The Advisory, Conciliation and Arbitration Service (ACAS) was charged with the task of defining which types of information disclosure could be regarded as 'good industrial relations practice'. Besides performing this particular task ACAS also suggested that employers and trade unions should seek to arrive at joint undertakings on how a policy of information disclosure could be effectively implemented. Ideally this was to be by means of 'information agreements' which specify the type of information to be disclosed, the form in which it is to be presented, the timing of disclosure, and to whom information should be disclosed.

Unfortunately for those favouring more open government by company management the apparent general intentions of the Act were largely overridden by the insertion of a number of exceptions to the main disclosure provisions. Prominent amongst these exceptions are clauses to the effect that the employer may refuse to diclose information on the grounds that:

● compilation of the information would involve an amount of work or expenditure out of reasonable proportion to the value of the information in the conduct of collective bargaining. (Thus the trade union is placed in the impossible position of having to demonstrate the value of an item of information in the context of collective bargaining without actually having seen it.)
● disclosure would cause substantial injury to the employer's undertaking for reasons other than its effect on collective bargaining.

The latter, 'substantial injury' clause has tended to be interpreted very widely by the Central Arbitration Committee (CAC), the tribunal set up to hear union complaints under the Act. A typical example of the approach adopted by the CAC concerns the dispute between Hoover Ltd and the General and Municipal Workers Union (Award No. 79/146, dated 26 February 1979). In this case it was held that although there was a strong case for disclosure to the union of information sufficient to enable trends in profitability of certain product lines manufactured at a particular plant to be ascertained, as without such information the union side could well be materially impeded in conducting collective bargaining, such data were of a highly sensitive commercial nature, hence the company was exempted from disclosing it.[3] Indeed in the vast majority of cases concerning financial information disclosure coming before the tribunal the employer has been able successfully to plead the substantial injury clause. In view of this fact, and the lengthy process the union has to go through in pursuing claims, which usually takes several months and involves a reference to ACAS for an attempt at conciliation prior to a formal hearing, it is perhaps not surprising that the disclosure provisions of the *Employment Protection Act* have been little utilized by unions in recent years.[4] However, this is not to say that trade unions are necessarily disinterested in the disclosure issue itself, as we shall see.

TRADE UNION REACTIONS TO THE ISSUE OF FINANCIAL INFORMATION DISCLOSURE

Traditionally trade union negotiators have tended to show more interest in factors such as changes in the cost of living, productivity and comparability with other groups of workers than the financial circumstances of particular companies. However, the 1970s saw the beginnings of a change in attitude, at least amongst national officials, towards the information disclosure issue. Certain unions, notably the General and Municipal Workers union (GMWU) began to seek, as a matter of policy, to secure information agreements with companies and indeed published advice for their shop stewards on what types of information to ask for (GMWU, 1978). Other unions such as the Transport and General Workers Union began to adopt the practice of using detailed financial arguments in pursuing certain 'prestige' national wage claims (e.g. TGWU, 1971, 1977).

A number of writers were led to comment most favourably on the level of professionalism in unions using 'ability to pay' arguments in wage bargaining (e.g. Palmer, 1977; Hawkins, 1979). Indeed, certain academic accountants and economists displayed a great deal of enthusiasm and ingenuity in constructing models of trade union decision making which implied a major role for corporate financial information (e.g. Climo, 1976; Cooper and Essex, 1977; Foley and Maunders, 1977; Pope and Peel 1981a, 1981b).[5]

Whereas many of the individual union initiatives in the disclosure field, and the academic modelling attempts mentioned above, focused on the wage bargaining issue, the Trades Union Congress (TUC) saw the disclosure issue in far broader terms, arguing that the provision of information direct to workers or negotiators could provide the potential basis for a degree of *de facto* control over aspects of a company's activities. An example of TUC ambitions in this field is provided by a 1982 report of the TUC – Labour Party Liaison Committee which calls for regular provision to the relevant trade unions of comprehensive information in the following areas:

- The financial position of the enterprise as a whole and of the individual subsidiaries and work-places. Information should cover cost structures, gross and net profits, cash flows, assets, liabilities, allocation of profits, details of government assistance, transfer prices, transactions with parent and subsidiary companies.
- Investment plans, details of actual or likely closures, takeovers or mergers, developments in the range of activities of the enterprise as a whole and subsidiary parts of it.
- Performance, output, productivity, orders and sales – again in relation to both the whole enterprise and parts of it.
- Pay and benefits, conditions of service and manning levels. In addition, information on future plans, the implications for employment and the corresponding manpower measures proposed should be disclosed.

The above demands for information provision are backed up by calls for sweeping changes in consultation and representation arrangements, designed to give workers and their trade union representatives a major role in corporate decision making.

Much interest in recent years has focused upon the extent to which the above evidence of apparent changes in union attitudes at the national level is reflected in individual company and plant-level bargaining. This interest reflects an appreciation of the major importance of the plant as a level of pay settlement.[6]

Early evidence produced by researchers suggested that corporate financial information was being increasingly accepted by union negotiators at the domestic level as possessing a potential usefulness which, however, tended to outweigh the existing provision of such data. Daniel (1976), for example, found that whereas the ability of employers to pay, as measured by trends in product demand, labour intensity, cash flow and the changing size of the work-force, appeared to have little influence over the wage increase agreed, financial circumstances influenced management priorities and hence the degree of difficulty associated with the negotiations. Furthermore, inability of the firm to pay was cited more frequently than any other argument put forward by management as being one that union negotiators felt to be persuasive. It is therefore somewhat surprising that Daniel found considerable evidence of management being disinclined to provide trade union officers with information on the financial side of the business.

A further study worthy of note is that of Cooper and Essex (1977) on the role of shop stewards. Surveying a sample of 230 stewards in the Greater Mamchester area, all members of the Amalgamated Union of Engineering Workers (AUEW), Cooper and Essex asked them to rank the important justifying factors used in pursuing a pay claim. They found that profits made by the firm ranked third in order of importance behind the cost of living and comparison with others in the same work-place. This marked a major departure from a ranking published in the 1968 Government social survey where profits of the firm appeared in ninth place. Cooper and Essex concluded that:

> Perhaps during the period between the two surveys shop stewards have come to regard accounting profits as a good predictor of a firm's willingness to pay a wage claim.   p. 214

A word of caution is necessary when interpreting the results of the Cooper and Essex study, the authors themselves emphasizing that their conclusions must be regarded as tentative in view of the forced choice questionnaire employed imposing a particular image of reality on respondents, and the relatively poor (24.8%) response rate achieved. This need for caution is reinforced when one considers the findings of some more recent major studies of the use made of company information by trade unions in collective bargaining, which produced little evidence of financial information being used by the union side (Mitchell *et al.*, 1980; Moore and Levie, 1981; Reeves and McGovern, 1981; Jackson-Cox *et al.*, 1984). Jackson-Cox *et al.*, for instance, found that:

> In general, management's provision of such information to trades union representatives was initiated in response to pressures arising out of constraints imposed by the environment in which firms operated, rather than in response to trade union pressures or requests.   p. 260

Similarly, Mitchell *et al.*, could find:

> no evidence to suggest that management had been under pressure from their work-forces to disclose information. Trade union leadership . . . had in general merely been permissive.   p. 55

These latter studies are particularly interesting in that, in common with the TUC approach considered earlier, they see a wider role for financial information acquisition than its use merely in wage bargaining. For example, they regard such information as being useful in order to arrive at an understanding of the rationale underlying management decisions, obtaining advance warning of issues or decisions, particularly those having repercussions on job prospects which may need to be negotiated, and furthermore in enabling unions to question the validity of certain management decisions or propose alternative courses of action. In other words, they see an important role for information acquisition in extending collective bargaining beyond the traditional areas of concern, terms and conditions of employment. Obviously trade unions need to seek such an extension of collective bargaining if they are to participate meaningfully in corporate decision-making in the areas of social performance which Cooper (1984) (amongst others) has argued are very much their legitimate area of concern. Also, of course, the above evidence of lack of union interest in acquiring and using financial information for such purposes has profound implications for future government legislative policy, and indeed potential developments in industrial democracy. It would therefore appear worthwhile to consider some possible explanations for the observed low rates of utilization of corporate financial information by union negotiators. Whereas one possible explanation may relate to the unhappy experiences of negotiators attempting to utilize the provisions of the *Employment Protection Act*, we would argue that there are other, more important factors involved which pose fundamental questions concerning the role of financial information itself in collective bargaining.

THE ROLE OF FINANCIAL INFORMATION IN COLLECTIVE BARGAINING

For corporate financial information to play a major role in the bargaining process one could argue that there must be a large measure of specific and shared calculative rationality inherent in union–management negotiations. Indeed many writers in this area appear to have based their analyses on just such a premiss. For example, Maunders (1981) has suggested that, where the union is regarded as acting as the labour market agent of employees, the economic arguments for disclosure are virtually identical to such arguments relating to shareholders, i.e. to facilitate the efficient allocation of resources. In the latter case the purpose of disclosure is to facilitate the efficient allocation of capital; in the former, labour. Further support for this rational view of the negotiating process is provided by Pope and Peel (1981a) who present a model of union decision-making which relies on expectations being formed 'rationally' and based on the 'optimal' use of information.

This assumption of specific and shared rationality has however come under recent attack, notably from Ogden and Bougen (1985) who argue that the bargaining process cannot usefully be modelled as a rational economic procedure concerned with efficient resource allocation. As well as pointing to the underlying antagonistic basis of capital–labour relations, they also question whether many conventional management decision-making processes within the organization are themselves the product of applied economic rationality. They draw our attention particularly to studies highlighting the anarchic tendencies of decision processes (Cohen *et al.*, 1972), the lack of complete knowledge on the part of management concerning alternative strategies (Wildavsky, 1965), and to decision-making processes under conditions of uncertainty concerning the objectives and cause–effect relationships of decision making (Thompson and Tuden, 1959). In the latter situation Burchell *et al.* (1980) point to the lack of scope for accounting systems to operate as 'answer machines' in the context of purely computational decision making, and argue that instead they are used as 'ammunition machines' to promote the positions of particular interested parties in situations of high uncertainty over organizational objectives, and as rationalization machines, legitimizing and justifying actions that have already been decided upon when there is a high degree of uncertainty over cause and effect relationships. Thus in the climate of uncertainty characterizing the collective bargaining arena accounting information can, as Bougen and Ogden (1981) rightly point out, function as an ideological mechanism for propagating and reinforcing managerial values and purposes rather than as an objective and neutral input. Such a role for accounting information may, of course, provide an acceptable 'rule of the game' for groups such as shareholders and creditors but cannot be acceptable to the union side when used in an industrial relations context.

The assumption of specific and shared rationality based on economic considerations, and the consequent acceptance of the importance of formal information flowing from the management information systems for collective bargaining purposes, may indeed be further questioned. For example, Earl and Hopwood (1980) cite the prevalence of informal planning and assessment practices in organizations, and the consequent incompleteness of formal rationality and 'routinization', leading to the development of powerful informal management networks for the formulation of corporate plans. As Batstone (1980) point out, these are networks from which workers and their representatives are excluded!

Some other factors which may be considered relevant when considering the potential for a financial information input into collective bargaining are as follows.

Union objectives

A number of researchers have looked at the provision of information for collective bargaining purposes in the context of the development of decision models for union representatives, a task which initially entails specifying union objectives. However, the search for universal objectives could well prove fruitless. It is quite likely, for example, that the objectives of a traditional craft union will differ considerably from those of a managerial white collar union: the former being primarily concerned with the protection of long-standing status and differentials, whilst the latter may actively seek changes giving them greater participation in decision making.

Furthermore, such generalized objectives as are specified may not indicate an increased role for corporate financial information in collective bargaining. For, as Cooper and Essex (1977) point out, it is unlikely that union objectives can be considered purely in terms of economic factors, a more fundamental interest may indeed centre on contesting managerial control (Ogden and Bougen, 1985).

As Batstone (1980) has indicated, such an interest can only be pursued by seeking to change the whole nature of organizational arrangements, by which is meant the rules and procedures by which the organization operates, together with the system of values, goals and priorities which permeate them. There appears little scope for using corporate financial information in this context, for very little can be achieved at individual organizational levels. Activity at a higher level is required as such objectives are most profitably pursued by attempting to change the economic, social, and political status quo, or to put it another way, seeking changes in the balance of power between classes in society (Cooper and Essex, 1977).

In so far as unions do pursue economic objectives, their aim here may well be to achieve a 'fair' settlement for all their members, regardless of the particular circumstances of the company they work for. As Lindop (1979) points out, people tend to judge incomes on the basis of other people carrying out similar jobs, this being the criterion on which fairness is determined. Thus he foresees a move away from plant bargaining towards larger bargaining units when economic circumstances worsen, as such agreements provide a 'safety net' for workers in plants adversely affected, who may then depend on the security of national or company-wide structures and the support of fellow trade unionists. Daniel (1981) indeed suggests that in seeking social justice unions would prefer to restrain the earnings of members in favourable circumstances rather than depress the relative pay of members in less favourable situations. Further evidence of the importance of the comparability factor for union negotiators is provided by Brown and Sisson (1975) and Blackaby (1978) who point to the union negotiator's concern with ensuring that the group he or she represents does not fall behind but gets at least the 'going rate'. The other major concern of union negotiators, to obtain wage increases for their members at least equal to the rise in the cost of living, may also reflect union concern with social justice. Such a concern with social justice suggests a very limited role for corporate financial data, produced from management information systems operating under profit maximization and cost minimization constraints, in the union negotiators decision model.

The potential for integrative bargaining
One of the strongest arguments commonly put forward in favour of a financial input into the collective bargaining process is that a move towards

integrative bargaining, which functions to find common or complementary interests and to solve problems confronting both parties to the negotiations, will thereby by encouraged.[7] Such a view owes much to the pluralist school of industrial relations which, whilst accepting conflict as being inherent in industrial societies, assumes that accommodation will be achieved between conflicting interest groups based on compromise (Fox, 1966).

Whereas some empirical support for the existence of integrative bargaining is provided by Morley and Stephenson (1977) other writers such as Dobson (1982) and Wilson *et al.* (1982) have questioned the degree of pluralism in industrial relations, pointing out that many managements adopt a unitarist approach, particularly in the realms of investment decisions, production methods, and business policy generally. Blackburn (1972) puts the point more strongly.

> To imagine that the personnel manager, production manager or supervisor has any choice other than to extract surplus value as efficiently as possible from his labour force is quite absurd. That is to say they seek to raise the value of what the worker produces as much as possible above the cost of hiring him.   p. 180

Thus it would appear possible to question the potential for integrative bargaining in many negotiating situations, particularly if one sees the interests of capital and labour as being diametrically opposed (Ogden and Bougen, 1985) or the union–management relationship as basically adversarial in nature (Craft, 1981).

Information as a power resource
The proposition that information is a power resource has attracted much support in the field of industrial relations, and probably explains the reluctance of some managers to lend their support to the principle of increased financial information disclosure. However, it should be realized that the mere possession of information does little to change the balance of power in union–management relations. As Pettigrew (1972) stresses:

> Power resources must not only be possessed by an actor, they must be controlled by him ... Control, may not be enough, there is also the issue of the skillful use of resources.   p. 202

Furthermore, Pettigrew argues that:

> The final decision outcome will evolve out of the process of power mobilituation attempted by each party in support of its demand.   p. 202

In the context of the above analysis one could point out that:

● Management controls the communication process, thus giving them a wide discretion over what to disclose, or not to disclose.
● Management possession of the means of production enables them to command decision-making procedures. In particular, empirical research by Wilson *et al.* (1982) has highlighted managerial control of strategic decision-making with the union side being restricted to a reactive stance, enabling them to merely impede implementation of decisions with no power to initiate and influence decision topics.

● There would appear to be a large difference in the degree of expert power in the use of information operating in favour of management and against the union side. For example, available evidence indicates that most union research departments are small and overworked (Marsh and Rosewell, 1976) and trade union education services are overstretched and under-financed (Cuthbert and Whitaker, 1977). Thus evidence provided by Lyall (1975) and Mitchell *et al.* (1980) pointing to a very low level of compre-hension of financial information by shop stewards should cause us little surprise. However, such findings should perhaps cause concern for those who see financial acquisition and use on the part of trade unions as an essential step in extending collective bargaining. Even though the studies by Lyall and Mitchell *et al.*, may be criticized on the grounds that they ascribed a purely 'answer machine' role to accounting systems, and tested the respondents accordingly, nevertheless it would appear necessary for union negotiators to understand the operation of present accounting systems if they are to appreciate their limitations, particularly their role as an ideological mechanism, and to develop suitable alternative systems and criteria.

● A number of studies (e.g. Reeves and McGovern, 1981; Jackson-Cox *et al.*, 1984) have highlighted lack of membership support as a crucial factor constraining union officials in their use of corporate financial information in collective bargaining. Thus the potential for the mobilization of mem-bership support behind demands based on detailed financial arguments appears very limited, particularly compared to support that could be mobilized behind comparability or cost of living claims.

Therefore there is a real danger that the mere possession of information by the union side without any corresponding power to influence decision mak-ing, due to their exclusion from key management policy-making networks, will merely lead to them beng 'sucked into management'. Indeed, as Jackson-Cox *et al.*, point out, management may adopt a policy of information dis-closure in order to increase employee identification with the company and hence lessen their identification with the union.

THE PROTECTION OF JOBS AS A UNION GOAL: A POSSIBLE MOTIVE FOR INFORMATION ACQUISITION AND USE

In the previous section we have looked at a number of factors which provide possible explanations for the generally low rates of utilization of corporate financial data by union negotiators, highlighted in recent research findings, despite apparent encouragement to the contrary from TUC pronouncements and national union policy statements.[8] However, this does not mean to say that we would deny the potential usefulness of such data, particularly if unions do have ambitions to extend collective bargaining into areas of corporate planning.

A starting point for our analysis is provided by a re-consideration of Pope and Peel's (1981b) thesis, referred to at the beginning of this chapter, that a major objective of a trade union is to maximize the employment prospects of its members. It is interesting to note in this context that a number of empirical studies have shown that the only general exception to an overall union disinterest in financial information at the domestic bargaining level occurs when security of employment becomes a major issue (e.g. Reeves and McGovern, 1981; Sherer *et al.*, 1981; Jackson-Cox *et al.*, 1984). In particular there is growing evidence of unions abandoning their traditional stance of merely reacting to managerial initiatives in favour of using information in order to positively extend collective bargaining in cases of threatened plant closure. Notable examples of trade unionists employing sophisticated finan-cial analysis in a bid to combat management-sponsored redundancy proposals are provided by the campaigns conducted against the closure of Dunlops Factory at Speke on Merseyside (described in Reeves and McGovern, 1981), and the closure of iron and steel-making at Corby.[9]

An unfortunate common feature of these latter efforts is that they came too late to have any effect. This is hardly surprising, for, as Jackson-Cox *et al.* indicate, union representatives are at a major disadvantage in dealing with non-routine issues, of which redundancy questions are a prime example, as they only become involved after management has taken the vital initial decisions. Bryer *et al.* (1984) have suggested that unions can only begin to grapple with this problem when they undertake sophisticated financial analy-sis exercises on a consistent basis, or, in Bryer *et al.*'s terminology, engage in 'shadow planning', which would enable them to understand and challenge managements plans. In the absence of such initiatives Batstone (1980) points out that workers are forced to employ a very limited range of arguments focusing essentially on potential profitability in the case of plant closure and redundancy situations. This is because in such situations the union side generally has to rely on information produced by the management infor-mation system, itself underpinned by restrictive assumptions and value judge-ments concentrating on profitability and cost minimization rather than, for example, job protection or social costs and benefits arising from production. This fact, together with the urgency of the situation, is enough to doom most union efforts in this field to inevitable failure.

For the union side to be able to anticipate and plan, rather than merely react to management plans, Cooper (1984) argues that union access to information is necessary, rather than a reliance on managerial disclosure initiatives. The 'access to information' approach implies that labour has a legitimate right to be involved in the management of the organization and, equally importantly assumes they are concerned with more than bargaining solely over pay and conditions. Reliance on disclosure alone is insufficient in these latter contexts as this leaves too much to the discretion of management.

Indeed, it should be noted here that the whole disclosure debate has been conducted virtually exclusively from a managerial perspective. This is apparent not only in the very restrictive provisions of the *Employment Protection Act* but also in the majority of disclosure models appearing in the accounting literature. As Ogden and Bougen (1985) point out, these tend to be concerned solely with the costs and benefits of disclosure as they affect management, and in so far as the interests of labour are considered they are assumed to be consistent with those of management. Thus the models only reflect a partial analysis of the disclosure issue from a societal viewpoint.[10] One notable attempt to redress the balance in the literature is provided by the work of Roy Moore and his colleagues at Ruskin College, which provides us with rigorous analysis of how the union side can use corporate financial information to extend collective bargaining. Their analysis, to which we now turn our attention has two distinct, but related strands, the 'constraints model' and the 'information scale'.

USE OF CORPORATE FINANCIAL INFORMATION BY TRADE UNIONS IN ORDER TO EXTEND COLLECTIVE BARGAINING

In an initial pilot study Moore *et al.* (1979) adopt what they term a 'user' approach, advising officials to:

> look to the use of information, not to the acquisition of more, when considering how to gain more influence within the enterprise. In particular ... information is a means to an end, it makes sense only within its context; it must be used within a strategy; and a wedge of the union or unions has to co-operate together to ensure its effectiveness   p. 34

In practice a number of constraints have to be overcome before trade unionists can use information effectively. Such constraints fall into two categories: firstly management constraints – managerial attitudes, the organization of industrial relations, company structure; and secondly union constraints – union servicing (i.e. education and research back-up), union policy, and union structure (including shop steward organization). In overcoming these constraints, union officials are urged to develop forward thinking, entailing the selection of objectives, the ordering of priorities and the choosing of strategies or means to achieve them. Only by developing forward thinking may trade unionists avoid the trap of being 'sucked into management'. In particular it is necessary for union officials to get to know and understand the company information system, as well as strengthening the union organization in the company, by developing a suitable structure, enabling a clear picture of all the activities and ramifications of the company to be obtained. The latter point is, of course, particularly important in that it is easy for shop stewards to develop an overly parochial approach to bargaining, whereas many issues facing them, such as investment strategy, are not confined to a particular plant and may best be tackled by the adoption of a multi-plant bargaining approach.

Moore and Levie's later (1981) project investigates in greater detail the context of disclosure and trade union use of company information. A further set of constraints is added to their original model, constraints created by the nature of the industry. Within this category the size and spread of employers, the nature of employment, employment traditions and relations between unions are specified as important factors.

The original constraints model, whilst accepted as a useful diagnostic tool in a particular industrial and company setting at a particular point in time, is criticized on the grounds that it is static, whereas disclosure and use of information are dynamic factors. Therefore Moore and Levie go on to identify crucial dynamic factors that can dramatically change disclosure and use of information. The factors identified are management style and strategy, the state of the economy (i.e. companies are more generally inclined to disclose information when things are going badly), and most importantly, the ambitiousness of union demands.

The basic thesis adopted is that as union demands become more ambitious in the context of developing collective bargaining, the union moves along an 'information scale'. Starting at the bottom of the scale, with an acceptance of company information as it comes, the union moves through points such as asking for additional information, seeking access to the management information system, and changing the system towards the ultimate point of developing its own trade union information system. The level of democracy in the union is considered to be the yardstick of its ability to improve its use of company information. Whereas formal democracy can be said to exist in all unions, the relationship between union officials and the membership resting ultimately on a voting nexus, decision making within the union in many cases has become an autocratic one-way process. Moore and Levie in their use of the term democracy are referring to the need for active, as opposed to merely formal, democratic procedures. This requires:

> a much higher level of involvement of the members and their representatives. It means a bargaining structure that is present at every level of the company. It implies a high level of co-operation, or at least discussion between and within unions. It means creating a new role for full time officers who no longer have to solve members' problems, but who enable them to solve their problems themselves. It means an active education and research programme that changes as collective bargaining develops. It means a flexible organisation that is capable of re-organising itself as the needs and problems of the members change.   p. 29

Whereas Moore *et al.*'s work makes a refreshing change to much of the literature in this area, being conducted very much within a trade union institutional context, and certainly highlights the magnitude of the task facing unions attempting to extend collective bargaining. There are two particular elements of the analysis that we would take issue with.

Firstly, the argument that union representatives should formulate objectives and strategies for using information before taking steps to acquire it, is somewhat over simplistic and therefore not entirely convincing. For, as Gospel (1978) has pointed out, the decision-orientated approach is not a one-way process whereby development of priorities leads to the identification and use of information, but is in fact a two-way process:

> For information itself provides a source of standards and criteria which can generate objectives. In other words, disclosure can activate objectives by changing perceptions of such things as pay discrepancies, job security prospects, managerial efficiency etc. In this way, the acquisition of information can lead to a stronger motivation for further disclosure of information.   p. 34

Jackson-Cox *et al.* take a similar line to Gospel, seeing company information as being particularly important in the development of 'intelligence' for the identification of new issues relating to the company and changes in management strategy which may give rise to issues which are not yet fully developed or disclosed.

Secondly, whilst recognizing union structure as a particular constraint on the effective use of information, Moore *et al.* nevertheless see union demands as being a universal change agent, notwithstanding the structural differences between different unions and within the same union in different locations. Whereas they suggest that trade union ambitions and trade union democracy are two dynamic variables that a union more or less controls itself, and can greatly enhance its use of information, Owen and Lloyd (1985) have argued that changes in these variables essentially hinge on roles played by individual union officials and their relationship to their constituent members. In other words, far more explicit attention should be paid to the possible importance of variations in the nature of the domestic organization.[11] There may well be major differences in approach to information usage, for example between full-time officials and shop stewards, blue collar and white collar representatives and, possibly most importantly stewards who are able to adopt a leadership role as opposed to those acting as delegates for membership aspirations. As we mentioned earlier, empirical studies have shown lack of membership support as a major constraint facing union representatives attempting to utilize financial information in bargaining. To the extent that the steward can 'lead' the membership, he may start to overcome this problem, particularly since, as Batstone *et al.* (1977) point out, strong bargaining relationships involving the exchange of confidential information are more likely to develop between managers and leader stewards than between managers and delegates.

Research by Owen and Broad (1983), based on a sample of shop stewards in two major engineering companies in the Greater Manchester area, all members of their respective union's negotiating committee, highlights the practical problems facing stewards attempting to implement the approach outlined by Moore *et al.* As well as illustrating a generally low level of ambitiousness of steward demands, with majorities of both blue and white collar stewards expressing the view that decisions relating to introduction of new products, investment plans, and drawing-up of financial budgets were management matters, despite the fact that such decisions exert a strong influence on job prospects (an area that the same stewards felt to be very much their concern), the study also indicates major current deficiencies in union structure and practices. Lack of knowledge of union policy relating to acquisition and use of corporate financial information, and inadequate training in its use, particularly on the blue collar side, were allied to problems of inter- and intra-union communication. In the former context many blue-collar stewards expressed little desire for co-operation with their white-collar counterparts, who were generally regarded as representing management views, whilst on the white-collar side fragmentation of bargaining arrangements posed a particular problem. Furthermore, communication between stewards and full-time officials appeared generally inadequate with a number of stewards, particularly on the white-collar side, expressing a strong degree of hostility towards full-time officials who, it was felt, did not show enough concern for particular company circumstances yet nevertheless expected to take a leading part in negotiations.

Such apparently poor relationships between shop stewards and full-time officials present a major obstacle to extending collective bargaining for, as Jenkins and Sherman (1977) point out, domestic bargainers need to be linked to the outside movement in order to give them the strength they need to match the employers economic power. Certainly, a closer, mutually supportive involvement of the union's full-time officials with shop stewards in different plants of the company would appear to be essential if the union side is to be properly equipped to bargain directly with managers responsible for corporate strategic decision making, rather than adopting a parochial plant-centred approach to bargaining.

Despite the above somewhat pessimistic picture regarding prospects for extending collective bargaining, some attempts have been made by trade unionists to achieve a degree of influence over matters such as investment and production policy. A notable example is provided by the Corporate Plan produced by the Lucas Aerospace Combine shop stewards committee, which, as well as highlighting the possibilities for the use of the corporate information where the union side operates with a particular purpose in mind, also illustrates the very real obstacles placed in the way of trade unionists attempting to achieve such influence.

The Lucas Plan[12]

The Lucas Aerospace Corporate Plan arose from the work of the combine shop stewards committee which, at the height of its power, was made up of stewards representing 14,000 union members in thirteen different unions at seventeen different company sites. Produced against a background of five thousand job losses in the company over a five-year period, the objectives of the plan were two-fold.

1. To protect union members' right to work by proposing a range of alternative products on which they could be engaged in the event of further cutbacks in the aerospace industry.
2. To ensure that amongst the alternative products were a number which would be socially useful to the community at large.

It should be stressed that the plan was far from being a hastily put together document produced in response to an immediate crisis (as was the case with the exercises we looked at in Chapter 7) but was in fact the product of over twelve months continuous effort. The idea was launched at a meeting the combine held with Tony Benn, the then Industry Minister, in November 1974, and the plan itself was not published until January 1976. In sum, it represented an attempt by the shop stewards to achieve some measure of control, or at least influence, over corporate decisions on investment and employment.

Backed by impressively detailed technical and economic supporting information, proposals were put forward for the development of approximately one hundred and fifty products in six major areas of technological activity. The criteria of social usefulness adopted were that:

● The product must not waste energy and raw materials, either in its manufacture or in its use.
● The product must be capable of being produced in a labour intensive manner so as not to give rise to structural unemployment.
● The product must lend itself to organizational forms within production which are non-alienating, and without authoritarian giving of orders. Instead, the work should be organized so as to link practical and theoretical tasks and allow for human creativity and enthusiasm.

In addition, a proposed Employee Development Programme was outlined which called for retraining and re-education schemes for both blue and white collar employees. It was stressed that the entire work-force, including semi-skilled and skilled workers, were capable of retraining for jobs which would greatly extend the range of work they could undertake. In the event of work shortages occurring before alternative products could be introduced, potential redundancies could be avoided by using re-education as a form of enlightened work sharing.

Reaction to the plan
Press reaction to the Corporate Plan was generally very favourable. The *Financial Times* (23.1.76) called the plan:

one of the most advanced yet prepared in the UK by a group of shop stewards. One of the most radical alternative plans ever drawn up by workers for their company . . .

whilst the *Engineer* (January 1976) felt it to be:

a twentieth century version of the industrial revolution.

Unfortunately the reaction of company management, the official trade union structure, and indeed the then Labour Government, was not equally enthusiastic.

The combine intended to put the plan forward in a negotiating framework in order to promote an extension of collective bargaining rather than the establishment of joint decision making or 'participation'. In the event, management refused to even discuss the plan with the combine, insisting instead that local consultative machinery be used, regarded by the union side as a normal divide and rule tactic (Lucas Aerospace Combine Shop Stewards Committee, 1979). Only very limited local victories were achieved by the combine. 'Mini' versions of the plan, for example, were successfully employed as a defensive measure to resist redundancy proposals at the Birmingham and Hemel Hempstead sites, and a small extension of collective bargaining was achieved at the Burnley site where a prototype heat pump was built. Also, certain ideas in the Corporate Plan were developed outside the main Aerospace division of the Lucas Company, but generally these diversification efforts were not backed with substantial resources and most have now been wound up.

Whereas certain sections of the wider trade union movement made encouraging noises and AUEW-TASS national officials went so far as to introduce elements of the plan into the 1976 round of wage bargaining, (unsuccessfully as it turned out), the general view appeared to be that existing collective bargaining machinery, represented by the Confederation of Shipbuilding and Engineering Unions (CSEU), was the only channel through which the company could be approached. However, communications addressed to the CSEU from the combine in the latter half of 1977 did not even meet with a reply.

The then Labour Government also provided little active help to the combine, despite a manifesto commitment to 'an irreversible shift of power towards working people'. Again they preferred to place the emphasis on existing collective procedures. In this particular case, of course, Government purchasing power could have been used as a lever against management if any will on the part of the Government to aid the combine had existed.

Despite its fate, the Lucas Workers Corporate Plan is nevertheless worthy of particular attention in that it represents a rare attempt to undermine in a practical, rather than purely theoretical, way the legitimacy of a system of production that gives priority to competitive success and profitability whilst ignoring matters such as the social costs of unemployment, the consequences of the productive process on the environment, and people's health and safety. It also challenged management's right to manage without accountability to the work-force. As Wainwright and Elliott (1982) point out, an extension of collective bargaining in this way, covering for example major investment and product decisions, opens up the possibility of corporate goals themselves being changed, and changed in the interests of groups other than shareholders. Possibly such an extension of collective bargaining is not possible on an individual company basis but would require action on a far broader front. This, more than anything, may explain the comparative failure of the Lucas initiative.

Nevertheless, the Corporate Plan does demonstrate the ability of trade unions to take a positive initiative rather than merely reacting to management proposals, and may therefore point the way forward to a real extension in collective bargaining in the future. Indeed the Lucas Plan has inspired some other, albeit less ambitious, attempts along the same lines (e.g. Beynon and Elliott, 1979; Speke Joint Shop Stewards Committee, 1979; Newcastle Trades Council, 1982). Elements of its underlying philosophy can also be detected in the 'Enterprise Plans' developed by Local Authority Enterprise Boards, notably the Greater London Enterprise Board (GLEB) which attempt to promote industrial democracy within firms seeking assistance, stressing the criteria of job security, equal opportunities, and training, as well as giving consideration to criteria including opportunities for socially useful applications of new technology.

SUMMARY AND CONCLUSIONS

In this chapter we have been concerned with assessing the role trade unions may play in broadening corporate social accountability. Whereas much of the material presented has inevitably had a more overtly 'political' flavour than is the norm in an accounting text, it must nevertheless be pointed out that many of the practical advances in social reporting both in the United Kingdom and Europe generally, discussed in earlier chapters, have tended to involve trade union interests either directly or indirectly. For this reason alone, whether one accepts or not the basic premiss that unions are closely concerned with many areas of a company's social performance, one cannot ignore the trade union aspect when considering issues of corporate social accountability and accounting.

Adopting a largely UK perspective we have attempted to assess the potential for trade unions to extend collective bargaining into areas previously excluded from its ambit, and how corporate financial information can be used to this end. Whilst empirical evidence generally points to low levels of utilization of financial data by union negotiators at present, possible reasons for which were analyzed in some detail, it was argued that the concern of trade unions with protecting member jobs, and hence combatting the social costs of unemployment, indicates a potentially greater role for such information in the future. However, the work of Moore *et al.* indicates that for unions to successfully extend the horizons of collective bargaining it would appear necessary for union structures and procedures to undergo radical reform. Nevertheless, the discussion of the Lucas Aerospace Corporate Plan does demonstrate the degree of challenge to traditional narrowly financial corporate objectives which unions are capable of mounting when the necessary degree of energy and initiative is present.

Whether initiatives such as that at Lucas Aerospace point the way forward to a real extension in collective bargaining or are merely isolated exercises doomed to inevitable failure is a question that can only be answered in the fullness of time. For the former to apply it would be necessary for unions to use existing collective bargaining machinery to negotiate access to management information systems as a matter of course, and may indeed require further legislation to legitimize union representatives having a say in corporate decision making, from which they are currently excluded. In any event, one can confidently predict that the issues raised in this chapter will remain very much on the political agenda in the foreseeable future: developments within the European Economic Community alone will see to that, and will involve the accounting profession – however reluctantly.

NOTES

1. Other pieces of legislation relevant in this context are the *Industry Act, 1975*, which gave powers to the Industry and Agriculture Ministers to compel firms deemed to be making a significant contribution to UK manufacturing industry to disclose certain types of economic and financial information to trade union representatives, and was subsequently repealed by the Conservative Government; and the *Health and Safety at Work Act, 1974*, discussed in Chapter 3.
2. The disclosure provisions in the *Employment Protection Act* closely resemble those appearing in the Labour Government's Industrial Relations Bill 1969 and the Conservative Government's *Industrial Relations Act, 1971*.
3. Specifically, data were requested in respect of each product manufactured in terms of sales in volume and by value, operating costs and contributions to net profit. Armed with such information the union could negotiate with the company on matters concerning investment, allocation of production work and wage rates to be paid.
4. For a comprehensive analysis see McSweeney (1983).
5. For a comprehensive discussion of the theoretical role of information as an input into models of the collective bargaining process see Foley and Maunders (1977) ch. 4.
6. For example, a study by Daniel (1976) which surveyed 254 plants, each employing over two hundred people drawn from the whole range of manufacturing industry, indicated that the plant represented, by a considerable margin, the most important level of bargaining over pay, particularly in engineering and metalworking.
7. The negotiation of a genuine productivity deal, which creates pay-offs for both management and workers, provides an example of such an integrative bargaining situation. Disclosure of information may also have a 'favourable' impact on the bargaining situation through its attitudinal structuring effects. See Foley and Maunders, particularly chapter 4, for a full discussion of this issue.
8. For a more substantial critique of these studies see Owen and Lloyd (1985) from which much of the analysis in this chapter is drawn.
9. See Bryer *et al.* (1982) particularly chapter 4, appendix 3, 'A financial appraisal of the future of iron and steelmaking at Corby'. See also Rowthorn and Ward (1979) for a study of the effects of closure on a number of important macroeconomic variables. Further case study evidence of redundancy campaigns is provided in Levie *et al.* (1984).

10. Models selected for particular analysis and criticism by Ogden and Bougen are those of Craft (1981), Foley and Maunders (1977), Palmer (1977), and Pope and Peel (1981b).

11. Marchington and Armstrong (1984) adopt a similar analysis in the context of joint consultation schemes, arguing that individual stewards face problems, such as role conflict, loss of contact with the membership, management unwillingness to disclose, and shopfloor apathy, to differing degrees and that for the union side:

> Consultation may have a rosier future where steward organisation is strong and where individuals gain experience both through union courses and through the support of their convenor.   p. 80

12. For a comprehensive, and highly readable, account of the full story behind the Lucas Aerospace Corporate Plan, which we have drawn upon heavily in this section, see Wainwright and Elliott (1982).

Chapter 10

Corporate social reporting – the way forward

Much of the earlier part of this book could be described as a 'state of the art' review, of both the practice of CSR and theory which relates either directly or indirectly to CSR. It will have been noticed that (for instance in Chapter 4) we have not merely tried to relay such theory but also to add to it. Selection of the examples of practice and the theories which were commented upon, whilst in part determined by space constraints, is in another, the personal responsibility of the authors, based on the values and beliefs which we articulated to some extent in the Introduction but which are further developed throughout the text. Despite our selectivity we are conscious that complexity, contradiction and potential confusion remains – which, indeed, fairly reflects the current state of the art in CSR. The purpose of this final chapter is thus, in part, to minimize one source of possible confusion by summarizing our own position on the direction we believe CSR in the UK *should* take and why.

As a group, and as individuals, the authors firmly believe that CSR, and the social responsibility which it is intended to reflect, is desirable. We do not, however, believe that it is sufficient merely to state a goal in this respect. Publication of *prescriptions* can, of course, affect the future in so far as they have an 'educational' or 'conditioning' effect on readers who are themselves social actors. But more may be achievable. A second part of this chapter, therefore, looks at the possible links between the publication of 'theories' (prescriptions) and changes in practice in CSR.

Finally, we use the concluding section of the book to indulge in some speculation about the likely future of CSR, asking some 'what if' questions as a form of sensitivity analysis of our forecasts and hence pointing to some of the critical determinants of the future of CSR.

SUMMARY OF PRESCRIPTIONS

The authors have no unqualified admiration for the status quo in society. We do not necessarily approve of the current distributions of income, wealth, and power – nor of the specific structures and processes (the 'capitalist system') which give rise to these. Indeed, a belief that there is a need to change the system, and particularly its induced neglect of non-market effects – pervades the book. But we also believe that change could and should be achieved by evolution and not revolution – which is what we mean when we say that our analysis starts by accepting the parameters of the status quo in society.

We also adopt a pluralistic view both of society and organizations – which enables us to talk in terms of 'stakeholder groups' who have competing as well as complementary interests in organizational impacts. Such a viewpoint, we accept, is partial in the sense that it ignores the question of how such interests have been determined and, more generally, how and why the 'parameters of the status quo' (such as the legal and political systems) may have come about and what causes them to be maintained. A possible explanatory long-term, world-view model for such issues is, for instance, offered by Marxism.

In comparison, our framework may be characterized as medium-term orientated and pragmatic. We do not want to deny the possibility that changes in CSR might induce evolutionary change in organizations/society which, in the manner of 'catastrophe theory', could become revolutionary in ultimate impact – but we would question CSR's instrumentality for this. In the now almost apocryphal remark: 'If we wanted to change society, we wouldn't start with accounting [or CSR].

Nevertheless, society is changing (continuously) and, we have argued, already contains its own seeds for change, for instance in the law. Thus, legal prescriptions can lead society to change (e.g. seat-belt wearing) whilst sometimes laws merely codify 'best practice' which has already been widely adopted. Hence our so-called empirical basis for identification of responsibility and accountability for corporate social performance is an evolutionary instrument. UK law and (past) legislative proposals *do* contain bases for identifying elements of social responsibility and accountability, whilst the corporate sector is replete (as we have shown) with examples of the voluntary acceptance of such accountability. Adoption of an empirical basis for accountability is thus consistent with both the democratic process – as determining the ability of elected representatives to pass 'leading' laws – and individual freedoms within the law.

On the strength of this observation we proceeded to ask how such accountability might best be fulfilled in terms of the identification, measurement and presentation of relevant information. One difficulty immediately faced was that, unlike in the case of 'economically rational' investors, there were no widely acceptable decision models available by means of which the relevance of information in CSR could be evaluated. Instead, we proposed that CSR presentations should contain their own statements of objectives, thus making possible a form of 'auto-evaluation'. At the same time, we suggested that these specific objectives should be constrained to refer to the overall social responsibility/accountability function of CSR.

Paralleling the debate which has taken place in financial reporting, we then examined the question of whether certain desirable attributes or 'qualitative characteristics' could be specified for CSR. Apart from the fairly obvious point that the information provided should relate to the objectives of its users, this didn't take us very far basically because of the much greater variety (of users, subject matter, purposes) associated with CSR as compared to financial reporting.

This very variety, however, led to the deduction that there is a need for greater user protection in CSR in the form of requirements that it consist of, as far as possible, unmanipulated (events) data, readable by a non-expert, and independently audited. These proposals are summarized in Figure 10.1.

---

1 Each report should include a statement of its objectives which allows (*inter alia*) the assessment of the:

   ● grounds for data selection
   ● reasons for form of presentation chosen.

2 The objective of a social report should be to discharge accountability in the spirit of improved democracy.

3 The information should be directly related to the objectives held for the particular groups to whom it is addressed.

4 The information should be unmanipulated and readable by a non-expert. It must be audited.

Figure 10.1 Required characteristics of a social report.

These prescriptions (in Chapter 4) to some extent anticipated the analyses of Chapters 5 and 6. From an accounting point of view, the most sophisticated form of social reporting might be considered as the production of fully articulated 'social accounts' (Chapter 6) which imitate the conventional final accounts of companies. But in order to arrive at such accounts, *valuation* of social performance items is required. It follows from the nature of an important class of these (externalities), however, that no objective market price can be put on them (since they are not traded). This does not preclude individuals or groups placing their own subjective valuations on them (as 'shadow' or 'accounting' prices) as is done in cost–benefit analysis, but we feel this should be left to the users of CSR, not the producers. As far as social performance outputs or impacts are concerned, therefore, we are in favour of their being reported in non-financial terms, in so far as financial quantification may usurp the evaluations of report users.

This is not to say that no financial information should appear in social reports. The relationships between an organization and society may be thought of in systemic terms, so that a full description of the system would have to cover inputs, outputs, processes and systems capacities (*inter alia*). If we use employee training as an illustration, this could mean providing representative data on, for example: numbers of man-hours of instruction; numbers and categories of qualifications achieved by trainees; range of courses run; and numbers of instructors available. Even listing such items is sufficient to trigger questions about their relevance and adequacy. Since there is, typically, insufficient specification of user-needs to identify one 'best' information set, it is probable that a number of alternative 'social indicators' for each aspect of the system may have to be provided. Amongst these, particularly on the inputs side, could well be financial information (e.g. amounts spent by the organization on training).

Problem with the use of social indicators are, indeed, the range of categories of such information, methods of measurement, and forms of representation which might be employed on plausible (conjectured) user-need grounds. As an alternative to getting bogged down in this particular morass, we stated a preference for the compliance with standards (CWS) approach. In this, standards of social performance derived from outside the reporting entity are used as yardsticks for the organization's own activities. A specimen layout for a CWS report is shown in Figure 10.2.

As will be seen, this is intended to conform with the required characteristics in Figure 10.1 and is consistent with the empirical identification of responsibility/accountability. Note that this approach would require a minimum degree of CSR (based on statutory and regulatory requirements) which would usually be in excess of that currently practised by organizations. In addition, the involvement of external parties (social auditors?) such as local authorities, trade unions, etc. would, we believe, encourage voluntary evolution on the part of companies in relation to both social performance and its reporting. Incremental organizational costs in reporting compliance with existing standards should be relatively insignificant, whilst any voluntary movement beyond this would presumably be based on cost–benefit comparison.

The penultimate section of the book (Chapters 7, 8 and 9) involves situations in which the foregoing prescriptions for 'general-purpose' CSR could be applied more specifically (to social audits on behalf of special interest groups, to employees, and to trade unions). Let us, however, continue to examine the possibilities for development of general purpose CSR.

Subject: Pollution (by location)

Air pollutants	Standard required	Source of standard	Organizational performance This year	Last year	Industry average
x					
x					
x					
x					

Narrative: to include – explanation of terms
                            – organizational performance reporting objectives
                            – Industrial Air Pollution Inspectorate report
                            – local authority report
                            – trade union response
                            – company response

(Repeated for, say, water pollution, work-place pollution; ambient and local noise, etc.)

Figure 10.2 Compliance with standard report.

THE MECHANISM OF IMPLEMENTATION

Our intention for CSR is that it should both reflect corporate social performance and influence it through affecting management's motivation towards such performance. The mechanism by which the latter may be achieved is through the 'information induction' effect, i.e. the observation that a reporter's behaviour is influenced by perceptions of how the report will be received. This can result in attention being given to aspects of organizational activities which were, perhaps, previously unconsciously neglected (because they were not measured), or improvements being made in relation to activities which were previously, consciously, differently performed (because they were not reported). In either event, social performance could 'improve'.

Alternatively, CSR could result in a reporting 'improvement' without any 'real' change in social performance. As we have seen, the state of the art in identification, measurement, and evaluation of social performance and the ready availability of alternative indicators is such as to make this a real possibility (albeit one which we have tried to minimize through the CWS approach). Much presumably depends upon the receptiveness of management towards the idea of social performance. In surveys of managerial attitudes, we have seen that some allocate it an independent value whilst others view it instrumentally (perhaps as a 'leading indicator' of financial performance). We should expect such attitudes – which are based upon individual value systems – to vary across cultures and over time. The latter is of most interest here in so far as it raises the possibility that managerial acceptance of social responsibility can change (or be changed).

An optimistic means of such change would be that of persuasion – via publications such as this – if not of the current then of the next generation of managers. But – to draw a parallel – for the most part, we who are teachers of accounting have waited (in some cases for decades) for evidence of this type of persuasion having an effect on the practice of financial and/or management accounting. In the light of what we now know about the quality of some of our earlier prescriptions, perhaps this is just as well. There is a commonsense explanation for this – when students become managers or accountants, they quite rapidly absorb the values and beliefs of their new professions (through 'social controls' like organizational induction courses, specialist professional education, work-group 'socialization', etc). In addition, they are influenced by the values and beliefs of society in general (as opposed to the educational system in particular).

So, while it is possible that theory (prescriptions) can lead practice (at least in the social sciences,) this is unlikely unless the theory is one 'whose time has arrived'. A more cynical view of this is embodied in the idea of accounting academia as a 'market for excuses' (Watts and Zimmerman, 1979): given the readiness of theorists to produce a range of competing prescriptions, the practitioner is always able to 'buy' that which supports his own interests, whatever its intrinsic merits. This leads to consideration of an alternative sequence – that practice may lead theory. In our area of concern, this could happen if managers were induced, either simultaneously or with a lag, by changes in society to change their own attitudes towards social responsibility/accountability, in turn leading to an increase in CSR. Whichever text happened to be authoritatively associated with this change could then be identified as the relevant 'theory'.

It seems to have been the belief of writers on social accounting in the 1970s, particularly in the USA, that they had caught such a moment. CSR *was* apparently increasing, social responsibility *was* a fashionable ancillary organizational objective. But it seems to have been a false dawn (and one which was less bright even then in the UK) – so where does CSR go from here?

THE FUTURE OF CSR

We write at a time (during the second Thatcher Government) when the omens for increased recognition of corporate social responsibilities and accountability through CSR could hardly look more unpromising. Financial efficiency and value for money are stressed as the keys to future social prosperity. Socially accountable organizations have been privatized. Control of inflation has brought record levels of bankruptcies and unemployment. Concern for the welfare of individual employees appears to have been downplayed in favour of policies designed to control labour costs and 'reduce the power of the unions'. In this setting, it is hardly surprising if, at organizational level, managers focus on financial performance (which may be critical for short- and medium-term survival) and seek to re-establish unilateral control of the labour process (the phenomenon known as the managerial resurgence). If practice does lead theory, this book is not apparently likely to command an immediate premium in the 'market for excuses'. On this line of reasoning, forecasting the future of CSR is bound up with general economic and political forecasting – and we do not want to get involved in that, except to point out that periodic changes of direction have been a predictable outcome of the democratic process in the UK for some time now.

What can be said is that *if* more favourable economic and political changes do occur (recur), the signs are that CSR could quickly recapture its former position and move ahead. Grounds for this belief are:

● From Chapter 3 – there remains a minority of large and potentially influential companies who continue the practice of CSR even in these unpromising times – they could be the springboard for future growth.
● From Chapter 2 – the practice and theory of CSR continues to be developed overseas, most notably in Europe, which is important in legislative influence terms for the UK.
● From Chapter 7 – paradoxically, the very factors which have apparently restricted general purpose CSR (financial cutbacks, unemployment) have added to its pragmatic and theoretical development by extending its range of application (e.g. in the form of local authority social audits, trade union sponsored closure evaluation reports).
● Increased access to education, improved standards of living and mass media communication are all factors which may be claimed to have assisted long-term changes in societal values and beliefs in the UK in this century. These have taken the form, *inter alia*, of expectations of greater involvement in decision making and more access to information. This trend may have been interrupted since 1979 but is arguably irreversible (to judge from comparable societies such as USA).

Quite apart from a possible role in 'preaching to the converted' (and helping them to develop their thoughts and practice), this text is designed to influence and prepare that much larger group of individuals and organizations which, we believe, will be involved in the *next* wave of corporate social reporting.

Bibliography

Abt, C.C. 1977. *The Social Audit for Management*. New York: Amacon.

Abt, C.C., and Associates. 1972 *et seq. Annual Report and Social Audit*.

Accounting Principles Board. 1970. *Basic Concepts and Accounting Principles Underlying Financial Statements of Business Enterprises*, Statement No. 4. New York: APB.

Accounting Standards Steering Committee. 1975. *The Corporate Report*. London: ASSC.

Acland, D. 1976. The effects of behavioural indicators on investor decisions: an exploratory survey. *Accounting, Organizations and Society*, Vol. 1, no. 2/3, pp. 133–42.

Advisory, Conciliation and Arbitration Service (ACAS). 1977. Code of Practice 2, *Disclosure of Information to Trade Unions for Collective Bargaining Purposes*. London: HMSO.

Alexander, B. 1978. Brush up your accounting theory. *Accountancy*. February, pp. 122–24.

Alexander, M.O. 1971. Investments in people. *Canadian Chartered Accountant*. July, pp. 38–45.

American Accounting Association. 1966. *A Statement of Basic Accounting Theory*. Evanston, Ill: AAA.

American Accounting Association. 1973a. Report of the Committee on Environment Effects of Organization Behavior. *Accounting Review Supplement*, pp. 72–119.

American Accounting Association. 1973b. Report of the Committee on Human Resource Accounting. *Accounting Review Supplement*, pp. 169–85.

American Accounting Association. 1975. Report of the Committee on Social Costs. *Accounting Review Supplement*, pp. 51–89.

American Accounting Association. 1977. *Statement on Accounting Theory and Theory Acceptance*. Sarasota, Fla: AAA.

American Institute of Certified Public Accountants. 1973. *Objectives of Financial Statements*. The Trueblood Report. New York: AICPA.

American Institute of Certified Public Accountants. 1977. *The Measurement of Corporate Social Performance*. New York: AICPA.

Anderson, J.C., and Frankle, A.W. 1980. Voluntary social reporting: an iso-beta portfolio analysis. *Accounting Review*. Vol. 55, no. 3, pp. 467–79.

Anderson, R.H. 1978. Responsibility accounting – how to get started. *Canadian Chartered Accountant Magazine*. September, pp. 46–50.

Anthony, R.W., and Young, D.N. 1984. *Management Control in Non-profit Organizations*, 3rd edn. Homewood, Ill: R.D. Irwin.

Arnold, J., and Hope, A.J.B. 1975. Reporting business performance. *Accounting and Business Research*. No. 18, pp. 96–105.

Arnold, J., and Moizer, P. 1984. A survey of the methods used by UK investment analysts to appraise investments in ordinary shares. *Accounting and Business Research*. No. 55, pp. 195–208.

Arrow, K.J. 1963. *Social Choice and Individual Values*. 2nd edn. New York: John Wiley.

Ashton, R.H. 1982. *Human information processing in accounting. Studies in Accounting Research No. 17* Sarasota, Fla: American Accounting Association.

Barnes, P.A. 1984. *The Myth of Mutuality*. London: Pluto Press.

Batstone, E. 1980. Systems of domination, accommodation and industrial democracy. In Burns, T., Karlsson, L., and Rus, V., eds, *Work and Power*. London: Sage.

Batstone, E., Boraston, I., and Frenkel, S. 1977. *Shop Stewards in Action*. Oxford: Blackwell.

Bauer, R.A., ed. 1966. *Social Indicators*. Cambridge, Mass: MIT Press.

Bauer, R.A. 1973. The state of the art of social auditing. In Dierkes, M., and Bauer, R.A., eds, *Corporate Social Accounting*. New York: Praeger.

Bauer, R.A., and Fenn, D.H. 1972. *The Corporate Social Audit*. New York: Russell Sage Foundation.

Baxter, W.T. 1982. Accounting standards – boon or curse? *Accounting and Business Research*. Vol. 13, no. 49, pp. 63–4.

Beams, F.A. 1970. Accounting for environmental pollution. *New York Certified Public Accountant*. August, pp. 657–61.

Beardshaw, V. 1981. *Conscientious Objectives at work*. London: Social Audit.

Beaver, W.H., Kennelly, J.W., and Voss, W.M. 1968. Predictive ability as a criterion for the evaluation of accounting data. *Accounting Review*. Vol. 43, no. 4, pp. 675–83.

Beaver, W.H. 1983. Research on monitoring the accounting standard setting process. In Bromwich, M. and Hopwood, A.G. eds, *Accounting Standards Setting*. London: Pitman.

Bedford, N.M. 1976. The *Corporate Report*: a discussion. *Accounting, Organizations and Society*. Vol. 1, no. 1, pp. 111–114.

Beesley, M., and Evans, T. 1978. *Corporate Social Responsibility: a reassessment*. London: Croom Helm.

Belkaoui, A. 1980. The impact of socio-economic accounting statement on the investment decision: an empirical study. *Accounting, Organizations and Society*. Vol. 5, no. 3, pp. 263–83

Belkaoui, A. 1984. *Socio-economic Accounting*. Connecticut: Quorum Books.

Bell, D. 1974. *The Coming of Post-industrial Society: a venture in social-forecasting*. London: Heinemann.

Benjamin, J.J., and Stranga, K.G. 1977. Differences in disclosure needs of major users of financial statements. *Accounting and Business Research*. No. 27, pp. 187–92.

Benston, G.J. 1982. Accounting and corporate accountability. *Accounting, Organizations and Society*. Vol. 7, no. 2, pp. 87–105.

Berry, T., Capps, T., Cooper, D., Hopper, T., and Lowe, T. 1985. NCB accounts – a mine of misinformation. *Accountancy*. January, pp. 10–12.

Beynon, H., and Elliott, H. 1979. *Workers Report on Vickers*. London: Pluto Press.

Bierman, H. 1974. The implications to accounting of efficient markets and the capital asset pricing model. *Accounting Review*. Vol. 49, no. 3, pp. 557–62.

Bird, P., and Morgan-Jones, P. 1981. *Financial Reporting by Charities*, London: ICAEW.

Birnberg, J.G., and Ghandhi, N.M. 1976. Toward defining the accountant's role in the evaluation of social programs. *Accounting, Organizations and Society*. Vol. 1, no. 1, pp. 5–10.

Blackaby, F. 1978. The reform of the wage bargaining system. *National Institute Economic Review*. August, pp. 49–54.

Blackburn, R. 1972. The new capitalism. In Blackburn, R., ed., *Ideology in Social Science: readings in critical social theory*. London: Fontana.

Blake, D.H., Frederick, W.C., and Myers, M.S. 1976. *Social Auditing – evaluating the impact of corporate programs*. New York: Praeger.

Blum, R., Herxheimer, A., Stenzl, C., and Woodcock, J., eds. 1983. *Pharmaceuticals and Health Policy*. London: Social Audit.

Bougen, P. 1983. Value added. In Tonkin, D.J., and Skerratt, L.C.L. *Financial Reporting 1983–84*.

Bougen, P. 1984. Review of *Linking Pay to Company Performance* by T. Vernon-Harcourt. *British Accounting Review*. Vol. 16, no. 1, p. 96.

Bougen, P.D., and Ogden, S.G. 1981. Power in organisations: some implications for the use of accounting in industrial relations. *Managerial Finance*. Vol. 7, no. 2, pp. 22–6.

Bowman, E.H. 1973. Corporate social responsibility and the investor. *Journal of Contemporary Business*. Winter, pp. 21–43.

Bowman, E.H. and Haire, M. 1976. Social impact disclosure and corporate annual report. *Accounting, Organizations and Society*. Vol. 1, no. 1, pp. 11–12.

Bremmer, H. 1976. *Estimating the Social Costs of National Economic Policy, Achieving the Goals of the Employment Act of 1946. Vol. 1*. Paper 5, US Congress Joint Economic Committee.

Brilloff, A. 1984. Double entry, double think, double speak. In Tinker, A., ed., *Social Accounting for Corporations*. Manchester: Manchester University Press.

Briston, R.J., and Dobbins, R. 1978. *The Growth and Impact of Institutional Investors*. London: ICAEW.

Brockoff, K. 1979. A note on external social reporting by german companies: a survey of 1973 company reports. *Accounting, Organizations and Society*. Vol. 4, no. 1/2, pp. 77–85.

Brooks, L.J. 1980. An attitude survey approach to the social audit: the Southam Press experience. *Accounting, Organizations and Society*. Vol. 5, no. 3, pp. 341–55.

Brown, W., and Sisson, K. 1975. The use of comparisons in workplace wage determination. *British Journal of Industrial Relations*. Vol. 13, no. 1, pp. 23–51.

Brummett, R.L., Flamholtz, E.G. and Pyle, W.C. 1968. Human resource measurement – a challenge for accountants. *Accounting Review*. Vol. 43, no. 2, pp. 217–24.

Bryer, R.A., Brignall, T.J., and Maunders, A.R. 1982. *Accounting for British Steel*. Aldershot: Gower.

Bryer, R.A., Brignall, T.J. and Maunders, A.R. 1984a. The case for shadow planning. In Levie, H., Gregory, D., and Lorentzen, N., eds, *Fighting Closures*. Nottingham: Spokesman.

Bryer, R.A., Brignall, S., and Maunders, A.R. 1984b. The origins of plant closures in UK manufacturing industry. In Levie, H., Gregory, D., and Lorentzen, N., eds, *Fighting Closures*. Nottingham: Spokesman.

Burchell, S., 1980. Casting around for a firm report base. *Accountant's Weekly*. 1 August, pp. 24–5.

Burchell, S., Clubb, C., Hopwood, A.G., Hughes, H., and Naphapiet, J. 1980. The role of accounting in organizations and society. *Accounting, Organizations and Society*. Vol. 5, no. 1, pp. 5–27.

Burchell, S., Cooper, D., and Sherer, M. 1982. Conceptual framework – one step forward, two back. *Accountancy*. May, p. 15.

Butcher, B. 1973. Anatomy of a social performance report. *Business and Society Review*. Autumn, pp. 246–252.

Buzby, S.L., and Falk, H. 1978. A survey of the interest in social responsibility information by mutual funds. *Accounting, Organizations and Society*. Vol. 3, no. 3/4, pp. 191–201.

Buzby, S.L., and Falk, H. 1979. Demand for social responsibility information by university investors. *Accounting Review*. Vol. 54, no. 1, pp. 23–37.

Centre for Alternative Industrial and Technological Systems. 1984. *Public Costs of Unemployment*. London: CAITS.

Chandra, G. 1974. A study of the consensus on disclosure among public accountants and security analysts. *Accounting Review*. Vol. 49, no. 4, pp. 733–42.

Chapman-Findlay, III M. 1977. On market efficiency and financial accounting. *Abacus*. December.

Chenhall, R.H. and Juchau, R. 1977. Investor information needs – an Australian study. *Accounting and Business Research*. No. 26, pp. 111–19.

Cherns, A.B. 1978. Alienation and accountancy. *Accounting, Organizations and Society*. Vol. 3, no. 2, pp. 105–14.

Churchill, N.C. 1974. Toward a theory for social accounting. *Sloan Management Review*. Spring 1974, pp. 1–17.

CIPFA/AHST. 1982. *Local Accountability*, London: CIPFA.

Climo, T. 1976. Disclosure of information to employees representatives: a wage bargaining decision model. Unpublished. University of Kent.

Cmnd. 3437. 1967. *The Nationalised Industries*. London: HMSO.

Cmnd. 5391. July 1973. *Company Law Reform*. London: HMSO.

Cmnd. 6225. 1975. *Inflation Accounting*. The Sandilands Report. London: HMSO.

Cmnd. 6525. 1976. *International Investment – Guidelines for multinational enterprises*. London: HMSO.

Cmnd. 6888. 1977. *The Future of Company Reports – a consultative document*. London: HMSO.

Cmnd. 7131. 1978. *The Nationalised Industries*, London: HMSO.

Cmnd. 7233. 1978. *Code of Conduct for Companies with Interests in South Africa*. London: HMSO.

Cmnd. 7654. 1979. *Company Accounting and Disclosure*. London: HMSO.

Cohen, M.D., March, J.G., and Olsen, J.P. 1972. A garbage can model of organizational choice. *Administrative Science Quarterly*. March, pp. 1–25.

Confederation of British Industry. 1973. *The Responsibilities of The British Public Company*. London: CBI.

Confederation of British Industry. 1975. *The Provision of Information to Employees – guidelines for action*. London: CBI.

Confederation of British Industry. 1976. *Response to Aims and Scope of Company Reports*. London: CBI.

Confederation of British Industry. 1981. *Company Responses to Unemployment*. London: CBI.

Confederation of British Industry. 1982. *Unemployment – a challenge for us all*. London: CBI.

Consultative Committee of Accounting Bodies. 1976. *Response to Aims and Scope of Company Reports*. London: CCAB.

Cooper, D. 1984. Accounting for labour. In Carsberg, B.V., and Hope, A., eds. *Current Issues in Accounting*. 2nd edn. Oxford: Philip Allen.

Cooper, D., and Essex, S. 1977. Accounting information and employee decision making. *Accounting, Organizations and Society*. Vol. 2, no. 3, pp. 201–17.

Cooper, D., and Sherer, M. 1984. The value of corporate accounting reports – arguments for a political economy of accounting. *Accounting, Organizations and Society*. Vol. 9, no. 3/4, pp. 207–32.

Corbett, P.G. 1980. Twenty years from now – the reality. *Accountant's Weekly*. 16 May, pp. 28–31.

Corcoran, W., and Leininger, W.E. 1970. Financial statements – who needs them? *Financial Executive*. August, pp. 34–8, 45–7.

Council for Economic Priorities. 1973. *Environmental Steel*. New York: CEP.

Counter Information Services. 1972 *et seq*. *Anti-Reports*. 9 Poland Street, London.

Cowton, C.J. 1983. Political and charitable contributions. In Tonkin, D.J., and Skerratt, L.C.L., eds. *Financial Reporting 1983–84*, pp. 117–23. London: ICAEW.

Craft, J.A. 1981. Information disclosure and the role of the accountant in collective bargaining. *Accounting, Organizations and Society*. Vol. 6, no. 1, pp. 97–107.

Craig, R., and Hussey, R. 1980. *Employee Reports – an Australian study*. Sydney: Enterprise Australia.

Cuthbert, M.H., and Whitaker, A. 1977. Disclosure of information and collective bargaining – a re-examination. *Journal of Business Finance and Accounting*. Vol. 4, no. 3, pp. 373–8.

Dahl, R.A. 1972. A prelude to corporate reform. *Business and Society Review*. Spring 1972 pp. 17–23.

Daniel, W.W. 1976. *Wage Determination in Industry*. Political and Economic Planning (PEP) Report, No. 563. London: PEP.

Daniel, W.W. 1981. Influences on the level of wage settlements in manufacturing industry. In Blackaby, F., ed., *The Future of Pay Bargaining*. London: Heinemann.

Danziger, R., and Scheid, J. 1980. Two years of application for the French law on the 'Bilan Social'. *Social Accounting Newsletter*. Vol. 2, no. 3, p.6.

Davis, K., and Blomstrom, R.L. 1975. *Business and Society: environment and responsibility*. Kogahusha: McGraw Hill.

Delmot, A. 1983. *Social Reporting in Belgium*. Paper presented to the European Accounting Association Sixth Annual Congress, University of Glasgow.

Department of Trade. 1976. *Aims and Scope of Company Reports*. London: HMSO.

Dickson, D. 1974. *Alternative Technology and the Politics of Technical Change*. London: Fontana.

Dierkes, M. 1979. Corporate social reporting in Germany – conceptual developments and practical experience. *Accounting, Organizations and Society*. Vol. 4, no. 1/2, pp. 87–107.

Dierkes, M., and Antal, A.B. 1985. The usefulness and use of social reporting information. *Accounting, Organizations and Society*. Vol. 10, no. 1, pp. 29–34.

Dierkes, M., and Bauer, R.A. 1973. *Corporate Social Accounting*, New York: Praeger.

Dierkes, M., and Preston, L.E. 1977. Corporate social accounting for the physical environment – a critical review and implementation proposal. *Accounting, Organizations and Society*. Vol. 2, no. 1, pp. 3–22.

Dilley, S.C., and Weygandt, J.J. 1973. Measuring social responsibility – an empirical test. *Journal of Accountancy*. September, pp. 62–70.

Dobbins, R., and Trussell, P. 1975. The valuation of human resources. *Management Decision*. Vol. 13, no. 3, pp. 155–69.

Dobson, J.R. 1982. What is good industrial relations? *Employee Relations*. Vol. 4, no. 2, pp. 5–10.

Dowling, J., and Pfeffer, J. 1975. Organisational legitimacy – social values and organisational behaviour. *Pacific Sociological Review*. January, pp. 122–36.

Downes, D., and Dyckman, T.R. 1973. A critical look at the efficient market empirical research literature as it relates to accounting information. *Accounting Review*. Vol. 43, no. 2, pp.300–17.

Drucker, P.F. 1980. *Managing in Turbulent Times*. London: Heinemann.

Dyckman, T.R., Downes, D.H., and Magee, R.P. 1975. *Efficient Capital Markets and Accounting – a critical analysis*. Englewood Cliffs, NJ: Prentice-Hall.

Earl, M.J., and Hopwood, A. 1980. From management information to information management. In Lucas, H.C., and Land, F.F., Lincoln, T.J., and Supper, K., eds, *The Information Systems Environment*. Amsterdam: North-Holland.

Elias, N.S. 1972. The effects of human asset statements on the investment decision. *Empirical Research in Accounting – Selected Studies*. pp. 215–23.

Epstein, M.J., Epstein, J.B., and Weiss, E.J. 1977. *Introduction to Social Accounting*. California: Western Consulting Group Inc.

Ernst & Ernst. 1976 *et seq*. *Social Responsibility Disclosure*. Cleveland, Ohio: Ernst & Ernst.

Estes, R.W. 1976. *Corporate Social Accounting*. New York: Wiley-Interscience.

Fanning, D. 1979. Employment reports – an appraisal. *Employee Relations*. Vol. 1, no. 4, pp. 8–12.

Fanning, D., ed. 1981. *Pension Funds – issues in accounting and finance*, Bradford: MCB Publications.

Flamholtz, E.G. 1971. A model for human resource valuation – a stochastic process with service rewards. *Accounting Review*. Vol. 46, no. 2, pp. 253–67.

Flamholtz, E.G. 1972. Toward a theory of human resource value in formal organizations. *Accounting Review*. Vol. 47, no. 4, pp. 666–78.

Flamholtz, E.G. 1973. Human resource accounting – measuring positional replacement costs. *Human Resource Management*. Spring, pp. 1–12.

Flamholtz, E.G. 1974. *Human Resource Accounting*. Encino, Calif.: Dickenson.

Flamholtz, E.G. 1976. The impact of human resource valuation on management decisions – a laboratory experiment. *Accounting, Organizations and Society*. Vol. 1, no. 2/3, pp. 153–65.

Fogler, H.R., and Nutt, F. 1975. A note on social response and stock valuations. *Academy of Management Journal*. Vol. 18, no. 1, pp. 155–60.

Foley, B.J. and Maunders, K.T. 1977. *Accounting Information Disclosure and Collective Bargaining*. London: Macmillan.

Fox, A. 1966. Managerial ideology and industrial relations. *British Journal of Industrial Relations*. Vol. 4, no. 3, pp. 366–78.

Francis, M.E. 1973. Accounting and the evaluation of social programs – a critical comment. *Accounting Review*. vol. 48, no.3. pp. 245–57.

Frankel, M. 1978. *The Social Audit Pollution Handbook*. London: Macmillan.

Frankel,M. 1981. *A Word of Warning* London: Social Audit.

Frankel, M. 1982. *Chemical Risk*. London: Pluto Press.

Friedman, M. 1962. *Capitalism and Freedom*. Chicago: University of Chicago.

Friedman, M. 1970. The social responsibility of business to increase its profits. *The Sunday Times Magazine*. 13 September, pp. 32–3.

Friedman, M. 1971. Does business have a social responsibility? *Bank Administration*. April.

Galbraith, J.K. 1974. *Economics and the Public Purpose*. London: Andre Deutsch.

Gambling, T. 1974. *Societal Accounting*. London: George Allen and Unwin.

Gambling, T. 1977a Accounting to society. In Carsberg, B.V., and Hope, A.J.B., eds, *Current Issues in Accounting*. Oxford: Phillip Allen.

Gambling, T. 1977b. Magic, accounting and morale. *Accounting, Organizations and Society*. Vol. 2, no. 2, pp. 141–51.

Gambling T. 1978a. The evolution of accounting man. *Accountant's Weekly*. 10 November, pp. 30–1.

Gambling, T. 1978b. *Beyond the Conventions of Accounting*. London: Macmillan.

General and Municipal Workers Union. 1978. *Disclosure of Information Guide*. Esher: GMWU.

Giles, W.J., and Robinson, D.F. 1972. *Human Asset Accounting*. London: Institute of Personnel Management.

Glatzer, W. 1981. An overview of the international development in macro social indicators. *Accounting, Organizations and Society*. Vol. 6, no. 3, pp. 219–34.

Glautier, M.W.E. 1976. Human resource accounting – a critique of research objectives for the development of human resource accounting models. *Journal of Business Finance and Accounting*. Vol.3, no. 2, pp. 3–21.

Glautier, M.W.E., and Roy, J.L. 1981. Social responsibility reporting. In Lee, T.A., ed, *Developments in Financial Reporting*. Oxford: Philip Allan.

Glautier, M.W.E., and Underdown, B. 1976. *Accounting Theory and Practice*. pp. 673–716. London: Pitman.

Glyn, A. 1985. *The Economic Case Against Pit Closures*. Sheffield: National Union of Mineworkers.

Glyn, A., and Harrison, J. 1980. *The British Economic Disaster* London: Pluto Press.

Glynn, J. 1985. *Value for Money Auditing in the Public Sector*. Hemel Hempstead: Prentice-Hall/ICAEW.

Gospel, H. 1978. The disclosure of information to trade unions: approaches and problems. *Industrial Relations Journal*. Vol. 9, no. 3, pp. 18–26.

Gray, D.H. 1973. One way to go about inventing social accounting. In Dierkes, M., and Bauer, R.A., eds, *Corporate Social Accounting*. New York: Praeger.

Gray, R.H. 1980. An evaluation of the current UK practice in external social reporting with special reference to Social Audit and Counter Information Services. M.A. (Econ) dissertation, University of Manchester.

Gray, R.H. 1981 The compliance with statute audit and report. Unpublished. University College of North Wales, Bangor.

Gray, R.H. 1983a. Accountability, financial reporting and not-for-profit organisations. *The British Accounting Review*, Vol. 15, no. 1, pp 3–23.

Gray, R.H. 1983b. Problems of accountability. *Public Finance and Accountancy*. November, pp. 29–31.

Gray, R.H. 1983c. Research and development. In Tonkin, D.J. and Skerratt, L.C.L. eds, *Financial Reporting 1983–4*. London: ICAEW, pp. 125–37.

Gray, R.H. 1984a. Uncharitable view of accounting. *Accountancy*. August, p. 84.

Gray, R.H. 1984b. The NHS Treasurer and accountability. *Public Finance and Accountancy*. April, pp. 30–2.

Gray, R.H. 1985. Review of *Social Accounting for Corporations* by A.M. Tinker (ed.). *British Accounting Review*. Vol. 17, no. 1, pp. 77–8.

Gray, R.H., and Hope, A.J.B. Disclosure: Where auditors are failing. *Accountancy*, December, pp. 19–20.

Gray, R.H., and Perks, R.W. 1982. How desirable is social accounting? *Accountancy*. April, pp. 101–103.

Gray, S., and Maunders, K.T. 1980. *Value Added Reporting: uses and measurement*. London: The Association of Certified Accountants.

Grojer, J., and Stark, A. 1977. Social accounting: a Swedish attempt. *Accounting, Organizations and Society*. Vol. 2, no. 4, pp. 349–86.

Gross, B.M. 1966. The state of the nation: social systems accounting. In Bauer, R.A., ed. *Social Indicators*. Cambridge, Mass: MIT Press.

Grove, H.D., Mock, T.J., and Ehrenreich, K.B. 1977. A review of human resource accounting measurements systems from a measurement theory perspective. *Accounting, Organizations and Society*. Vol. 2, no. 3, pp. 219–36.

Groves, R.E.V. 1981. Human resource accounting and reporting. In Lee, T.A., ed. *Developments in Financial Reporting*. Oxford: Philip Allan.

Hammill, A.E. 1979. *Simplified Financial Statements*. London: Institute of Chartered Accountants in England and Wales.

Hargreaves, B.J.A., and Dauman, J. 1975. *Business Survival and Social Change – a practical guide to responsibility and partnership*. London: Associated Business Programmes.

Harrell, A.M. and Flick, H.D. 1980. Comparing the impact of monetary and non-monetary human asset measures on executive decision making. *Accounting, Organizations and Society*. Vol. 5, no. 4, pp. 393–400.

Harte, G.F., and Owen, D.L. 1986. Fighting de-industrialisation – the role of local government social audits. *Accounting, Organizations and Society* (forthcoming).

Hatfield, H.R. 1927. *Accounting*, New York: D. Appleton & Co.

Hawkins, K. 1979. The future of collective bargaining. *Industrial Relations Journal.* Vol. 10, no. 4, pp. 10–21.

Heard, J.E., and Bolce, W.J. 1981. The political significance of corporate social reporting in the USA. *Accounting, Organizations and Society*, Vol. 6, no. 3, pp. 247–54.

Hekimian, J.S., and Jones, C.H. 1967. Put people on your balance sheet. *Harvard Business Review.* January/February, pp. 105–113.

Hermanson, R.H. 1964. *Accounting for Human Assets.* Occasional Paper No. 14, Bureau of Business & Economic Research, Graduate School of Business Administration, Michigan State University, East Lansing, Mich.

Hetherington, J.Â.C. 1973. *Corporate Social Responsibility Audit: – A Management Tool for Survival.* London: The Foundation for Business Responsibilities.

Hilton, A. 1978. *Employee Reports.* Cambridge: Woodhead Faulkner.

Hines, R.D. 1984. The implications of stock market reaction (non-reaction) for financial accounting standard setting. *Accounting and Business Research.* Vol. 15, no. 57, pp. 3–14.

Hird, C. 1983. *Challenging the Figures.* London: Pluto Press.

HMSO. 1981. *Local Authority Annual Reports.* London: Welsh Office, HMSO.

Hofstede, R. 1976. Behavioural accounting research – pathologies, paradigm and prescription. *Accounting, Organizations and Society.* Vol. 1, no. 1, pp. 43–58.

Hope, A.J.B. and Gray, R.H. 1982. Power and policy making – the development of an R & D standard. *Journal of Business Finance and Accounting.* Vol. 9, no. 4, pp. 531–58.

Horn, R.V. 1980. Social indicators – meaning methods and applications. *International Journal of Social Economics.* Vol. 7, no. 8.

House of Lords. 1982. *Report from the Select Committee on Unemployment.* London: House of Lords.

Hughes, J. 1981. Britain in crisis – de-industrialization and how to fight it. Nottingham: Spokesman.

Humble, J. 1973. *Social responsibility audit – a management tool for survival.* London: The Foundation for Business Responsibilities.

Humble, J., and Johnson, M.A. 1978. *Corporate Social Responsibility – the attitudes of European business leaders.* Brussels: Management Centre Europe.

Hussey, R. 1978. France has a social audit. *Accountancy.* February, pp. 111–12

Hussey, R. 1979. *Who Reads Employee Reports?* Oxford: Touche Ross.

Hussey, R. 1981. Developments in employee reporting. *Managerial Finance.* Vol. 7, no. 2, pp. 12–16.

Ijiri, Y. 1975. Theory of accounting measurement. *Studies in Accounting Research No. 10.* Evanston, Ill.: AAA.

Imberg, D., and MacMahon, P. 1973. Company law reform. *Social Audit.* Vol. 1, no. 2, pp. 3–17.

Imke, F.J. 1966. Relationships in accounting theory. *Accounting Review.* Vol. 41, no. 2, pp. 318–22.

Ingram, R.W. 1978. An investigation of the information content of (certain) social responsibility disclosures. *Journal of Accounting Research.* Vol. 16, no. 2, pp. 270–85.

Jackson-Cox, J., McQueeney, J., and Thirkell, J.E.M. 1984. The disclosure of company information to trade unions – the relevance of the ACAS Code of Practice on disclosure. *Accounting, Organizations and Society.* Vol. 9, no. 3, pp. 253–73.

Jacoby, N.H. 1973. *Corporate Power and Social Responsibility.* London: Collier Macmillan.

Jaggi, B. 1980. An analysis of corporate social reporting in Germany. *International Journal of Accounting, Education and Research.* Vol. 15, no. 2, pp. 35–45.

Jenkins, C., and Sherman, B. 1977. *Collective Bargaining*. London: Routledge & Kegan Paul.

Jensen, R.E. 1976. Phantasmagoric accounting. *Studies in Accounting Research No. 14*. Sarasota, Florida: AAA.

Jeuda, B. 1980. Deserving a better fate – The Corporate Report. *Accountancy* February, pp. 76–8.

Johnson, H.L. 1979. *Disclosure of Corporate Social Performance*. New York: Praeger.

Jones, D.M.C. 1978. *Disclosure of Financial Information to Employees*. London: Institute of Personnel Management.

Jones, D.M.C. 1977. The path to disclosure. *Management Decision*. Vol. 15, no. 4, pp. 410–19.

Jonson, L.C. Jonsson, B., and Svensson, G. 1978. The application of social accounting to absenteeism and personnel turnover. *Accounting, Organizations and Society*. Vol. 3, no. 3/4, pp. 261–8.

Jurkus, A.F. 1979. The uncertainty factor in human resources accounting. *Personnel*. November/December, pp. 72–5.

Kempner, T.K., MacMillan and Hawkins, K.H. 1976. *Business and Society*. Pelican: Harmondsworth.

Kern, W. 1975. The accounting concept in German labour-oriented business management. *International Journal of Accounting*. Vol. 10, no. 2, pp. 23–35.

Kjellen, B. 1980. *Employee consultants and economic information for employees*. Research Report, University of Stockholm.

Layard, R. 1972. *Cost Benefit Analysis – selected readings*. Harmondsworth: Penguin.

Lee, T.A. 1974. Enterprise income – survival or decline and fall. *Accounting and Business Research*. No. 15, pp. 178–92.

Lee, T.A. 1985. *Income and Value Measurement*. 3rd edn. Reading: Van Nostrand Reinhold.

Lee, T.A., and Tweedie, D.P. 1977. *The Private Shareholder and the Corporate Report*. London: ICAEW.

Lee, T.A., and Tweedie, D.P. 1981. *The Institutional Investor and Financial Information*. London: ICAEW.

Lessem, R. 1977. Corporate social reporting in action – an evaluation of British, European and American practice. *Accounting, Organizations and Society*. Vol. 2, no. 4, pp. 279–94.

Lev, B., and Schwartz, A. 1971. On the use of the economic concept of human capital in financial statements. *Accounting Review*. Vol. 46, no. 1, pp. 103–11.

Levie, H., Gregory, D., and Lorentzen, N., eds. 1984. *Fighting Closures*. Nottingham: Spokesman.

Lewis, N.R., Parker, L.D., and Sutcliffe, P. 1984a. Financial reporting to employees – the pattern of development 1919 to 1979. *Accounting, Organizations and Society*. Vol. no. 2/3. pp. 275–89.

Lewis, N.R., Parker, C.D., and Sutcliffe, P. 1984b. Financial reporting to employees – towards a research framework. *Accounting and Business Research*. Vol. 14, no. 55, pp. 229–39.

Libby, R. 1981. *Accounting and Human Information Processing*. Englewood Cliffs, NJ : Prentice-Hall.

Lieberman, A.Z., and Whinston, A.B. 1975. An event-accounting information system. *Accounting Review*. Vol. 50, no. 2, p. 249.

Likierman, A., 1979. Performance measures for the nationalised industries. *Accountancy*. May, p. 117.

Likert, R. 1967. *The Human Organization*. New York: McGraw-Hill.

Lindop, E. 1979. Workplace bargaining – the end of an era. *Industrial Relations Journal*. Vol. 10, no. 1, pp. 12–21.

Lindblom, C. 1984. The accountability of private enterprise – private–no: enterprise–yes. In Tinker, A., ed., *Social Accounting for Corporations*. Manchester: Manchester University Press.

Linowes, D.F. 1972a. An approach to socio-economic accounting. *Conference Board Record*. November, pp. 58–61.

Linowes, D. 1972b. Let's get on with the social audit – a specific proposal. *Business and Society Review*. Winter, pp. 39–42.

Lucas Aerospace Combine Shop Stewards Committee. 1979. *Democracy Versus the Circumlocution Office*. Institute for Workers Control Pamphlet No. 65, Nottingham.

Lyall, D. 1975. Opening the books to the workers. *Accountancy*. Vol. 86, no. 2, pp. 42–4.

Lyall, D. 1981. Financial reporting for employees. *Management Decision*. Vol. 19, no. 3, pp. 33–8.

Lyall, D. 1982. Disclosure practices in employee reports. *Accountants Magazine*. July, pp. 246–8.

McAdam, T.W. 1973. How to put corporate responsibility into practice. *Business and Society Review*. No. 6, pp. 8–16.

McComb, D. 1978. Some guidelines on social accounting in the US. *Accountancy*. April, pp. 50–2.

MacPherson, C.B. 1973. *Democratic Theory – essays in retrieval*. Oxford: Oxford University Press.

McSweeney, B. 1983. *The Influence of Legislation on the Disclosure and use of Financial Information in UK Collective Bargaining*. London: Association of Certified Accountants.

Macve, R. 1981. *A Conceptual Framework for Financial Accounting and Reporting*. London: The Institute of Chartered Accountants in England and Wales.

Maitre, P. 1978. The measurement of the creation and distribution of wealth in a firm by the method of surplus accounts. *Accounting, Organizations and Society*. Vol. 3, no. 3/4, pp. 227–36.

Marchington, M., and Armstrong, R. 1984. Employee participation – some problems for some shop stewards. *Industrial Relations Journal*. Vol. 15, no. 1, pp. 68–81.

Marlin, J.T. 1973. Accounting for pollution. *Business and Society Review*. February, pp. 41–6.

Marques, E. 1976. Human resource accounting – some questions and reflections. *Accounting, Organizations and Society*. Vol. 1, no. 2/3, pp. 175–8.

Marsh, A., and Hussey, R. 1979. Survey of employee reports. *Company Secretary's Review*. Tolley.

Marsh, A., and Rosewell, R. 1976. A question of disclosure. *Industrial Relations Journal*. Vol. 7, no. 2, pp. 4–16.

Mathews, M.R. 1984. A suggested classification for social accounting research, *Journal of Accounting and Public Policy*. Vol. 3, pp. 199–221.

Maunders, K.T. 1981. Social reporting and the employment report. In Skerratt, L.C.L., ed., *Financial Reporting 1981–82*, pp. 217–27. London: ICAEW.

Maunders, K.T., 1982a. Simplified and employee reports. In Skerratt, L.C.L. and Tonkin, D.J., eds, *Financial Reporting 1982–83*, pp. 173–7. London: ICAEW.

Maunders, K.T., 1982b. Social reporting and the employment report. In Tonkin, D.J., and Skerratt, L.C.L., eds, *Financial Reporting 1982–83*, pp. 178–87. London: ICAEW.

Maunders, K.T. 1984. *Employment Reporting – an investigation of user needs, measurement and reporting issues and practice*. London: ICAEW.

Maxwell, S.R. and Mason, A.K. 1976. *Social Responsibility and Canada's Largest Corporations*, ICRA Occasional Paper No. 9. Lancaster: University of Lancaster.

Medawar, C. 1976. The social audit – a political view. *Accounting, Organizations and Society*. Vol. 1, no. 4, pp. 389–94.

Medawar, C. 1978a. *Insult or Injury*. London: Social Audit.

Medawar, C. 1978b. *The Social Audit Consumer Handbook*. London: Macmillan.

Medawar, C. 1978c. What is accountability? *The Accountant's Magazine*. November, pp. 472–4.

Medawar, C. 1979. *The Consumers of Power*. London: Social Audit.

Medawar, C. 1984. *The Wrong Kind of Medicine*. Consumers' Association. London: Hodder & Stoughton.

Medawar, C., and Freese, B. 1982. *Drug Diplomacy*. London: Social Audit.

Mesarovic, M., and Pestel, E., 1975. *Mankind at the Turning Point*. Club of Rome. London: Hutchinson. 1975.

Mirvis, P.H. and Macey, B.A. 1976. Accounting for the costs and benefits of human resource development programs – an interdisciplinary approach. *Accounting, Organizations and Society*. Vol. 1, no. 2/3, pp. 179–93.

Mishan, E.J. 1975. *Cost Benefit Analysis – an informal introduction*. 2nd edn. London: George Allen & Unwin.

Mitchell, F., Sams, K.T., Tweedie, D.P., and White, P.J. 1980. Disclosure of information – some evidence from case studies. *Industrial Relations Journal*, Vol. 11, no. 5, pp. 53–62.

Moore, R., Gold, M., and Levie, H. 1979. *The Shop Stewards Guide to the Use of Company Information*. Nottingham: Spokesman.

Moore, R., and Levie, H. 1981. *Constraints upon the Acquisition and Use of Company Information by Trade Unions*. Occasional Paper No. 67. Trade Union Research Unit, Ruskin College, Oxford.

Morley, I. and Stephenson, G. 1977. *The Social Psychology of Bargaining*. London: George Allen & Unwin.

Morley, M.F. 1978. *The Value Added Statement*. Edinburgh: The Institute of Chartered Accountants of Scotland.

Newcastle Trades Council. 1982. *Jobs for a Change – alternative production on Tyneside*. Newcastle: Newcastle Trades Council.

Nikolai, L.A., Bazley, J.D., and Brummett, R.L. 1976. *The Measurement of Corporate Environmental Activity*. New York: National Association of Accountants.

Ogden, S.G., and Bougen, P.D. 1985. A radical perspective on disclosure of information to trade unions. *Accounting, Organizations and Society*. Vol. 10, no. 2, pp. 211–24.

OECD, 1980. *Draft Synthesis Report of Working Party on Social Indicators*. Paris.

Owen, D.L. 1984. Can UK meet the challenge of social reporting? *Accountancy*. August, pp. 73–4.

Owen, D.L. 1985. Europe leads on social reporting. *Certified Accountant*. January, pp. 39–40.

Owen, D.L., and Broad, G. 1983. Information disclosure – views from the shopfloor. *Employee Relations*. Vol. 5, no. 3, pp. 28–32.

Owen, D.L., and Harte, G.F. 1984. Reporting on corporate accountability to the workforce. *The Accountant's Magazine*. May, pp. 184–7.

Owen, D.L., and Lloyd, A.J. 1985. The use of financial information by trade union negotiators in plant level collective bargaining. *Accounting, Organizations and Society*. Vol. 10, no. 3, pp. 329–50.

Packard, V. 1962. *The Hidden Persuaders*. Harmondsworth: Pelican.

Packard, V. 1963. *The Waste Makers*. Harmondsworth: Penguin.

Palmer, J.R. 1977. *The Use of Accounting Information in Labour Negotiations*. New York: National Association of Accountants.

Parke, R., and Peterson, J.L. 1981. Indicators of social change – developments in the USA. *Accounting, Organizations and Society*. Vol. 6, no. 3, pp. 235–46.

Parker, L.D. 1976. Social accounting – don't wait for it. *The Accountant's Magazine*. February.

Parker, L.D. 1977. *The Reporting of Company Financial Results to Employees*. London: ICAEW.

Paton, W.A. 1922. *Accounting Theory*. New York: The Ronald Press.

Paton, W.A., and Littleton, A.C. 1940. *An Introduction to Corporate Accounting Standards*. Monograph No. 3. Evanston, Ill.: AAA.

Patterson, N. 1976. *Nuclear Power*. Harmondsworth: Penguin.

Pearce, D.W. 1971. *Cost Benefit Analysis*. London: Macmillan.

Perks, R.W., and Butler, L. 1977. Accounting standards in practice – the experience of SSAP2. *Accounting and Business Research*. No. 29, pp. 25–33.

Perks, R., and Glendinning, R. 1981. Little progress seen in published performance indicators. *Management Accounting*. December, pp. 28–30.

Perks, R.W., and Gray, R.H. 1978. Corporate social reporting – an analysis of objectives. *British Accounting Review*. Vol. 10, no. 2, pp. 43–59.

Perks, R.W., and Gray, R.H. 1979. Beware of social accounting. *Management Accounting*. December, pp. 22–3.

Pettigrew, A.M. 1972. Information control as a power resource. *Sociology*, Vol. 6, pp. 187–204.

Pope, P.F., and Peel, D.A. 1981a. Information dislosure to employees and rational expectations. *Journal of Business Finance and Accounting*. Vol. 8, no. 1, pp. 139–46.

Pope, P.F., and Peel, D.A. 1981b. The optimal use of information, collective bargaining and the disclosure debate. *Managerial Finance*, Vol. 7, no. 2, pp. 17–21.

Popoff, B. 1972. Postulates, principles and rules. *Accounting and Business Research*. No. 7, pp. 192–3.

Prakash, P., and Rappaport, A. 1977. Information inductance and its significance for accounting. *Accounting, Organizations and Society*. Vol. 2, no. 1, pp. 29–38.

Preston, L.E. 1981. Research on corporate social reporting – directions for development. *Accounting, Organizations and Society*. Vol. 6, no. 3, pp. 255–62.

Preston, L.E., and Post, J.E. 1975. *Private Management and Public Policy – the principle of public responsibility*. Englewood Cliffs, NJ: Prentice-Hall.

Preston, L.E., Rey, F., and Dierkes, M. 1978. Comparing corporate social performance – Germany, France and Canada and the US. *California Management Review*. Summer, pp. 40–9.

Pryke, R. 1981. *The Nationalised Industries*. Oxford: Martin Robertson.

Purdy, D. 1981. The provision of financial information to employees – a study of the reporting practices of some large public companies in the United Kingdom. *Accounting, Organizations and Society*. Vol. 6, no. 4, pp. 327–38.

Puxty, A.G. 1986. Social accounting as imminent legislation – a critique of technist ideology. *Advances in Public Interest Accounting*. Vol. 1, no. 1.

Ramanathan, K.V. 1976. Toward a theory of corporate social accounting. *The Accounting Review*. Vol. 51, no. 3, pp. 516–28.

Rawls, J. 1972. *A Theory of Justice*. Oxford: Oxford University Press.

Reeves, T.K., and McGovern, T. 1981. *How Shop Stewards Use Company Information – Ten Case Studies of Information Disclosure*. London: Anglian Regional Management Centre.

Renshall, J.M. 1976. Changing perceptions behind the Corporate Report. *Accounting, Organizations and Society*. Vol. 1, no. 1, pp. 105–109.

Renshall, M. 1979. Three roads worth exploring. *Accountant's Weekly*. 23 February, p. 21.

Renshall, M., Allan, R., and Nicholson, K. 1979. *Added Value in External Financial Reporting*. London: ICAEW.

Rey, F. 1978. Corporate social responsibility and social reporting in France. In Schoenfeld, H., ed., *The Status of Social Reporting in Selected Countries*. Urbana, Ill.: University of Illinois.

Robertson, J. *The Sane Alternative*. London: James Robertson.

Rockness, J.W. 1985. An assessment of the relationship between US corporate environmental performance and disclosure. *Journal of Business Finance and Accounting*. Vol. 12, no. 3, pp. 339–54.

Rowthorn, B., and Ward, J. 1979. How to run a company and run down an economy – the effects of closing down steel-making in Corby. *Cambridge Journal of Economics*. Vol. 3, pp. 329–40.

Russell, P. 1981. *Social Indicators and Social Accounting – Concepts, Methods and Application*. Working Paper 8103. Universtity of Manchester.

Rutherford, B.A. 1977. Value added as a focus of attention for financial reporting – some conceptual problems. *Accounting and Business Research*. No. 27, pp. 215–20.

Rutherford, B.A. 1980. A published statement of value added – a survey of three years experience. *Accounting and Business Research*. Vol. 11, no. 41, 15–28.

San Miguel, J.G., Shank, J.K., and Govindarajan, V. 1977. Extending corporate accountability – a survey and framework for analysis. *Accounting, Organizations and Society*, Vol. 2, no. 4, pp. 333–47.

Schoenfeld, H.W. 1978. Social reporting – its present development. In Schoenfeld, H., ed., *The Status of Social Reporting in Selected Countries*. Urbana, Ill.: University of Illinois.

Schreuder, H. 1979. Corporate social reporting in the Federal Republic of Germany – an overview. *Accounting, Organizations and Society*. Vol. 4, no. 1/2, pp. 109–22.

Schreuder, H. 1981. Employees and the corporate social reports – the Dutch case. *Accounting Review*. Vol. 56, no. 2, pp. 294–308.

Schreuder, H. 1985. Suitable research – on the development of a positive theory of the business suit. *Accounting, Organizations and Society*. Vol. 10, no. 1, pp. 105–10.

Schreuder, H., and Ramanathan, K.V. 1984a. Accounting and corporate accountability – an extended comment. *Accounting, Organizations and Society*. Vol. 9, no. 3/4, pp. 409–15.

Schreuder, H., and Ramanathan, K.V. 1984b. Accounting and corporate accountability – a postscript. *Accounting, Organizations and Society*. Vol. 9, no. 3/4, pp. 421–3.

Schumacher, E.F. 1973. *Small is Beautiful*. London: Abacus.

Schwan, E.S. 1976. The effects of human resource accounting data on financial decisions – an empirical test. *Accounting, Organizations and Society*. Vol. 1, no. 2/3, pp. 219–37.

Seidler, L.J. 1973. *Dollar Values in the Social Income Statement World*. Spring, pp. 16–23. London: Peat, Marwick, Mitchell & Co.

Seidler, L.J., and Seidler, L.L. 1975. *Social Accounting Theory Issues and Cases*. Los Angeles: Melville.

Shanks, M. 1978. What is social accounting? *Social Accounting*. London: CIPFA.

Sherer, M., Southworth, A., and Turley, S. 1981. An empirical investigations of disclosure, usage and usefulness of corporate accounting information. *Managerial Finance*. Vol. 7, no. 2, pp. 6–11.

Shocker, A.D., and Sethi, S.P. 1973. An approach to incorporating societal preferences in developing corporate action strategies. *California Management Review*. Summer, pp. 97–105.

Singh, D.R., and Ahuja, J.M. 1983. Corporate social reporting in India. *International Journal of Accounting*. Vol. 18, no. 2, pp. 151–70.

Skerratt, L.C.L., and Tonkin, D.J. 1982. *Financial Reporting 1982–83*. London: ICAEW.

Snowball, D. 1980. On the integration of accounting research on human information processing. *Accounting and Business Research*. Vol. 10, no. 39, pp. 307–18.

Social Audit. 1974. *Social Audit No. 4*. London: PIRC.

Social Audit. 1973–1976. *Social Audit Quarterly*. London: PIRC.

Solomons, D. 1974. Corporate social preferences – a new dimension in accounting reports? In Edey, H. and Yamey, B.S., eds, *Debits, Credits, Finance and Profits*, pp. 131–41. London: Sweet & Maxwell.

Sorter, G.H. 1969. An 'events' approach to basic accounting theory. *Accounting Review*. Vol. 44, no. 1, pp. 12–19.

Speke Joint Shop Stewards Committee. 1979. *Dunlop – Jobs for Merseyside*. Centre for Alternative Industrial and Technological Systems.

Spicer, B.H. 1978a. Accounting for corporate social performance – some problems and issues. *Journal of Contemporary Business*. Vol. 7, no. 1, pp. 151–70.

Spicer, B.H. 1978b. Investors, corporate social performance and information disclosure – an empirical study. *The Accounting Review*. Vol. 53, no. 1, pp. 94–111.

SSRC. 1976. *The Social Responsibilities of Business – a report to the Social Science Research Council by an SSRC advisory panel*. London.

Steeds, D. 1976. Changes in social values and the role of the profession. *Accountancy*. August, pp. 76–9.

Stephenson, L. 1973. Prying open corporations – tighter than clams. *Business and Society Review*. Winter, pp. 66–73.

Sterling, R.R. 1970. On theory construction and verification. *Accounting Review*. Vol. 45, no. 3, pp. 444–57.

Sterling, R.R. 1972. Decision oriented financial accounting. *Accounting and Business Research*. Summer, pp. 198–208.

Stewart, J.D. 1984. The role of information in public accountability. In Hopwood, A., and Tomkins, C., eds, *Issues in Public Sector Accounting*. Oxford: Philip Allen.

Stock Exchange. 1976. *Commentary on the Department of Trade's Consultative Paper*. London: The Stock Exchange.

Stone, C.D. 1975. *Where the Law Ends*. New York: Harper & Row.

Strier, F. 1980. The business manager's dilemma I–III. *Journal of Enterprise Management*. Vol. 2, pp. 5–10, 11–26, 119–26.

Taylor, A.H. 1976. Presenting financial information to employees. *Managerial Finance*. Vol. 2, no. 1, pp. 17–18.

Teoh, H.Y., and Thong, G. 1984. Another look at corporate social responsibility and reporting – an empirical study in a developing country. *Accounting, Organizations and Society*. Vol. 9, no. 2, pp. 189–206.

The Ecologist. 1972. *A Blueprint for Survival*. Harmondsworth: Penguin.

Theunisse, H. 1979. *Corporate social reporting in Belgium*. Working Paper 79/08. State University Centre of Antwerp, Faculty of Applied Economics.

Thompson, E.R., and Knell, A. 1979. *The Employment Statement in Company Reports*. London: The Institute of Chartered Accountants in England and Wales.

Thompson, J.D., and Tuden, A. 1959. Strategies, structures and processes of organizational decision. In Thompson, J.D. *et al.*, eds, *Comparative Studies in Administration*. Pittsburgh: University of Pittsburgh Press.

Tinker, A. ed. 1984a. *Social Accounting for Corporations*. Manchester: Manchester University Press.

Tinker, A. 1984b. Theories of the State and the state of accounting – economic reductionism and political voluntarism in accounting regulation theory. *Journal of Accounting and Public Policy*. Vol. 3, pp. 55–74.

Tinker, A. 1985. *Paper Prophets – a social critique of accounting*. Eastbourne: Holt Saunders.

Tomkins, C., and Groves, R.E.V. 1983. The everyday accountant and researching his reality. *Accounting, Organizations and Society*. Vol. 8, no. 4, pp. 361–74.

Tonkin, D.J., and Skerratt, L.C.L. 1983. *Financial Reporting 1983–84*. London: ICAEW.

Trades Union Congress. 1974. *Industrial Democracy*. London: TUC.

Trades Union Congress – Labour Party Liaison Committee. 1982. *Economic Planning and Industrial Democracy – the framework for full employment*. London: The Labour Party.

Transport and General Workers Union. 1971 & 1977. *The Ford Wage Claim*. London: TGWU.

Tricker, R.I. 1983. Corporate responsibility, institutional governance and the roles of accounting standards. In Bromwich, M., and Hopwood, A.G., eds, *Accounting Standards Setting – An International Perspective*. London: Pitman.

Trotman, K.T. 1979. Social responsibility disclosure by Australian companies. *The Chartered Accountant in Australia*. March, pp. 24–8.

Tweedie, D.P. 1981. Standards, objectives and the *Corporate Report*. In Leach, R., and Stamp, E., eds, *British Accounting Standards – The First Ten Years*. Cambridge: Woodhead-Faulkner.

UEC Working Party on Social Reporting. 1983. *Socio-economic Information*. A report prepared for the 9th UEC Congress, Strasbourg.

Ullmann, A. 1979. Corporate social reporting – political interests and conflict in Germany. *Accounting, Organizations and Society*. Vol. 4, no. 1/2, pp. 123–33.

United Nations. 1954. *Report on International Definitions and Measurement of Standards and Levels of Living*. New York: United Nations.

United Nations. 1975. *Towards a system of social and demographic statistics*. Studies in Methods, Series F, No. 18. New York: United Nations.

United Nations commission on Transnational Corporations. 1982. *Draft United Nations Code on Transnational Corporations*. New York: United Nations.

Votaw, D. 1973. The nature of social responsibility. *Journal of Contemporary Business*. Winter, pp. 1–20.

Wainwright, H., and Elliott, D. 1982. *The Lucas Plan – a new trade unionism in the making?* London: Allison & Busby.

Ward, S. 1985. Minority enterprises take a helping hand. *Accountancy Age*. 17 January, p. 17.

Watts, R.L., and Zimmerman, J.L. 1979. The demand for and supply of accounting theories – the market for excuses. *Accounting Review*. Vol. 54, no. 2, pp. 273–305.

Wells, D. 1985. Barclays is losing its fight with a shadow on points. *Accountancy Age*. 9 May, pp. 9–10.

Wildavsky, A. 1965. *The Politics of the Budgetary Process*. Boston: Little Brown.

Wilders, M., and Heller, F. 1981. Company information to employees. In Marsh, A., and Hussey, R., eds, *Employees, Trade Unions and Company Information*. Oxford: Touche Ross.

Williams, P.F. 1980. The evaluative relevance of social data. *Accounting Review*. Vol. 55, no. 1, pp. 62–77.

Wilson, D.C., Butler, R.J., Cray, D., Hickson, D.J., and Mallory, G.R. 1982. The limits of trade union power in organisational decision making. *British Journal of Industrial Relations*. Vol. 20, no. 3, pp. 322–41.

Wiseman, J. 1982. An evaluation of environmental disclosures made in corporate annual reports. *Accounting, Organizations and Society*. Vol. 7, no. 1, pp. 53–63.

Wright, R. 1970. Managing man as a capital asset. *Personnel Journal*. April, pp. 290–8.

Index